Credits

Author

Joseph Labrecque

Reviewers

Sajith Amma

Deborah Gray

Darrell Heath

Acquisition Editors

Wilson D'souza

Mary Nadar

Lead Technical Editors

Hithesh Uchil

Unnati Shah

Technical Editors

Prasanna Joglekar

Manmeet Singh Vasir

Project Coordinator

Joel Goveya

Proofreader

Aaron Nash

Indexer

Rekha Nair

Graphics

Aditi Gajjar

Production Coordinator

Melwyn D'sa

Cover Work

Melwyn D'sa

About the Author

Joseph Labrecque is primarily employed by the University of Denver as Senior Interactive Software Engineer specializing in the Adobe Flash Platform, where he produces innovative academic toolsets for both traditional desktop environments and emerging mobile spaces. Alongside this principal role, he often serves as adjunct faculty communicating upon a variety of Flash Platform solutions and general web design and development subjects.

In addition to his accomplishments in higher education, Joseph is the Proprietor of Fractured Vision Media, LLC, a digital media production company, technical consultancy, and distribution vehicle for his creative works. He is founder and sole abiding member of the dark ambient recording project *An Early Morning Letter, Displaced,* whose releases have received international award nominations and underground acclaim.

Joseph has contributed to a number of respected community publications as an article writer and video tutorialist. He is also the author of *Flash Development for Android Cookbook, Packt Publishing* (2011), *What's New in Adobe AIR 3, O'Reilly Media* (2011), *What's New in Flash Player 11, O'Reilly Media* (2011), *Adobe Edge Quickstart Guide,* Packt Publishing (2012) and co-author of *Mobile Development with Flash Professional CS5.5 and Flash Builder 4.5: Learn by Video, Adobe Press* (2011). He also serves as author on a number of video training publications through video2brain, Adobe Press, and Peachpit Press.

He regularly speaks at user group meetings and industry conferences such as Adobe MAX, FITC, D2W, 360 | Flex, and a variety of other educational and technical conferences. In 2010, he received an Adobe Impact Award in recognition of his outstanding contribution to the education community. He has served as an Adobe Education Leader since 2008 and is also an Adobe Community Professional.

Visit him on the Web at http://josephlabrecque.com/.

Thanks to my family, friends, and benefactors for your continued support.

Superabundant thanks to Leslie, Paige, and Lily!

About the Reviewers

Sajith Amma has been working as a Technology Consultant for various UK and Indian companies since 2005. He is a hardcore PHP Programmer and a passionate Web Developer working on cutting-edge technologies, especially in the mobile platform. He has received his Masters degree in Business Information Systems from the University of East London. He uses his technical blog (`sajithmr.me`) to share his findings and interesting articles related to programming.

Sajith is the co-founder of MobMe Wireless Solutions, an Indian company, which is listed in the top 100 as one of the best innovation companies in India. He has worked as a Technology Consultant for companies such as Vodafone UK, Orange UK, and T-Mobile UK. He is currently working as a Solution Architect for a UK-based company, Muzicall Ltd.

> I would like to thank Muzicall Ltd. for giving me the opportunity to work with HTML5 and Adobe Edge. I would also like to thank Joseph Labrecque for giving me the opportunity to review this book.

Deborah Gray has been in the design business for 20 years, having started in the 1980s in the newspaper business. For the last seven years, she has run a successful Sonoma County design agency, Deborah Gray Design (http://deborahgraydesign.com/). She has designed and developed hundreds of websites and print campaigns for clients in the San Francisco Bay Area and worldwide.

Deborah specializes in frontend development and WordPress. Her early experience as a Print Designer created a passion for design and typography that is clean, simple, and withstands the test of time.

Darrell Heath has an education in Applied Information Technology. He is an experienced Visual Artist, and for the past nine years has been a freelance Web Developer through various local IT consultants. Since 2005, he has been a tutorialist for the National Association of Photoshop Professionals (NAPP), Layers Magazine, and Planet Photoshop.

Darrell has also provided a technical review for *Adobe Edge: The Missing Manual, Chris Grover, O'Reilly Media*. He is an active member in a number of Adobe community forums, and is a co-moderator for NAPP's private membership board.

Visit him on the Web at http://www.heathrowe.com.

www.PacktPub.com

Support files, eBooks, discount offers and more

You might want to visit www.PacktPub.com for support files and downloads related to your book.

Did you know that Packt offers eBook versions of every book published, with PDF and ePub files available? You can upgrade to the eBook version at www.PacktPub.com and as a print book customer, you are entitled to a discount on the eBook copy. Get in touch with us at service@packtpub.com for more details.

At www.PacktPub.com, you can also read a collection of free technical articles, sign up for a range of free newsletters and receive exclusive discounts and offers on Packt books and eBooks.

http://PacktLib.PacktPub.com

Do you need instant solutions to your IT questions? PacktLib is Packt's online digital book library. Here, you can access, read and search across Packt's entire library of books.

Why Subscribe?

- Fully searchable across every book published by Packt
- Copy and paste, print and bookmark content
- On demand and accessible via web browser

Free Access for Packt account holders

If you have an account with Packt at www.PacktPub.com, you can use this to access PacktLib today and view nine entirely free books. Simply use your login credentials for immediate access.

Table of Contents

Preface   **1**

Chapter 1: Introducing Adobe Edge Animate   **13**

The history of Adobe Edge Animate   **14**

The inner workings of Edge Animate   **15**

  HTML, CSS, and JavaScript   15

    HTML   15

    CSS   16

    JavaScript   16

  How jQuery is used in Edge Animate   16

  JSON   17

  The Adobe Edge Animate Runtime   18

Adobe Edge Animate and Adobe Flash Professional   **19**

  Is Edge Animate a competing product to Flash Professional?   20

  Comparisons with Flash Professional   20

    Stage   21

    Timeline   21

    Keyframes   21

    Labels   22

    Symbols   22

    Library   22

    Actions   22

Installing Adobe Edge Animate and getting started   **23**

  Installing Edge Animate   23

  The Edge Animate welcome screen   27

  Creating a new Edge Animate project   28

    Save   30

    Save As...   31

  File structure in the Edge Animate project   32

    Edge includes   33

Application interface overview	33
The application window	34
Customizing the Edge Animate panel layout	35
Managing workspaces	36
The Edge Animate application menu	38
The Edge Animate toolbar	38
Panels in Edge Animate	41
Adobe Edge Animate keyboard shortcuts	49
Keyboard Shortcuts dialog	50
Adobe Edge Animate menu items	50
File	51
Window	52
Help	53
Summary	**53**
Chapter 2: Drawing and Adjusting Composition Elements	**55**
Adobe Edge Animate drawing tools	**56**
Background Color and Border Color	56
Rectangle tool	56
Rounded Rectangle tool	57
Ellipse tool	57
Drawing elements upon the Stage	**57**
The Selection tool	58
Working with the Rectangle tool	58
Using the Rectangle tool	59
Working with the Rounded Rectangle tool	60
Using the Rounded Rectangle tool	60
Working with the Ellipse tool	63
Using the Ellipse tool	63
Properties unique to rectangle and ellipse elements	**64**
Properties of elements	65
Background Color	65
Border Color	66
Border Thickness	66
Border Style	66
Border Radii	66
Border Radii units	66
Modifying rectangle elements	66
Modifying properties of rectangle elements	67
Duplicating drawing elements	68
Copying a rectangle element with the Selection tool	69
Layout and guidance tools	70
Layout Preferences tool	70
Rulers	72
Guides	72
Smart Guides	74

Adobe Edge Animate menu items   **75**
    Edit   75
    View   76
    Modify   76
Summary   **77**
Chapter 3: Selecting and Transforming Elements   **79**
  Locating the Selection and Transform tools   **79**
  The Selection tool   **80**
    Using the Selection tool   81
  The Transform tool   **82**
    Using the Transform tool   83
    Manipulating the Transform Point   84
  The Edge Animate Stage   **88**
    Manipulating the Stage   89
      Rulers and Guides   89
      Center the Stage   90
      Zoom controls   90
  Building responsive compositions   **91**
    Making a document responsive   91
    Making elements responsive   92
      Global versus Applied   92
      Responsive presets   94
    Simulating various screen sizes   95
  The Elements panel   **95**
    Element visibility   96
    Locking elements   97
    Managed versus unmanaged elements   98
      Managed   98
      Static   98
    Reordering elements   99
    Renaming elements   99
    Grouping elements   100
  Properties shared by all element types   **102**
    Element properties   102
      ID   103
      Class   103
      Actions   103
      Visibility   103
      Overflow   103
      Opacity   104
    Position and Size properties   104
      Position   104
      Size   104

Transform properties	104
Scale	105
Skew	105
Transform Origin	105
Rotate	105
Cursor properties	105
Cursor	106
Shadow properties	106
Shadow type	106
Shadow color	106
Shadow horizontal offset	106
Shadow vertical offset	106
Blur radius	106
Spread	107
Clip properties	107
Clip	107
Accessibility properties	107
Title	107
Tab Index	107
Stage properties	108
Document title	108
Width	108
Height	108
Background color	108
Overflow	109
Autoplay	109
Composition ID	109
Poster	109
Down-level Stage	109
Preloader	109
Adobe Edge Animate menu items	**110**
View	110
Summary	**111**
Chapter 4: Using Text and Web Fonts	**113**
Locating the Text tool	**113**
The Text tool	**114**
Text element types	114
Creating text elements on the Stage	**116**
Creating text elements	117
Point text versus Paragraph text	118
Point text	118
Paragraph text	118
Text property retention	119
Properties unique to text elements	**120**
Main text element properties	120

Secondary text element properties   121
Text shadows   **122**
Using web fonts in Adobe Edge Animate   **122**
About web fonts   123
Generic font definitions   123
Microsoft's core fonts for the Web   124
Hosted web font services   124
Applying web fonts to an Edge Animate project   125
Using local fonts from your collection   127
Managing fonts in the Edge Animate Library   **130**
Viewing fonts within {projectname}_edge.js   131
Summary   **132**
Chapter 5: Importing External Assets   **133**
Importing external assets   **133**
Image element types   134
Properties unique to image elements   134
Image Source   135
Swap Image   135
Background Position Offset X   135
Background Position Offset Y   135
Background Position Units   136
Background Size Width   136
Background Size Height   136
Background Size Units   136
More about image elements   136
Reveal in Finder/Explorer   136
The alt attribute   137
Scalable Vector Graphics   **137**
Importing SVG images   138
SVG notifications   140
Bitmap images   **140**
Types of bitmap images   141
Portable Network Graphics   141
Joint Photographic Experts Group   141
Graphics Interchange Format   142
Importing bitmap images   142
Using animated GIFs   144
Working with imported assets   **144**
Considerations when working with imported assets   145
Managing assets within the Library   146
Asset instance creation   146
Swapping assets   146
Importing Symbol Libraries   **147**

Exporting assets from other Creative Suite applications   **148**

Exporting from Illustrator   149

Exporting from Adobe Photoshop   151

Exporting from Fireworks   152

     Using the Edge Animate extension for Fireworks   153

     Using the extension   155

Exporting from Flash Professional   158

Summary   **159**

Chapter 6: Creating Motion Through the Timeline   **161**

Animation within Edge Animate   **161**

The Edge Animate Timeline   **162**

Playback controls   162

     Time   163

     Timeline options   163

     More about the Show Grid control   164

Timeline controls   165

     The Playhead   165

     The Pin   165

     Zoom controls   166

Keyframes   166

     Keyframe navigation   167

Creating motion   **167**

Inserting keyframes   167

     Adding keyframes through the Properties panel   168

     Adding keyframes through the application menu   168

     Using the Timeline keyframe buttons   169

     Using right-click for keyframe insertion   170

Animating with the Playhead   170

Animating with the Pin   173

Editing transitions   **174**

Transition delay   175

Transition duration   175

Transition end   175

Modifying element properties based on transition   175

Transition easing controls   176

Transition easing types   177

Shifting transitions   178

Changing transition duration   178

Selecting transition keyframes   178

Selecting multiple transitions   179

Copy and paste keyframes   179

Generating transitions through keyframes   179

Expanding and contracting composition duration   180

Animating a website header   **180**
  Project setup, asset import, and general layout   181
  Performing the animation of elements   182
    Animating the background   183
    Animating the cover art (do this for each cover
    art image)   183
    Animating the title text   184
    Finishing up!   184
Automated animation techniques   **185**
  Pasting motion   185
    Paste Transitions To Location   185
    Paste Transitions From Location   185
    Paste Inverted   186
    Paste Actions   186
    Paste All   186
  Automation example   186
    Initial state   186
    Transition begin state   187
    Transition end state   188
Adobe Edge Animate menu items   **189**
  Edit   190
  Timeline   191
Summary   **192**
Chapter 7: Interactivity with Actions, Triggers, and Labels   **193**
Working with Edge Animate actions   **194**
  The Actions panel   195
    Preferences in Actions panel   196
  Applying actions to the Stage   196
  Applying actions to individual elements   198
Changing the mouse cursor   **198**
  Cursor types   199
Triggers   **201**
  The Timeline Actions layer   202
  Working with triggers   202
  Working with labels   203
  Jumping to labels   203
The Code panel   **206**
  Full Code view   207
  Code Error warnings   207
Action and trigger breakdown   **208**
  Composition actions   209
  Mouse actions   210
  Touch actions   211

jQuery actions 211
Action and trigger events 212
Adding interactivity to a website header **214**
Creating the text element 214
Adding interactivity to the title 216
Adding interactivity to the album art 216
Completing the final website header composition 218
Using touch actions for mobile devices **219**
Adobe Edge Animate menu items **222**
Edit 222
Summary **222**
Chapter 8: Making Use of Symbols, Nested Elements,
and Grouping **223**
What are Symbols in Edge Animate? **223**
Differences between Symbols and other elements 224
Symbols are self-contained 224
Symbols exist within the Library panel 225
Symbols are instantiated upon the Stage 225
Symbols have their own Timeline 226
Symbols can employ Playback Actions 227
Comparison of Symbols in Edge Animate with Symbols
in Flash Professional 228
Similarities 229
Differences 229
Creating and managing Symbols **229**
Converting assets into Symbols 231
Managing Symbols through the Library panel 233
Edit 233
Delete 233
Rename 234
Duplicate 234
Export... 234
Sharing Symbols across Edge Animate compositions **234**
Exporting a Symbol 235
Importing a Symbol 236
Properties unique to Symbol instances **236**
Instance ID 237
Symbol name 237
Scrub toggle 237
Playback Actions 238
Using Playback Actions to control Symbol playback 238
Available Playback Commands 240

Internal Symbol properties 241
Symbol-level events 242
Nesting elements **242**
How nesting works 243
Nesting assets 244
Nesting text 246
Controlling nested content 248
Grouping and ungrouping within Edge Animate 252
Adobe Edge Animate menu items **253**
Modify 253
Summary **254**
Chapter 9: Advanced Animation Techniques **255**
Clipping **255**
Clip properties 256
The Clipping tool 257
Image elements and the Clipping tool 258
Revealing image and text elements through clipping 259
Animating with sprite sheets **263**
Generating sprite sheets from Flash Professional CS6 264
Using a sprite sheet within Edge Animate 266
Animating with PNG sequences **268**
Generating PNG sequences from Flash Professional CS6 268
Using PNG sequences in Edge Animate 270
Summary **274**
Chapter 10: Publishing Edge Animate Compositions **275**
Publishing an Edge Animate composition **275**
Publish Settings **276**
Targeting the Web / Optimized HTML 277
Using the Frameworks via CDN option 278
Using the Google Chrome Frame for IE 6, 7, and 8 option 278
Using the Publish content as static HTML option 280
Targeting InDesign/DPS/Muse 281
Targeting iBooks / OS X 284
Capturing a poster image **285**
Saving a poster image 286
Down-level Stage **287**
Editing the Down-level Stage panel 287
Using a poster image 288
Image properties 289
Text properties 290
Creating custom Down-level Stage 291

Using project preloaders	**293**
Using a built-in preloader	294
Creating a custom preloader	296
Publishing a composition	**300**
Before publishing	301
After publishing	301
Summary	**301**
Chapter 11: Further Explorations with Adobe Edge Animate	**303**
The Adobe Edge Animate Runtime API	**303**
Modifying existing web content in Edge Animate	**305**
Animating existing web content	305
Integrating Edge Animate content into existing websites	**308**
Embedding a composition	309
Embedding content	310
Embedding with static content	310
Packaging with <iframe>	311
Embedding more than one Edge Animate composition within a web page	**311**
Measuring page load through Chrome Developer tools	**313**
Network	314
Audits	314
Other development tools	315
Advanced CSS treatments in Edge Animate	**316**
Video support in Adobe Edge Animate	**318**
The HTML5 <video> tag	319
MP4	319
WebM	319
OGG	319
Adobe Flash Player	320
Embedding a YouTube video within an Edge Animate composition	320
Compositional audio integration	**324**
The HTML5 audio tag	325
Working with audio	326
Using Adobe Edge Inspect with Edge Animate	**328**
Summary	**331**
Index	**333**

Preface

Adobe Edge Animate is an all new tool from Adobe which seeks to enable the authoring of motion and interactive experiences through HTML5, CSS3, and JavaScript in a manner consistent with Creative Suite applications. Edge Animate is able to create such experiences at this time, due to advancements in browser technology and the need for a consistent, cross-platform solution which is able to function across desktop and mobile operating systems.

Why do we need Adobe Edge Animate?

Some may ask for an explanation: why do we need Edge Animate when we have tools such as Flash Professional which also create animation and interactive content for the Web? There are a number of reasons for this, which we will now attempt to illustrate.

Adobe Flash Player restrictions

Traditionally, those of us designing animated or highly interactive content for the Web have been able to rely on Adobe Flash Player to display this content without issue across Windows, Mac, and Linux. In fact, Adobe and many independent entities still reports that Flash Player is installed on 96 to 99 percent of desktop machines. There are problems though, as we must now account for mobile operating systems which place restrictions upon the Flash Player, or even outright ban it entirely. The most problematic of these platforms is Apple iOS.

It is worth noting that the Google Android, Windows 8 (desktop and mobile), BlackBerry 10, and BlackBerry Tablet OS mobile operating systems all have robust Flash Player 11 support. However, Adobe has halted any further development for the mobile Flash Player after version 11.1 as of the publication of this book. Others do have the option of licensing Flash Player and integrating it into their systems, as RIM continues to do for their QNX-based systems such as BB10 and PlayBook.

Since Flash content is restricted from running within the mobile iOS Safari browser, designers have been searching for alternative ways of delivering experiences to these devices.

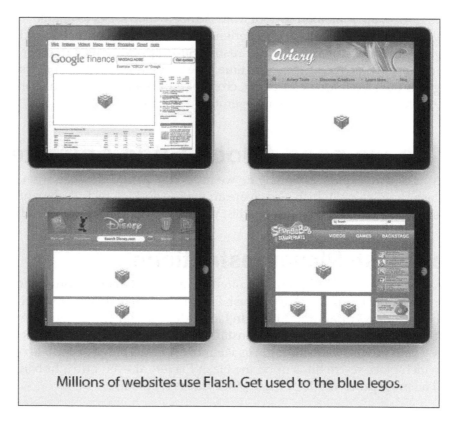

Millions of websites use Flash. Get used to the blue legos.

Image courtesy of Lee Brimelow

Though Apple iOS has banned Flash Player in the browser, Flash content can be distributed through the Apple App Store in the form of compiled applications which target this platform. Similarly, other mobile operating systems such as Google Android, Windows 8, RIM BlackBerry 10, and Tablet OS also include full support for Flash-based projects through Adobe AIR.

HTML technology maturity

For much of its history, HTML has provided a way for web designers to creatively markup content for rendering within a browser. With the draft HTML5 specification currently under development, this role has been expanded in some ways which attempt to move beyond simple textual markup and into the rich media space.

Three tags often cited as examples of this include the following:

- `<video>`: For simple video playback in HTML
- `<audio>`: For simple audio playback in HTML
- `<canvas>`: For programmatically rendering bitmap visuals in HTML through JavaScript APIs

Along with the core HTML specification in development are related specifications such as CSS3 and a variety of additional specifications meant to extend the core technologies of the Web. We have also seen great increases in the speed of JavaScript engines over the past couple of years, enabling greater use of the basic scripting language for the Web. Add a number of frameworks (such as the popular jQuery [http://jquery.com/] framework) to this environment and we have quite the revolution in core web technologies!

Shifting roles

Adobe Flash Player has always served as an extension to core web technologies such as HTML, CSS, and JavaScript—enabling experiences within the browser that were just not possible using these technologies on their own. With the recent expansions we've already detailed, some of the capabilities of Flash Player have now been made possible in other technologies.

Primary among these is the ability to create motion and animated objects employing core web technologies using tools such as Adobe Edge Animate.

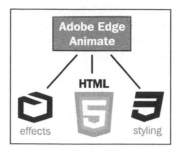

Although it is now possible to create website intros, rich ads, and other motion content using a tool such as Edge, designers should be careful not to replicate the nuisances of the past. The Web doesn't need more "Skip Intro" landing pages.

While HTML and related technologies have adopted some of what designers used the Flash Player for years ago, it is important to consider that the Flash Platform has also grown quite a bit over the last few years. The role of Flash has shifted from enabling motion and rich interactivity on the Web to providing rich video experiences, enterprise applications, advanced web modules, and console-quality games with Flash Player 11. The Flash Platform itself has expanded from the browser and onto desktop and mobile operating systems using Adobe AIR: smartphones, tablets, and even television units and automobile dashboards have benefitted from this shift in technology.

Interested in what lies in the future for the Flash runtimes? Adobe has published a white paper that outlines the roadmap for the next two years and sets the foundation for technological advances for the next decade.

Read the Adobe roadmap for the Flash runtimes at
http://www.adobe.com/go/flashplayer_roadmap/.

While web browser technology (as seen in Chrome, Firefox, Safari, Opera, and Internet Explorer 10) is evolving to provide web professionals with more choices in what technology is used to create content for the browser, Flash Player still holds a strong place in this environment and the two sets of technologies will work together to expand the Web, just as they have done for the past 15+ years.

Mobile deployment

Perhaps the single largest driving factor in the rapid evolution of core web technologies over the past two years has been the prevalence of advanced browsers on mobile devices. Due to the fact that mobile computing is still so new, users are not coming into this environment with old technology. This enables browser makers and device manufacturers to bundle web browsers with these systems that take full advantage of HTML5, CSS3, and advanced JavaScript rendering engines.

Most mobile browsers are based upon the open source WebKit [http://www.webkit.org/] rendering engine. Couple this with the fact that prominent desktop browsers such as Google Chrome and Apple Safari also use WebKit for their rendering engines and we have a widely adopted baseline to lean upon when developing experiences using newer technologies.

 Note that WebKit is the rendering engine for the actual Edge Animate application environment, offering a true WYSIWYG experience during composition authoring. WebKit is also used in integrated runtimes such as Adobe AIR, furthering the reach of this popular HTML rendering codebase.

What can Adobe Edge Animate be used for?

Generally, Edge Animate can be used to create many of the same types of animations and interactions that we would have expected Flash Player to handle on the Web in the mid to late 1990s.

This includes the movement of visual objects across the stage and basic mouse interactions.

Web animation

Edge Animate uses an all-new timeline for producing motion which borrows a lot from other applications such as Adobe After Effects. Through the use of keyframes along the timeline, designers have very fine-grained control over many object properties and can easily enable easing algorithms, which provide an additional flair to animated content. Edge Animate offers a unique approach to creating and accessing page level elements, their properties, and animating them on the timeline.

Interactive content

Edge Animate is not just about making things move. The Edge Animate Runtime also includes a robust API to enable interactivity through mouse, touch, and time-based actions. These interactive commands can be applied to individual, visible objects upon the stage, or used along the timeline in the form of triggers. Interactivity can modify aspects of the stage timeline, modify the properties of other objects within an Edge Animate project, or even invoke calls to content outside of the project.

Is Adobe Edge Animate for me?

While this book will often make reference to other applications such as Flash Professional or After Effects, you will not need to have prior experiences with these applications to get the most out of Edge Animate. So long as you understand the basics of HTML, CSS, and JavaScript—and have a desire to learn a worthwhile motion and interaction tool which targets these standards, then you should be all set!

Let's get started!

We have now taken a look at some ways in which the Web landscape is changing, specifically when talking about the roles of the primary technologies used to create motion and interactive design in the browser. The content produced by Edge Animate would only have been possible using Flash Player in years past. HTML, CSS, and JavaScript have advanced to the point that this sort of content can now be produced using core web technologies. At the same time, Adobe Flash Player and the wider Flash Platform have expanded beyond these roles. We've also had a high level view of Adobe Edge Animate and some of the content types which are enabled through use of this authoring tool.

Throughout this book, we'll be taking a complete look at the Animate application interface, demonstrate how to create and import project assets, and use those assets in the creation of compositions which feature advanced motion and interactivity using web standards.

What this book covers

Chapter 1, Introducing Adobe Edge Animate, provides a comprehensive overview of the entire Edge Animate application interface. This overview includes a look at the panels, tools, menus, and other application elements we will need to familiarize ourselves with when using Animate.

Chapter 2, Drawing and Adjusting Composition Elements, delves into the drawing tools contained within the Animate application to allow the creation of simple rectangular elements and assorted other objects.

Chapter 3, Selecting and Transforming Elements, provides a look at the Selection and Transform tools, their uses, and unique attributes. We also have a good overview of the Properties panel and its use across element types.

Chapter 4, Using Text and Web Fonts, demonstrates the creation of text elements within an Edge Animate project and provides detailed examples of using web fonts for even more expressive textual content.

Chapter 5, Importing External Assets, will show how to import and use an abundance of external assets within our Edge Animate compositions.

Chapter 6, Creating Motion Through the Timeline, demonstrates how simple it is to build a composition which involves a number of animated elements and presents a unique toolset for dealing with motion on the Web.

Chapter 7, Interactivity with Actions, Triggers, and Labels, will expand upon the motion-based topics of the previous chapter through the addition of interactive elements within an Edge Animate project. We'll also have a look at some of the more complex uses of the Adobe Edge Animate Runtime APIs.

Chapter 8, Making Use of Symbols, Nested Elements, and Grouping, provides a deep analysis of the powerful Symbol architecture within Edge Animate and demonstrates a variety of uses for Symbol instances. We also take a look at nested elements and provide some example projects.

Chapter 9, Advanced Animation Techniques, delves into the world of clipping, sprite sheets, and image sequences in extending much of the core motion functionality through the use of external assets and additional techniques.

Chapter 10, Publishing Edge Animate Compositions, examines the many options available to us when preparing and publishing an Edge Animate composition for the Web or other supported targets.

Chapter 11, Further Explorations with Adobe Edge Animate, contains many techniques which are either too general in nature, or are too expansive to fit within any of the other chapters.

What you need for this book

To use this book effectively, you will need to acquire Adobe Edge Animate from Adobe. Edge Animate is available with a subscription to the Creative Cloud service.

Adobe Edge Animate can be acquired from `http://html.adobe.com/edge/animate`.

Who this book is for

This book is for anyone who wants to get started using Adobe Edge Animate to create engaging, interactive content for the Web. It isn't necessary that you have any prior knowledge of website or motion design.

Conventions

In this book, you will find a number of styles of text that distinguish between different kinds of information. Here are some examples of these styles, and an explanation of their meaning.

Code words in text are shown as follows: "These elements will default to a `<div>` HTML element, but can be changed to employ the following HTML elements instead."

A block of code is set as follows:

```
(function(symbolName) {
Symbol.bindElementAction(compId, symbolName, "${_fvm001}",
"mouseover", function(sym, e) {
// Change an Element's contents.
//  (sym.$("name") resolves an Edge element name to a DOM
//  element that can be used with jQuery)
sym.$("Info").html("August (2000)");
});
```

When we wish to draw your attention to a particular part of a code block, the relevant lines or items are set in bold:

```
Symbol.bindElementAction(compId, symbolName, "${_Rectangle}",
"mousedown", function(sym, e) {
sym.playReverse();
// insert code for mousedown here
});
//Edge binding end
```

New terms and **important words** are shown in bold. Words that you see on the screen, in menus or dialog boxes for example, appear in the text like this: "The first option is to simply click on **Create New** on the welcome screen".

 Warnings or important notes appear in a box like this.

 Tips and tricks appear like this.

Reader feedback

Feedback from our readers is always welcome. Let us know what you think about this book—what you liked or may have disliked. Reader feedback is important for us to develop titles that you really get the most out of.

To send us general feedback, simply send an e-mail to feedback@packtpub.com, and mention the book title through the subject of your message.

If there is a topic that you have expertise in and you are interested in either writing or contributing to a book, see our author guide on www.packtpub.com/authors.

Customer support

Now that you are the proud owner of a Packt book, we have a number of things to help you to get the most from your purchase.

Downloading the example code

You can download the example code files for all Packt books you have purchased from your account at http://www.packtpub.com. If you purchased this book elsewhere, you can visit http://www.packtpub.com/support and register to have the files e-mailed directly to you.

Errata

Although we have taken every care to ensure the accuracy of our content, mistakes do happen. If you find a mistake in one of our books—maybe a mistake in the text or the code—we would be grateful if you would report this to us. By doing so, you can save other readers from frustration and help us improve subsequent versions of this book. If you find any errata, please report them by visiting http://www.packtpub.com/support, selecting your book, clicking on the errata submission form link, and entering the details of your errata. Once your errata are verified, your submission will be accepted and the errata will be uploaded to our website, or added to any list of existing errata, under the Errata section of that title.

Piracy

Piracy of copyright material on the Internet is an ongoing problem across all media. At Packt, we take the protection of our copyright and licenses very seriously. If you come across any illegal copies of our works, in any form, on the Internet, please provide us with the location address or website name immediately so that we can pursue a remedy.

Please contact us at copyright@packtpub.com with a link to the suspected pirated material.

We appreciate your help in protecting our authors, and our ability to bring you valuable content.

Questions

You can contact us at questions@packtpub.com if you are having a problem with any aspect of the book, and we will do our best to address it.

1
Introducing Adobe Edge Animate

This chapter will delve into Adobe Edge Animate, concentrating on the history of the Edge Animate project, looking at the technologies behind Edge Animate, comparing Edge Animate with Flash Professional (as the two applications share many similarities), providing a full overview of many Edge Animate application interface features, and finally taking a brief look at the Edge Animate welcome screen and how to create a new project.

Adobe Edge Animate boasts a modern, designer-friendly user interface that should be somewhat familiar to long-time users of the Adobe Creative Suite applications. We will run through each aspect of the interface including the following options:

- Interface features
- Application menus
- The toolbar
- Stage
- Timeline
- Edge Animate panels

After processing the information presented here, we should have a clear understanding of the interface as a whole and also the usefulness of its individual aspects.

The history of Adobe Edge Animate

During the Adobe MAX 2010 conference in Los Angeles, California, Adobe engineers got on stage in front of over 5000 attendees to present a software prototype built in Adobe AIR. This software allowed a user to adjust the properties of imported assets in a way very similar to the workflow of Flash Professional, but instead of outputting to SWF to target the Flash Player, the Adobe Edge Prototype actually output content to HTML, CSS, and JavaScript for playback in a web browser, without the need for any additional plugins.

 Adobe AIR is a solution for creating desktop and mobile applications built on Flash Platform technology. Many Adobe products are built using AIR, including the new touch applications for use on tablets and Adobe Muse. Visit http://www.adobe.com/products/air.html.

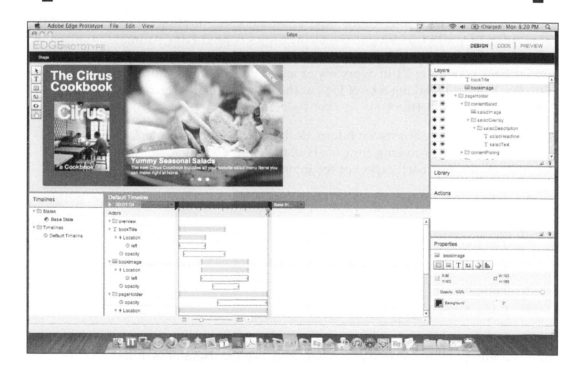

While the Edge Prototype certainly appeared very different from what we know today as **Adobe Edge Animate**, MAX attendees went wild over the prospects of such a tool. This was the first glimpse of what would eventually become the product we know today as Adobe Edge Animate. Since that time, Adobe has released periodic updates to the Adobe Edge Preview releases on Adobe Labs, with the intent to gather user feedback early and often in order to make the product conform to user expectations and become a useful addition to the Creative Suite.

With Adobe's long history of motion and interactivity in products such as Director, After Effects, and Flash Professional, Edge Animate has an excellent lineage behind it, and while creating content like this which targets HTML is quite new, the tools and techniques for authoring this material comes to us along a well-tread path.

The inner workings of Edge Animate

Adobe Edge Animate relies heavily on three related technologies: HTML5, CSS3, and JavaScript. The default doctype for Edge Animate created projects is HTML5; all the 2D transforms, translate(), rotate(),scale(), and skew() for example, are rendered as CSS3 (for modern browsers). There are also specific JavaScript libraries that play an essential role in making all of this work together. These include jQuery and the Adobe Edge Animate Runtime.

In order for Edge Animate content to work successfully, all of these components must be in their correct place and there are certain files which should not be edited once generated by the application. The Edge Animate application itself also requires a .an file type to be present in order to author and edit a project.

 Any .html file can also be opened up within Edge Animate and be worked upon. A .an file and associated imports will be created upon save and publication.

HTML, CSS, and JavaScript

Edge Animate primarily targets HTML for display, supported by both CSS and JavaScript. Why? Well, the fact of the matter is these technologies have finally become capable of handling rich motion and interactive content and as these are the core technologies of the Web, it makes sense to use them whenever we can.

Let's take a quick look at these three specifications in light of their primary function on the Web and relation to one another.

HTML

Hyper Text Markup Language (HTML) is the core of the Web. With the HTML5 specification (still in draft), we not only have an organic evolution of the language through additional semantic tags, but also a new set of APIs that can allow elements within the documents to be greatly influenced through JavaScript.

CSS

Cascading Style Sheets (CSS) determine to a great extent how a website is visually structured and designed. With the CSS3 specification (still in draft), designers can still use these specifications in all modern browsers to influence the way certain elements behave.

JavaScript

The **JavaScript** language is a superset of **ECMAScript (ECMA-262) Edition 3**, formalized by ECMA International, a worldwide standards body. The latest version of the language is JavaScript 1.8.5 but the real improvements in recent years have come from the browser manufacturers themselves, as they seek to improve JavaScript execution through the development of faster JavaScript engines.

So when we look into an HTML document produced by Edge Animate, we see the following code:

```
<div id="Stage" class="EDGE-1632861112">
  </div>
```

This is the stage symbol element within which all other elements are injected upon runtime, through the use of JavaScript libraries.

 This may be the only HTML element you will ever see produced by Edge Animate. Everything else is handled via JSON objects and specialized JavaScript includes(features). There is an option to render other elements as static HTML, but that is optional.

How jQuery is used in Edge Animate

It is no exaggeration to state that jQuery is the most popular JavaScript framework in use today. Many similar JavaScript frameworks arose in 2007 with the emergence of **Asynchronous JavaScript and XML (AJAX)** and more dynamic HTML data transfer methods. At one point, there were over 250 of these frameworks, but with the passing of time, only a handful remain in active development.

As stated on the project website,

> *jQuery is a fast and concise JavaScript Library that simplifies HTML document traversing, event handling, animating, and Ajax interactions for rapid web development.*

In a nutshell, jQuery aims to make using JavaScript more accessible to non-programmers or those who are not familiar with the language, make it more consistent across browsers, and more powerful in its simplicity. Documentation for jQuery can be found online at `http://docs.jquery.com/`.

Adobe Edge Animate leverages jQuery and builds upon it within the Adobe Edge Animate Runtime and also makes use of the jQuery easing library when dealing with motion. When opening any HTML document generated by Edge Animate, we can see these includes in the head of our published document through the library preloader:

```
<!DOCTYPE html>
<html>
<head>
  <meta http-equiv="Content-Type" content="text/html; charset=utf-8">
  <meta http-equiv="X-UA-Compatible" content="IE=Edge"/>
  <title>AnimateProject</title>
<!--Adobe Edge Runtime-->
    <script type="text/javascript" charset="utf-8"
src="AnimateProject_edgePreload.js"></script>
    <style>
        .edgeLoad-EDGE-1159339764 { visibility:hidden; }
    </style>
<!--Adobe Edge Runtime End-->

</head>
<body style="margin:0;padding:0;">
    <div id="Stage" class="EDGE-1159339764">
    </div>
</body>
</html>
```

 Other Adobe products, such as Adobe Dreamweaver, also make heavy use of jQuery. In fact, Adobe actively contributes back to the jQuery and jQuery Mobile libraries.

JSON

JavaScript Object Notation (JSON) is a data-interchange format used to exchange data from one system to another. Over the past few years, it has been adopted by a variety of languages and systems for both data transmission and storage. In some ways, it is very similar to XML. Unlike XML, JSON is not a markup language but rather stores data in objects and structures represented in name/value pairs.

Edge Animate uses JSON to store element definitions and attributes with a project. For example, the following JSON fragment represents a rectangle on the Stage:

```
content: {
  dom: [
    {
    id:'Rectangle',
    type:'rect',
    rect:['25px','40px','211px','147px','auto','auto'],
    fill:["rgba(192,192,192,1)"],
    stroke:[0,"rgba(0,0,0,1)","none"]
    }],
  symbolInstances: [
  ]
  }
```

To learn more about JSON, visit `http://www.json.org/`.

The Adobe Edge Animate Runtime

The set of JavaScript libraries used in an Edge Animate project is collectively referred to as the **Adobe Edge Animate Runtime**. Normally, when we think of a runtime, we are talking about a piece of software like Adobe Flash Player, the **Adobe Integrated Runtime (AIR)**, or the **Java Runtime Environment**. These are all self-contained pieces of software which enable the playback of applications and other content that targets these specific runtimes. The Adobe Edge Animate Runtime is very different in that it is a set of files that supports the content defined through the Adobe Edge Animate application, but even these libraries rely upon another piece of software for them to run properly: the web browser.

If you look within an HTML file produced by Edge Animate, you will see a JavaScript **include** that handles the runtime libraries included within the head of that document, as shown in the following code:

```
<!--Adobe Edge Runtime-->
    <script type="text/javascript" charset="utf-8"
src="AnimateProject_edgePreload.js"></script>
    <style>
        .edgeLoad-EDGE-1159339764 { visibility:hidden; }
    </style>
<!--Adobe Edge Runtime End-->
```

Adobe Edge Animate and Adobe Flash Professional

Many have called for the death of Flash Player since the 2010 letter *Thoughts on Flash* by the late Steve Jobs of Apple, Inc. It has always seemed a foolish proposition; HTML is the standard and Flash Player is the mechanism which is able to push beyond that standard. Both technologies were never meant to be in competition with one another, but should rather be thought of as complementary.

This is still the case today, even though HTML has, at this point, finally taken on some of the responsibilities that Flash Player has long been the bearer of. Flash has also evolved with recent versions of the runtime to focus on advanced video, console-quality gaming, and rich mobile applications through Adobe AIR.

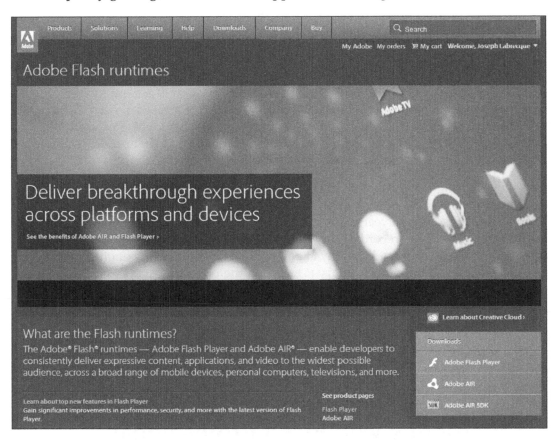

In terms of Edge Animate, we have a product that aims to take some of these tasks from Flash Player and make them truly cross-platform—even across operating systems that have no support for the browser-based Flash Player, such as Apple iOS or Windows Phone 7. The beauty of Edge Animate as an application is that it borrows much from the structures and paradigms that have been established by Flash Professional, making skills easily transferable from one application to another.

 While Adobe Flash Player has been made available for many Android devices, Adobe has made the decision to halt engineering efforts for the mobile Flash Player which runs in the browser. This does not impact the availability of the runtime upon existing supported devices, but does pose a challenge when considering upcoming hardware and operating system requirements.

Is Edge Animate a competing product to Flash Professional?

This depends upon the type of project we are working with. If we are looking to create a website landing page, rich menuing system, or advertisement, then yes, Edge Animate is definitely a competitor to Flash Professional. However, it is important to recall that Adobe produces many different tools that produce similar output; just look at Photoshop and Fireworks for an obvious examples of this.

When evaluating Edge Animate in comparison to Flash Professional, we must take into account how new Edge Animate and the concepts around it actually are. Flash Professional has over 15 years of history behind it. It is unrestrained by standards bodies and has a track-record of rapid innovation when pushing web-based content beyond what HTML is traditionally capable of. Flash Player also benefits from compiling to a self-contained binary (.swf) and the powerful ActionScript 3.0 programming language.

While Flash Professional and Edge Animate can do some things in a very similar way, and can produce similar output in terms of motion and basic interactivity, for anything that goes beyond what HTML and related technologies can handle upon their own, Flash-based content is still a powerful extension for console-quality games, advanced video solutions, and other specific use cases.

Comparisons with Flash Professional

With the expectation that many designers approaching Edge Animate will be coming to it with experience in Flash Professional, much of the tooling in Edge Animate shares both functional and naming conventions used in that application.

Stage

The **Stage** panel can be thought of as the canvas upon which we are able to paint our scenes, or the frame within which all our action takes place. The Stage panel in Edge Animate differs from this in Flash Professional, in the way that its dimensions are controlled and the background color is applied because in Edge Animate, the Stage is just another symbol.

Timeline

While Flash Professional and Edge Animate do share the concept of a Timeline, that is where the similarities end. The Flash Professional timeline is frame-based while Edge Animate includes a time-based timeline, similar to what is found in After Effects. In the end, these are just two ways of working with motion across time—in essence, this is what we are dealing with in either case.

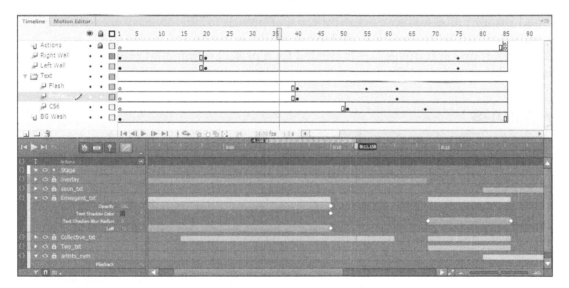

Keyframes

Both Flash Professional and Edge Animate give the user the ability to define keyframes across the project. Timeline **keyframes** are points of distinction which define or modify various properties of an element across time. This is the most basic way in which motion is achieved in either program. Keyframes in Edge Animate behave to a great degree like those from Adobe After Effects.

Labels

Labels are a mechanism by which we can mark up the Timeline at certain points. These can be used for both visual reference while authoring, or through code to navigate to certain areas of the Timeline based upon the label itself.

Symbols

Symbols are reusable assets whose instances can be used across a project. In Flash Professional, these may be **MovieClip**, **Button**, or **Graphics** symbols. In Edge Animate, there is no such distinction—though Edge Animate symbols are most similar to Flash **MovieClip** symbols in execution.

Library

Flash Professional organizes symbols, fonts, and assets within the project library. The **Library** panel takes an organizational approach to provide easy access to the symbols. With Edge Animate, we have a similar concept which also stores any symbols, fonts, and image assets created for a project within that project library, exposed through the **Library** panel.

Actions

Actions in Edge Animate can be compared with those in Flash Professional (Macromedia Flash 4). Each program has an **Actions** panel which can be opened and closed as needed to access simple program instructions. In Edge Animate, we can apply **Actions** to elements on the Stage, and to the Timeline through triggers. As we can see from the following screenshot, many of the panels present in Edge Animate are derived from those that exist in Flash Professional. This makes the transition simpler for Flash designers than it would otherwise be.

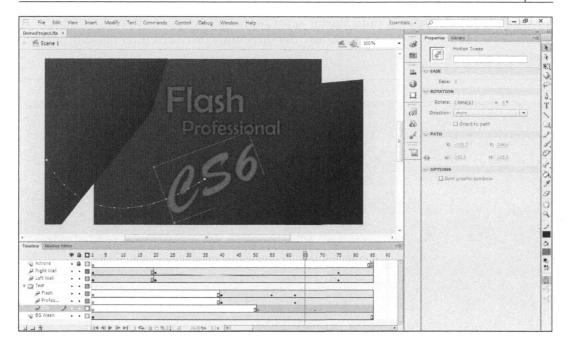

Installing Adobe Edge Animate and getting started

Before moving on, we'll want to be sure that Adobe Edge Animate is installed and running properly on our system. We'll also have a brief look at the Edge Animate interface and see how to create a new project.

Installing Edge Animate

To complete the demonstrations and examples included in this book, you'll need to acquire a copy of Adobe Edge Animate itself. Edge Animate 1.0 can be installed at no charge as part of a free Creative Cloud subscription.

To download Edge Animate with an existing subscription, you may use `http://creative.adobe.com/`.

To create a new Creative Could starter account free of charge, go to `http://html.adobe.com/edge/animate/` and follow the directions provided after clicking on the **Get Started** button.

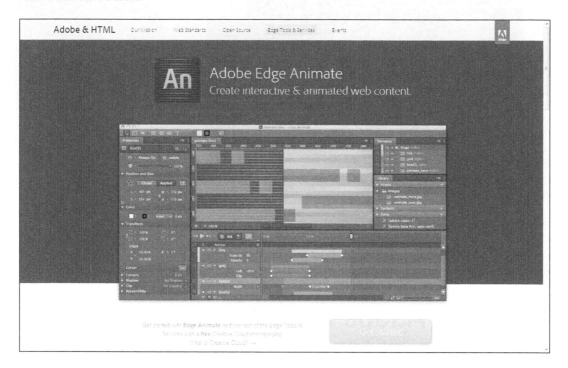

Adobe Edge Animate can be installed on the following systems:

- Microsoft Windows 7
- Apple Mac OS X [10.6]

 Installing Edge Animate on Microsoft Windows XP or Apple MAC OS X [10.5] is not supported in any way.

To download and install Edge Animate on a local computer, we must utilize the Adobe download manager available to us through the Creative Cloud.

1. Sign in to Creative Cloud through `https://creative.adobe.com/` and click on **Apps**. You will see the following window:

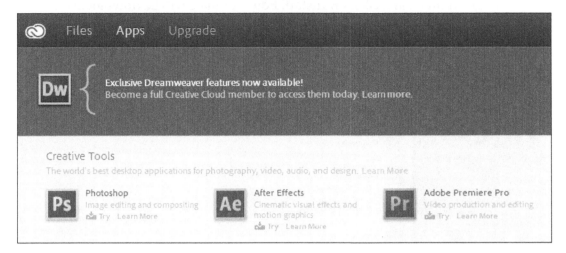

2. We will now be at the Apps screen. Scroll down to see **Edge Tools & Services** and locate the entry **Edge Animate**:

3. Click on **Download** and **Adobe Application Manager** will download and install to your local computer. Scroll down the list of applications to locate Edge Animate and click on **Install**. Edge Animate will be downloaded and installed automatically.

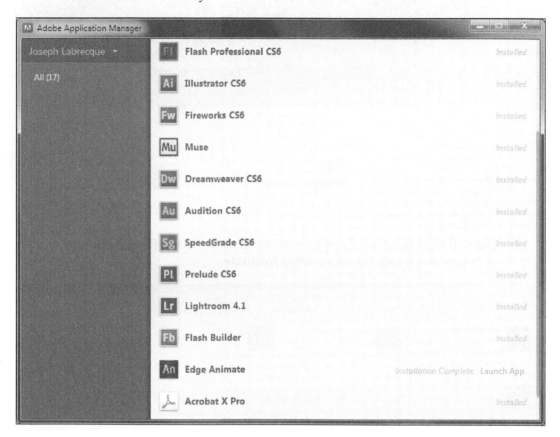

We are now ready to begin using Adobe Edge Animate. Locate the startup icon on your machine to run the application or simply click on **Launch App** from the download manager.

 Note that we can also download trials of many Creative Cloud applications through this same interface, if desired.

The Edge Animate welcome screen

When starting the Adobe Edge Animate application, we'll be presented with a welcome screen. This is very similar to the welcome screens available in other Adobe applications as it will present a number of options for us to get started using the product:

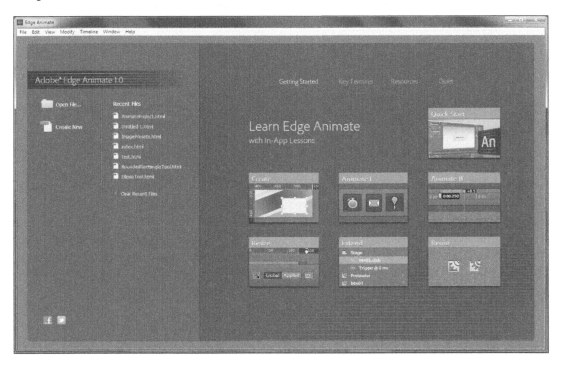

These options include the following:

- **Open File...**: When we choose this option, a dialog showing the local file system will be opened for us. This allows us to browse the file system to locate Edge Animate projects that are already under construction. Edge Animate documents have the file extension .an.

- **Create New**: This option will enable us to create a brand-new Edge Animate project. We will detail the specifications of this in the next topic.

- **Recent Files**: Any Edge Animate projects that were previously opened within the application will be listed here. Opening these projects is as simple as clicking upon the project name.

- **Clear Recent Files**: Choosing this option will clear the recent files list from both the welcome screen and the application menu.

- **Getting Started**: This area displays a number of lessons that can be accessed from within Edge Animate itself. Selecting any of these lessons will open the **Lessons** panel and allow us to step through a sample project, learning as we go.

- **Key Features**: This lists out a number of the features Edge Animate presents for our use and provides a link to the full release notes.

- **Resources**: This provides access to a number of online resources, including documentation, discussion forums, project samples, and more.

- **Quiet**: This option simply quiets the welcome screen and removes any items within this area from view.

- **Other Options**: The welcome screen also includes some social media buttons that allow users to connect with the Edge Animate team on Facebook and Twitter.

Creating a new Edge Animate project

There are two ways in which we can create a new Edge Animate project. The first option is to simply click on **Create New** on the welcome screen. This will immediately create a new Edge Animate project with a blank stage. The second method of creating a new Edge Animate project is through the file menu. Simply clicking on **File** and then on **New** will have the exact same effect.

 Alternatively, we can use the keyboard shortcut: *Ctrl + N* (for Windows) or *Command + N* (for Mac).

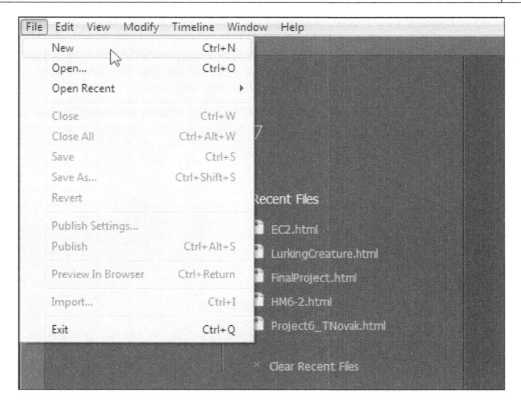

Whenever we create a new document, the width and height of the Stage will automatically be sized to the resolution of 550px in width by 400px in height.

Whichever method you choose, you will now have a new project opened within Edge Animate. This project will look quite scarce to begin with, as it basically consists of a single, blank Stage symbol. This Stage is representative of the single `<div>` HTML element we can locate within the HTML file that Edge Animate produces upon saving it, as shown in the following screenshot:

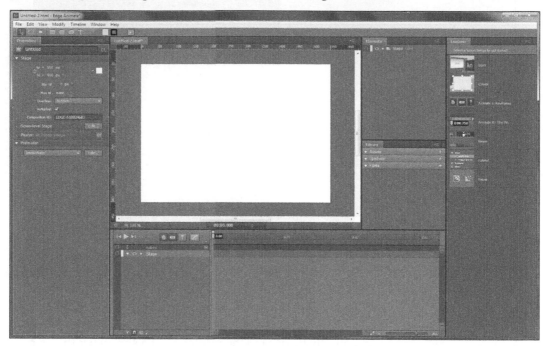

After our project has been created, the first order of business is to actually save the document. To save a document in Adobe Edge Animate, we can go to the **File** menu and choose either the **Save** or **Save As...** options.

Save

This option will either save the current document if it has been previously saved to the file system, or it will prompt the user to provide a filename and location to save the document if this happens to be a new project.

The keyboard shortcut for this option is *Ctrl + S* (for Windows) or *Command + S* (for Mac).

Save As...

Similar to the **Save** option, this provides the same functionality but will always prompt the user for a filename and location through a system dialog. This is useful when saving separate versions of the same project, or when you simply want to save the project to a new location.

The keyboard shortcut for this option is *Ctrl + Shift + S* (for Windows) or *Command + Shift + S* (for Mac).

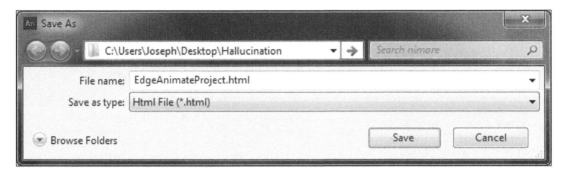

In the case of a new project, either option will provide us with a file system dialog. We see from the previous screenshot that what we are saving is, in actuality, a `.html` file. This is an important thing to remember about Edge Animate projects—when we are working in the Edge Animate authoring environment, we are really working in real time with the content that is being produced.

Downloading the example code

You can download the example code files for all Packt books you have purchased from your account at `http://www.packtpub.com`. If you purchased this book elsewhere, you can visit `http://www.packtpub.com/support` and register to have the files e-mailed directly to you.

File structure in the Edge Animate project

As soon as we save our Edge Animate project, a number of files are produced and included in the location we specified when naming the initial .html file. We'll have a look at each of these files, and what their specific purpose is within our project:

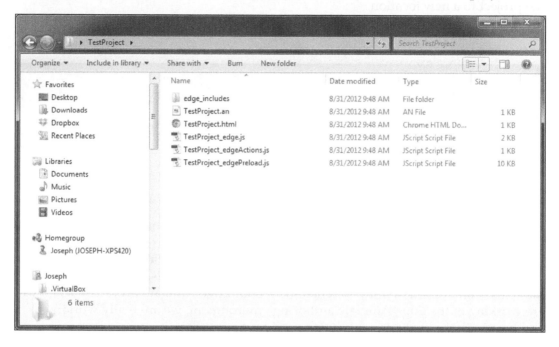

The files produced by Edge Animate include the following types (the project_name in the curly brackets represents the name of the project you use to save your work):

- {project_name}.an: The .an file produced along with the project simply preserves properties within the authoring environment. Examples of these properties include whether certain elements are twirled down through the **Elements** panel, specific colors, and fonts used in the project. This file allows environment settings to be preserved across sessions.

- {project_name}.html: This .html file serves many purposes. It is the file used within an Edge Animate project that serves to bind all of the Edge Animate Runtime and project-specific files together. This is also the file which is effectively opened within the authoring environment. Finally, running this file in a browser allows us to preview our full project.

- {project_name}_edge.js: This is actually a file containing all of the JSON structures associated with an Edge Animate project, along with some code which binds the Edge Animate Stage to a specified HTML element and initializes the runtime.

- `{project_name}_edgeActions.js`: This JavaScript file contains all the instances of actions defined within the Edge Animate application.

- `{project_name}_edgePreload.js`: This JavaScript file serves to load in all of the other files and bind them to the project upon runtime.

 In the pre-release versions of Edge Animate, the `.an` file was actually given the extension `.edge` — we may encounter compositions in this book or on the Web which use the older extension. Either can be opened within Edge Animate.

Edge includes

The `edge_includes` directory contains the jQuery and Adobe Edge Animate Runtime files necessary for this all to work correctly. None of the files within this directory should ever be modified manually.

- `jquery-{version}.min.js`: This is the minimized jQuery library packaged along with the Edge Animate Runtime

- `jquery.easing.{version}.js`: This is the minimized jQuery easing library packaged along with the Adobe Edge Animate Runtime

- `edge.{version}.min.js`: This is the minimized Adobe Edge Animate Runtime library

- `json2.js`: This is a helper file for older browsers

Application interface overview

Being primarily focused on motion and interactivity, the Edge Animate interface places a great emphasis upon modifying element properties over time. We will discover that the Edge Animate application configures many useful sections of the interface such as the Stage, Timeline, and **Properties** panels in plain view in order to make these tools readily available in our work.

The application window

Whether running Edge Animate on Windows or OS X, the application window will appear very similar across platforms. In many of Adobe's creative products, the windowing on OS X is very different than it is on Windows, as the desktop will actually show through the application — though this behavior can be toggled in recent versions as shown in the following screenshot:

With Adobe Edge Animate, the operating mode is the same across platforms — so while the reader will notice that most of the screenshots in this book feature the Windows version of Edge Animate, there should be very little difference when running the application on Mac OS X.

The application window itself is broken into a variety of separate modules. Most of these modules fall under the category of panels and can be toggled on and off, collapsed, combined with other panels, or anchored to different areas of the application window. Most of these actions are done through mouse actions and dragging.

Customizing the Edge Animate panel layout

Any panel in Edge Animate can be anchored to the application window or can be made to float within a small utility window. Floating panels are useful if placing them across different monitors on a full workstation, whereas docking these panels can preserve space on a smaller laptop display, as you can see in the following screenshot:

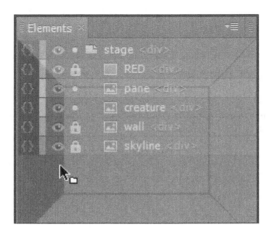

To tear a panel out of the main application window and create a floating panel, simply click upon the grippes next to an anchored panel's name. While the mouse button remains pressed, pull the panel from its present location. We will see the panel has now changed state. Have a look at the following screenshot:

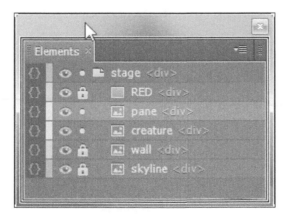

At this point, as we move our cursor amongst other interface elements, we will see a grid appear from time to time with portions of the grid highlighted in a violet color. This color indicates that the panel may be dropped in this location to be anchored in that particular position. Release the mouse button to dock the panel, or when there is no highlighted portion of the grid to allow the panel to remain in a floating state.

> Dragging a panel totally off the application window and releasing it will ensure that we create a floating panel.

Managing workspaces

In a similar fashion to other Creative Suite applications, Edge Animate provides the ability to customize the workspace and preserve a variety of these customizations through the concept of application workspaces.

The ability to easily switch between different workspaces is useful when moving between the layout, animation, and interactivity portions of a project, as the relevant panels and other interface structures can be given more prominence, and those which are not needed for certain tasks can be either dismissed or placed in a smaller role.

To create a new workspace, we will perform the following actions:

1. First locate the **Workspace** selection option within the **Window** application menu. Click on it to reveal the drop-down choices as shown in the following screenshot:

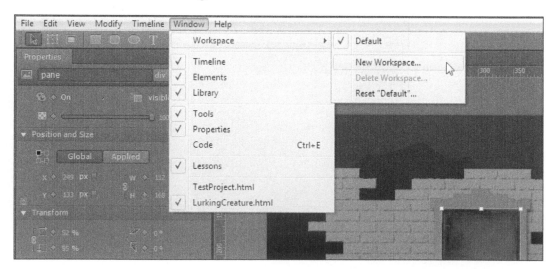

2. Select **New Workspace** and provide a name for your custom workspace in the **Name** field. Select **OK** once you are finished:

3. To verify that your workspace has been saved, return to the **Workspace** drop-down menu and click on it once again. Your new workspace will appear in the list of choices. Switching between this and other workspaces is now as simple as performing a quick selection using this drop-down control:

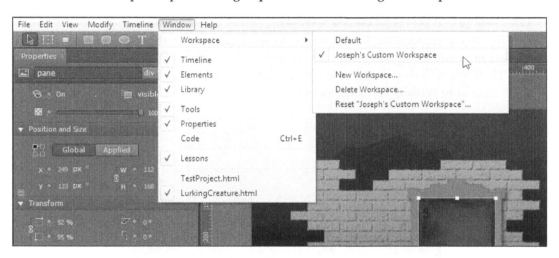

We have a few other options for managing our workspaces aside from **New Workspace**. We also have **Delete Workspace,** which deletes the currently selected workspace from memory. In the case that while working, we have modified our workspace to assist with any specific task, it is useful to be able to reset the workspace to its default configuration. To reset a workspace that has been modified, simply choose the **Reset "Default"...** option (the workspace you are working on will be mentioned in this option instead of default workspace). This allows us to quickly revert to our saved workspace instead of manually moving things back to how they were.

The Edge Animate application menu

Most computer programs have a standard menu system that includes choices such as **File**, **Edit**, and **View**, along with a variety of application-specific choices. Edge Animate is no different in this regard, as you can see in the following screenshot:

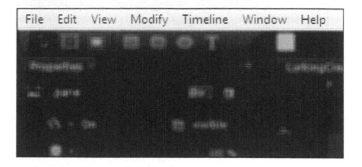

The Edge Animate toolbar

The Edge Animate toolbar, by default, is located along the top left-hand side of the application window and contains an assortment of tools used when interacting with Stage. Here we will discover a selection tool, vector element creation tools, and a text tool for working within the Stage panel, as shown in the following screenshot:

Stage

The Stage panel in an Edge Animate project is the fundamental starting point of our element structure. Any additional elements created or imported will reside within and be animated upon this Stage. The following screenshot shows you the Stage panel:

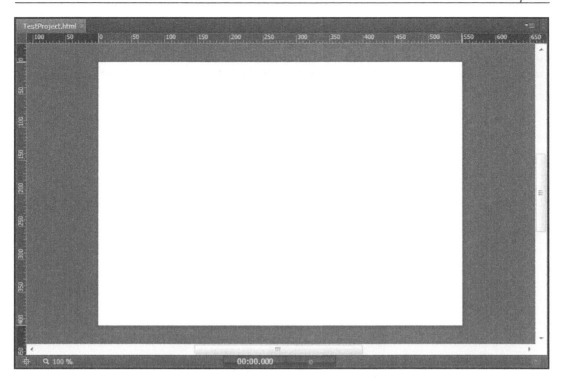

Stage itself is actually just another symbol within Edge Animate. The element which represents Stage is the only HTML element which can be seen when viewing the source code of the `.html` file produced by Edge Animate. Refer to the following code:

```
<!DOCTYPE html>
<html>
<head>
    <meta http-equiv="Content-Type" content="text/html;
charset=utf-8">
    <meta http-equiv="X-UA-Compatible" content="IE=Edge"/>
    <title>AnimateProject</title>
<!--Adobe Edge Runtime-->
    <script type="text/javascript" charset="utf-8"
src="AnimateProject_edgePreload.js"></script>
    <style>
        .edgeLoad-EDGE-1159339764 { visibility:hidden; }
    </style>
<!--Adobe Edge Runtime End-->
</head>
<body style="margin:0;padding:0;">
    <div id="Stage" class="EDGE-1159339764">
    </div>
</body>
</html>
```

The Stage element for any particular Edge Animate project will always have a unique `class` attribute called **Composition ID,** which is bound to JavaScript functionality contained within the project's main JavaScript file. In the case of the previous code, the `class` value is **EDGE-1159339764** and the JavaScript file preloader is `AnimateProject_edgePreload.js`:

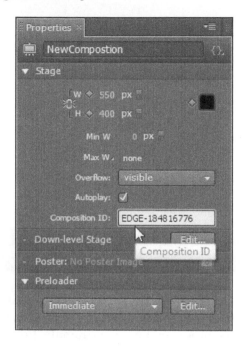

 Composition ID is editable from within the contextual properties panel.

 Users coming to Edge Animate from Flash Professional will undoubtedly notice some similarities here, as Flash Professional also has the concept of a stage.

Though there are many differences between the two types, in Edge Animate, the Stage is much more easily controlled through the motion engine, allowing us to resize or change the background color at will. In Flash Professional, the Stage is much more static. For instance, the background color cannot be animated in any such way.

Timeline

The **Timeline** feature in Edge Animate defines the various elements that are at play over time and exposes changes related to these elements in a visual way. The Edge Animate Timeline is robust, yet simple to use. It inherits many of its attributes and behaviors from other applications such as After Effects and Flash Professional—yet it makes a good attempt to refine these concepts as well, as shown in the following screenshot:

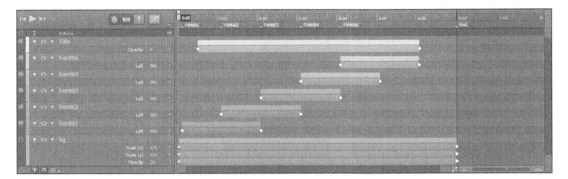

Panels in Edge Animate

For those familiar with other applications in the Adobe Creative Suite, the concept of panels will be quite familiar. As an example, here we see panels as implemented in what is perhaps one of the most popular applications in the Creative Suite: Photoshop.

Panels are defined sets of functionality exposed through the application **graphical user interface** (**GUI**). Generally, the panels in Adobe Edge Animate can be closed, combined, moved, resized, and collapsed as needed. Any panels which are not present in a particular workspace configuration, can be opened through the commands in the **Window** menu.

To maximize any panel in Edge Animate, simply click on the panel option icon in the upper-right corner of the panel in question and choose **Maximize Frame** as shown in the following screenshot:

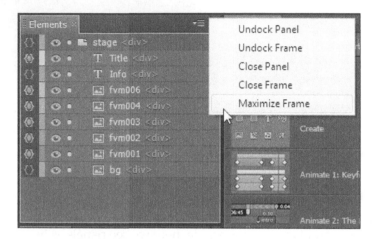

Once a panel has had its frame maximized, the workspace layout can be easily restored by clicking on the panel option icon in the upper-right corner and choosing **Restore Frame Size**.

Lessons

When starting out with Adobe Edge Animate, we can get a jump start by accessing tutorials within the **Lessons** panel. This panel displays a set of common scenarios dealing with symbols, animation, interactivity, and so on. Each lesson will step the user through a series of actions and provide a full set of example files as well.

 The **Lessons** panel can be accessed or dismissed through the application menu by selecting **Window** | **Lessons**.

Elements

The **Elements** panel is a representation of all the HTML elements included as part of our Edge Animate project. Every element is always nested within the Stage and elements like this, which contain sub-elements can be twirled down to expose those elements. We may also toggle visibility of particular elements by toggling the eye icon on and off, as well as the lock icon.

When an element is locked, Edge Animate will prevent us from modifying the properties of that particular element. Refer to the following screenshot:

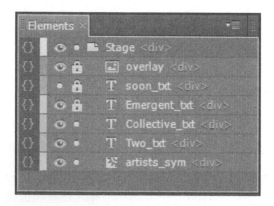

 To reorder elements, we can drag-and-drop individual elements within the **Elements** panel. This will effectively modify the z-index of each element accordingly.

When editing HTML content that was *not* produced in Edge Animate, a small `</>` HTML element next to certain elements indicates that those elements would be limited in what we can do through Edge Animate. We will never see this indicator when dealing with compositions created entirely in Edge Animate.

Library

The **Library** panel includes a listing of imported **Assets**, such as bitmap and SVG images, and also a list of symbols in the **Symbols** menu that have been created within Edge Animate, and font definitions in the **Fonts** menu, which can be employed through text elements. The first two of these elements are added to the **Library** panel once they are included within an Edge Animate project, and can be added to the Stage from this panel. The font definitions are added through this interface and then referenced through **Text** elements within the **Properties** panel. Refer to the following screenshot:

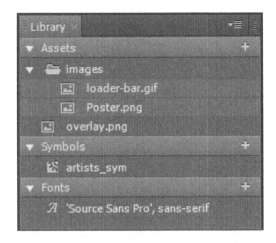

By clicking on the plus button attributed to either category, we can either add new **Assets** through a file browse dialog or create a new symbol from selected elements. Web fonts can also be defined in the **Fonts** menu through the **Library** panel in this manner.

Properties

The contextual properties panel (**Properties** panel, herein) is one of the most important panels within Edge Animate, as this is where all of the properties of an element can be modified. The properties available to us will depend upon the element which has been selected. For instance, the Stage will have very few properties in comparison to a rectangle or text element.

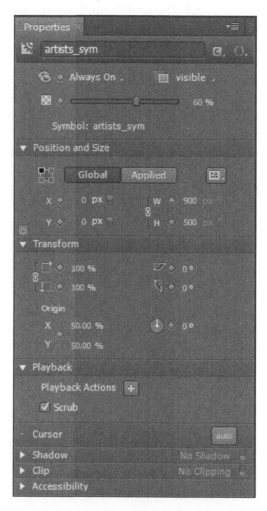

Many of the Adobe Creative Suite applications include the concept of a properties panel. Applications such as Flash Professional, which have been inherited from Macromedia, normally feature this panel quite prominently among the various application panels.

Actions

The **Actions** panel in Edge Animate allows us to insert small bits of JavaScript code into our compositions. This code comes in the form of triggers (in **Triggers**), events (in **Events**), and actions (in **Actions**). The basic idea is that we are either able to write JavaScript here which conforms to the Edge Animate Runtime API, or we can alternatively employ the buttons along the left-hand side of the panel to insert preconfigured bits of code onto an element, as shown in the following screenshot:

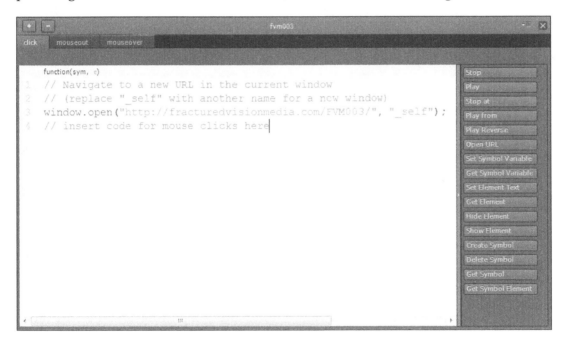

 Depending upon whether we are inserting code along the Timeline as a trigger or upon an element or Small symbol as an event, determines the options available for us in the options stack.

The **Actions** panel in Edge Animate functions very closely to the early actions panels in Flash Professional. For comparison, in the following screenshot we can see how the **Actions** panel in Flash Professional appears. Again, the engineers working on Edge Animate have gone to great lengths to make users of Flash Professional feel comfortable within this new environment.

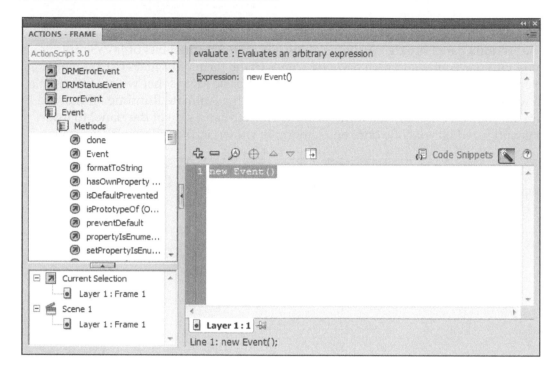

Code

The **Code** panel serves a number of useful functions within Edge Animate. Truly, anything we can do within the **Actions** panel can also be done within the **Code** panel—so there is some replication of functionality here. What makes this panel unique is that it provides us with a view of the entire composition and the code bits scattered throughout in one place.

For those familiar with Flash Professional, this is a lot like the Movie Explorer in that application, though the presentation here is much more useful as we do not have to click down through a number of objects and filters to get to each individual piece. We will notice many small things like this in Edge Animate which are improvements over ideas and workflow options present within older Adobe products. This is a good thing. Embrace it!

Adobe Edge Animate keyboard shortcuts

Edge Animate ships with a defined set of keyboard shortcuts to help us work more quickly within the application. Many of these shortcuts can be seen within the various contextual menus that can be accessed upon various elements or through the application menu. These shortcuts range from the standard copy and paste, to specialized Edge Animate commands to toggle the pin or paste actions.

Keyboard Shortcuts dialog

To access the **Keyboard Shortcuts** dialog, from the application menu, choose **Edit | Keyboard Shortcuts…** and the dialog window will appear:

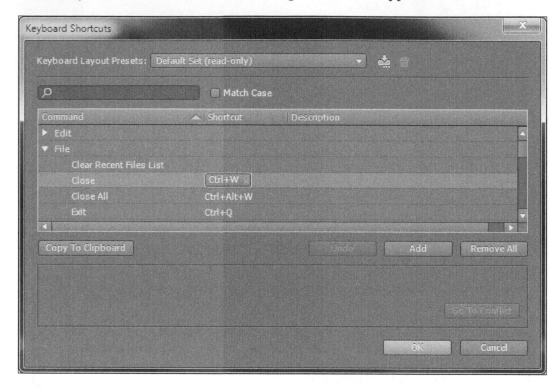

From this dialog, we can review all of the assigned shortcuts in the application, or even customize them to create our own set. Custom presets are stored as XML upon the local hard drive. The dialog also supplies us with a filter and the ability to copy all keyboard shortcuts to the system clipboard in order to paste them into a text editor or some other document in order to more easily recall them when learning the application.

Adobe Edge Animate menu items

We will have a look at some of the general project options available to us from the Edge Animate application menu and provide a brief overview of the function of each option. Menu options specific to certain other Edge Animate features will be introduced along with the feature or tool itself in later chapters.

File

The **File** menu option provides a number of options for working with Edge Animate files themselves:

Command	Description
New	This creates a new, blank project.
Open...	This opens a previously saved project.
Open Recent	This provides a list of recently opened projects that a user can select from. Selecting one of these projects will load it into Edge Animate, similar to the **Open** command.
Close	This command will close the current Edge Animate project, prompting the user to save the document first, through an application alert window.
Close All	This closes all projects which are currently open. Similar to the **Close** command, a dialog box requesting the uscr to save each project will appear in a sequence.
Save	This command saves the current project. It is only valid for previously saved projects.
Save As...	This opens a browse dialog prompting the user to provide a project filename and location to save the Edge Animate project. Previously unsaved projects are required to use this command.
Revert	This reverts an opened and modified Edge Animate project to its last saved state.
Publish Settings...	This allows access to specify the settings with which to publish an Edge Animate composition.
Publish	This performs a publish operation which adheres to the settings specified in **Publish Settings....** It also optimizes the composition for distribution.
Preview In Browser	While it is possible to preview certain things within the Edge Animate application itself, as projects become more complex, we will want to be sure and run them within a true browser environment. This command will launch a browser and load in the current project automatically.
Import...	This allows the import of `.png`, `.gif`, `.jpg`, and `.svg` files into a project. These imported files will appear in the project library and upon Stage.
Exit	This closes the entire application. If there are any unsaved projects open, Edge Animate will prompt the user to save the document first, through an application alert window.

Window

The **Window** menu provides the ability for an Edge Animate user to toggle various application panels on and off. Certain panels are off by default, and turning them on here will allow us to anchor them to the application window, or otherwise position them as floating panels. We are also given access here to workspace management commands.

Command	Description
Workspace	This provides a number of commands for managing Edge Animate workspaces.
Workspace | Default (also listed are any defined workspaces)	These are simply quick access commands to switch between defined workspaces.
Workspace | New Workspace	This command will save the current application window configuration as a named workspace for later recall.
Workspace | Delete Workspace	This deletes the currently selected workspace from application memory.
Workspace | Reset "Default"... (if there are any previously defined workspaces, they are also listed)	This command allows us to quickly revert to our saved workspace to its saved state.
Timeline	This toggles Timeline within the Edge Animate application window.
Elements	This toggles the **Elements** panel within the Edge Animate application window.
Library	This toggles the **Library** panel within the Edge Animate application window.
Tools	This toggles the **Tools** panel within the Edge Animate application window.
Properties	This toggles the **Properties** panel within the Edge Animate application window.
Code	This toggles the **Code** panel off and on.
Lessons	This toggles the **Lessons** panel off and on.

Help

The **Help** menu item contains information about Edge Animate as a product, and links to read about the APIs which exist when interacting with the runtime through JavaScript. The following table shows the various commands in this menu:

Command	Description
Edge Animate Help...	This opens the Edge Animate help pages in an Internet-connected web browser.
Edge Animate JavaScript API...	This provides an overview of the Adobe Edge Animate Runtime API.
Edge Animate Community Forums	This is the direct link to the forums on Adobe.com.
Change Language...	This switches the application language.
Adobe Product Improvement Program...	This is an opt-in to allow the user to participate in improving the product through the collection of anonymous usage statistics.
About Adobe Edge Animate...	Selecting this command will bring up information about Edge Animate—including specific version information.

Summary

In this chapter, we had a look at the history behind the Adobe Edge Animate application from its beginnings as a basic prototype and have looked into a number of the standard web technologies used by Edge Animate projects. We also discussed Edge Animate in relation to Flash Professional and many of the similarities between the two programs. If you are used to Flash Professional, picking up Edge Animate should be relatively simple! We also took a brief look at Edge Animate, including how to install the program, the options available to us using the Edge Animate welcome screen, and how to quickly create a new Edge Animate project.

We should now also be familiar with all of the menus, panels, and other interface elements available to us in the Adobe Edge Animate application window. While we have touched upon some basic functionality here, the remaining bulk of this book will detail a variety of ways in which we can use Edge Animate to create a variety of standards-based projects that leverage motion and interactivity to produce rich, engaging content for the Web.

In the next chapter, we'll look specifically at the various tools available to us within Edge Animate that allow us to create basic elements through the internal drawing tools.

2
Drawing and Adjusting Composition Elements

In order to perform any sort of animation or interactivity in an Edge Animate composition, we'll need to either create or import the elements necessary for any particular project. Adobe Edge Animate includes a limited number of drawing tools which can be used to create elements within our composition.

In this chapter, we'll have a look at a few of the tools available to us in Edge Animate, including the following tools with the keyboard shortcuts in parentheses:

- The **Rectangle** tool (*M*)
- The **Rounded Rectangle** tool (*R*)
- The **Ellipse** tool (*O*)
- The **Selection** tool (*V*)
- **Rulers**
- **Guides**
- **Layout preferences**

We'll also go through some basic examples of using these tools, and see how to modify their properties within a composition.

Adobe Edge Animate drawing tools

Basic rectangular elements can be easily produced using either the **Rectangle** tool or the **Rounded Rectangle** tool. To create ellipses and circles, we can utilize the **Ellipse** tool as well. These elements can eventually be used within an animation, allow user interaction, or even be converted into Edge Animate symbols.

The drawing tools can be accessed through a series of icons within the Edge Animate toolbar. By default, the toolbar is positioned at the very top of the application window, directly below the application menu.

 It is possible to move the toolbar around as it is a panel, and therefore share all of the options and attributes of any panel within the Edge Animate application interface.

Background Color and Border Color

While not a drawing tool per se, this set of swatches located within the toolbar directly influences the colors used within the drawing tools. It provides quick access to both element background and border color selectors from the toolbar. Normally, this can also be modified through the **Properties** panel when an element has been selected, as shown in the following screenshot:

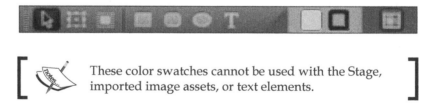

These color swatches cannot be used with the Stage, imported image assets, or text elements.

Rectangle tool

The **Rectangle** tool (*M*) shown in the following screenshot allows us to create rectangular elements upon the Stage, which can be animated through Timeline or have interactivity applied to them through the **Actions** panel. These elements will default to a `<div>` HTML element.

Rounded Rectangle tool

The **Rounded Rectangle** tool (R) shown in the following screenshot allows us to create rectangular elements with rounded corners upon the Stage, which can be animated through Timeline or have interactivity applied to them through the **Actions** panel. These elements will default to a `<div>` HTML element.

 The **Rounded Rectangle** tool behaves almost exactly like the **Rectangle** tool and elements produced with either tool are functionally identical.

Ellipse tool

The **Ellipse** tool (O) allows us to create both ellipses and circles upon the Stage, which can be animated through Timeline or have interactivity applied to them through the **Actions** panel. These elements will default to a `<div>` HTML element, as shown in the following screenshot:

 The **Ellipse** tool is located to the right-hand side of the **Rounded Rectangle** tool within the toolbar.

Drawing elements upon the Stage

Within Edge Animate, we are always working with browser **Document Object Model (DOM)** elements. The most basic elements in Edge Animate are ones that are produced through the application drawing tools—**Rectangle**, **Rounded Rectangle**, and **Ellipse**. Any of these will produce a basic element that has four sides and contains a background and stroke color.

The Selection tool

While we have reserved an entire chapter to discuss the **Selection** tool and **Transform** tool, it is necessary to mention the **Selection** tool here for the basic functionality it provides when dealing with the drawing tools. As shown in the following screenshot, it resembles an arrow in the left-most position in the toolbar:

The behavior of the drawing tools is such that when an element is created using any of the tools, the **Selection** tool will automatically activate, along with automatic selection of the element which has just been created. The reason for this is that it allows us to quickly modify the properties of an element without having to first choose another tool and then select the element manually. For more information on the **Selection** tool, have a look at *Chapter 3, Selecting and Transforming Elements*.

Working with the Rectangle tool

The **Rectangle** tool looks like a little rectangle in the toolbar. Selecting this tool allows us to create rectangular elements directly upon the Stage.

To create a new rectangle using this tool, we click on the Stage and drag the mouse across the area we wish the rectangle to appear over, finally releasing the mouse once we are finished:

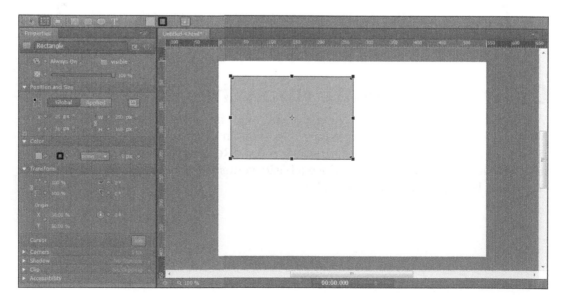

After a rectangle has been created, we can manipulate the small black diamonds at each corner (through use of the **Transform** tool) to form a rounded rectangle.

Using the Rectangle tool

To create a new element using the **Rectangle** tool, perform the following steps:

1. Create a new project and name it `RectangleTool.html`.

2. Select the **Rectangle** tool from the toolbar.

3. Hover over the Stage. Notice that the cursor now appears as a crosshair.

4. Click anywhere on the Stage and drag. Notice that as you do this, the rectangle will grow or shrink, depending upon how far you drag from your original point. When you are happy with the size of your rectangle element, release the mouse button to complete this task.

 Holding the *Shift* key while dragging will constrain a rectangular element to a square when using the **Rectangle** tool (*M*).

5. The **Selection** tool will automatically be activated for us and the rectangle element just created will be in a selected state. We can now modify the element that was just created through the **Properties** panel:

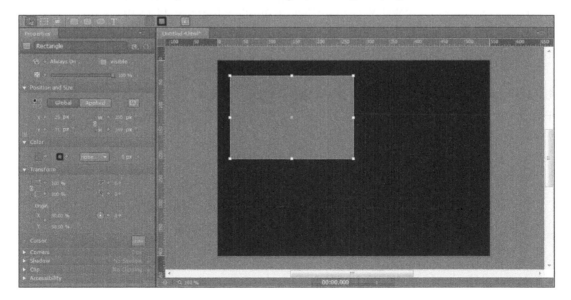

Working with the Rounded Rectangle tool

The **Rounded Rectangle** tool is almost identical to the **Rectangle** tool, except for the fact that it will retain the border radii settings from one instance to another as new rounded rectangles are created:

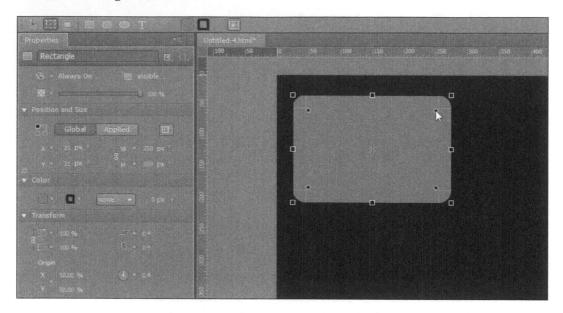

 As is the case with the **Rectangle** tool, after a rounded rectangle has been created, we can further manipulate the small black diamonds at each corner (through use of the **Transform** tool) to adjust the border radii.

Using the Rounded Rectangle tool

To create a new element using the **Rounded Rectangle** tool, perform the following steps:

1. Create a new project and name it RoundedRectangleTool.html.
2. Select the **Rounded Rectangle** tool from the toolbar.
3. Hover over the Stage. Notice that the cursor now appears as a crosshair.
4. Click anywhere on the Stage and drag. Notice that as you do this, the rounded rectangle will grow or shrink, depending upon how far you drag from your original point. When you are happy with the size of your rounded rectangle element, release the mouse button to complete this task.

Just as the case is with the **Rectangle** tool, holding the *Shift* key while dragging out a new rounded rectangle element will create a square instead of a rectangle.

5. The **Selection** tool will automatically be activated for us and the rectangle element just created will be in a selected state. We can now modify the element that was just created through the **Properties** panel:

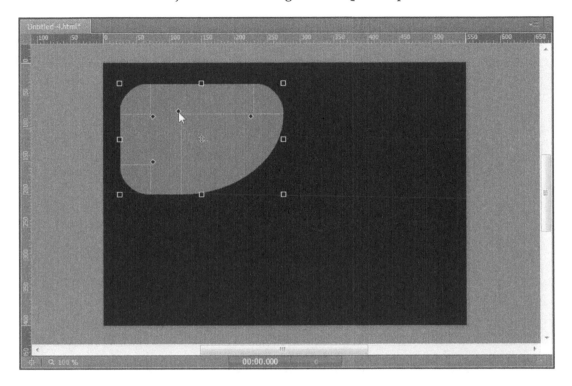

Holding the *Ctrl* or *Command* key and dragging any of the radius modifier, diamonds will allow us to modify only the selected corner in isolation from the rest.

Notice that the element created with the **Rounded Rectangle** tool looks a bit different from the previous rectangle element that was created with the **Rectangle** tool. This is because the **Rounded Rectangle** tool will create, by default, a rounded rectangle element whose border radius is 10 pixels at each corner. One other attribute unique to this tool is that it will remember the previous settings of radii upon subsequent use.

Let's modify the settings of the element we've just created in order to demonstrate this concept.

6. With the rounded rectangle element we just created selected, look over at the **Properties** panel.

7. Modify the border radius to be something other than the default 10 pixels.

8. Now select the **Rounded Rectangle** tool from the toolbar.

9. Draw out another rounded rectangle element upon the Stage.

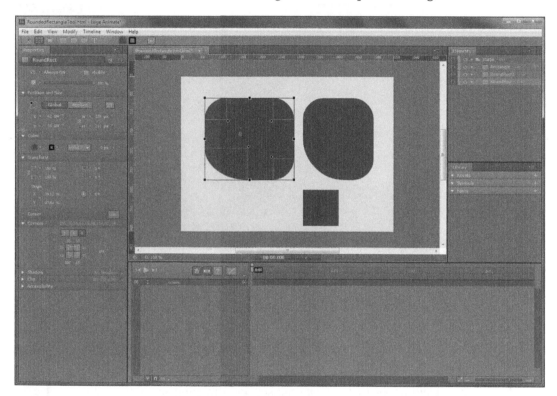

Notice that this new element retains all of the properties which were adjusted upon the previous rounded rectangle element. Even if we now select the **Rectangle** tool and create some elements with that, the **Rounded Rectangle** tool will still remember the previous settings used with that tool.

 Holding the *Shift* key and dragging any of the radius modifier diamonds will allow us to align all corner radii together while snapping to a 90-degree angle.

Working with the Ellipse tool

The **Ellipse** tool looks like a little circle in the toolbar. Selecting this tool allows us to create elliptical elements (including circles!) directly upon the Stage.

To create a new ellipse using this tool, we click upon the Stage and drag the mouse across the area we wish the ellipse to appear over, finally releasing the mouse once we are finished. This is just as we've done with the previous drawing tools.

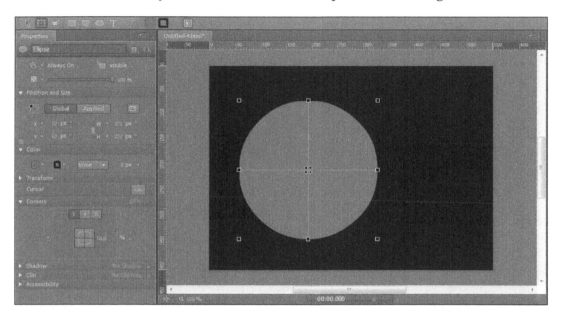

 After an ellipse has been created, notice we can still adjust the corner radii with the **Transform** tool as we can with other drawn elements.

Using the Ellipse tool

To create a new element using the **Ellipse** tool, perform the following steps:

1. Create a new project and name it `EllipseTool.html`.
2. Select the **Ellipse** tool from the toolbar.
3. Hover over the Stage. Notice that the cursor now appears as a crosshair.
4. Click anywhere on the Stage and drag. Notice that as you do so, the ellipse will grow or shrink, depending upon how far you drag from your original point. When you are happy with the size of your ellipse element, release the mouse button to complete this task.

Holding the *Shift* key while dragging will constrain an ellipse element to a circle when using the **Ellipse** tool (*O*).

5. The **Selection** tool will automatically be activated for us and the ellipse element just created will be in a selected state. We can now modify the element that was just created through the **Properties** panel:

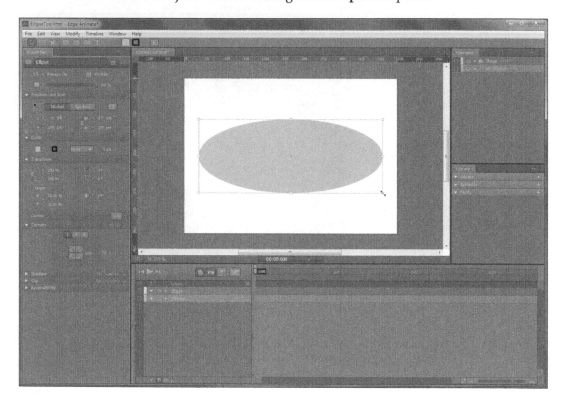

Properties unique to rectangle and ellipse elements

In this book, we will examine the properties unique to each element being discussed as we introduce it. Rectangle and ellipse elements have a number of unique properties for their type, which we will examine briefly here:

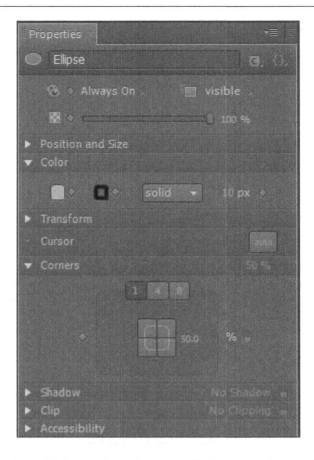

For a list of properties which are shared across all elements, have a look at *Chapter 3*, *Selecting and Transforming Elements*.

Properties of elements

The following properties are shared between all drawn elements. No matter whether we are working with drawing tool elements created with the **Rectangle**, **Rounded Rectangle**, or **Ellipse** tools—we will be able to adjust these properties through the **Selection** tool and **Properties** panel.

Background Color

This is the tool to apply color to our rectangle background in RGBA format—red, green, blue, and alpha.

Border Color

This is the tool to apply color to our rectangle border, if it exists, in RGBA format—red, green, blue, and alpha.

Border Thickness

This is the tool to change thickness of the border, if it exists, in pixels.

Border Style

This tool specifies the style of border around the rectangle element. It can be set to none, solid, or dashed.

Border Radii

This property specifies the roundness of the border radius. This property can be set to apply to all corners, individual corners, or even specific **X** and **Y** properties of individual corners. It is very flexible!

Border Radii units

These are the units the border radii are measured in. We can choose between pixels and percentages.

Modifying rectangle elements

Once a rectangle element is created, it can be easily modified through the **Properties** panel. General properties such as **Width, Height, Position,** and **Scale** are easily accessible alongside rectangle-specific properties such as **Background Color** and **Overflow**. Refer to the following screenshot:

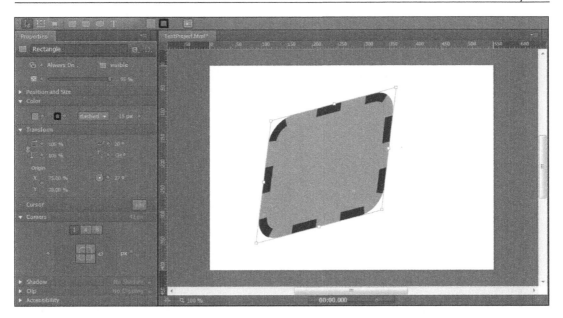

 Of course, this manner of element modification is not specific to drawing elements and can be used upon all sorts of visual elements within an Edge Animate composition.

Modifying properties of rectangle elements

Let's step through some simple modifications of a rectangle element through the **Properties** panel:

1. We're going to first need to create a rectangle element. Select the **Rectangle** tool (*M*) from the toolbar.

2. Now, simply click-and-drag out a rectangle element as we've done previously in this chapter.

3. Once we create the rectangle element, the **Selection** tool (*V*) will automatically be enabled with the element pre-selected for us. Depending upon our previous fiddling, our rectangle element could have any number of possible properties modified.

4. Using the **Properties** panel, modify the following properties. Notice that Animate defaults to the **Global** coordinate system for each element. We will leave this as such, unless otherwise indicated.

- ○ **Location X:** 60 px
- ○ **Location Y:** 40 px
- ○ **Width:** 255 px
- ○ **Height:** 170 px
- ○ **Background Color:** #900000
- ○ **Border Color:** #000000
- ○ **Border Style:** dashed
- ○ **Border Thickness:** 8 px
- ○ **Rotation:** 10 deg

 In order to adjust the width and height independently of one another, we must unlink the **Size** properties through use of the small chain-link icon.

All of these properties are simply suggestions to achieve a rectangle element similar to the one seen in the previous screenshot. At this point, have a go at playing with any of the other properties to see how they affect the element. There is much that can be done through the **Properties** panel.

Duplicating drawing elements

When laying out a number of similar elements in a composition, it is useful to be able to duplicate them all from a base element and then make small adjustments afterwards. This allows both consistencies in certain aspects of an element group, but also provides a simple method of forming these elements as unique entities within the composition.

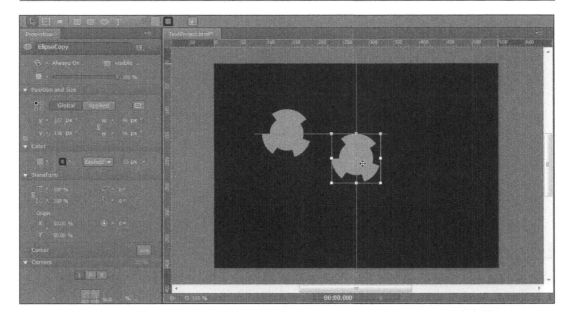

There are a few ways in which we can duplicate an element within Edge Animate. Perhaps the quickest of these methods is to simply perform a copy and paste operation. This can be accomplished through the following keyboard shortcuts:

- **Copy**: *Ctrl + C* (for Windows) or *Command + C* (for Mac)
- **Paste**: *Ctrl + V* (for Windows) or *Command + V* (for Mac)

A more manual way of accomplishing these same commands is to locate the appropriate entries within the **Edit** application menu.

Copying a rectangle element with the Selection tool

Aside from the Edge Animate menu commands and keyboard shortcuts, we can also duplicate elements already upon the Stage panel by using the **Selection** tool. Let's create a simple rectangle and duplicate it through the following steps:

1. We're going to first need to create a rectangle element. Select the **Rectangle** tool (*M*) from the toolbar.

2. Now, simply click-and-drag out a rectangle element as we've done previously in this chapter.

3. Once we create the rectangle element, the **Selection** tool will automatically be enabled with the element pre-selected for us.

4. At this point, we have the option of using the keyboard shortcuts for our menu commands as explained previously. Simply copy and paste to duplicate the rectangle element if this approach is desired.

5. Alternatively, we can use the mouse to perform the duplication. Hold down the *Alt* key and click upon our rectangle element.

6. While holding the mouse down, drag the element to a different location on the Stage panel and release. This will duplicate the element for us without much fuss and additionally allow us to choose the placement of the new rectangle.

Layout and guidance tools

When working with any element on the Stage, it is useful to have some tools which assist in the layout and positioning of the elements in question. Edge Animate comes equipped with a number of tools which assist us in this task—the **Layout Preferences** tool, **Rulers**, and **Guides**.

Layout Preferences tool

The **Layout Preferences** tool allows us to make some decisions around the default properties of certain element types when created or imported. The tool itself is located on the toolbar, to the right-hand side of the default color swatches. It appears as a small ruler in the toolbar, indicating layout:

When this tool is activated, a small overlay appears which allows us to set a number of layout preferences for the current project. Most of these preferences have to do with how elements are measured, using either pixels or percentage units:

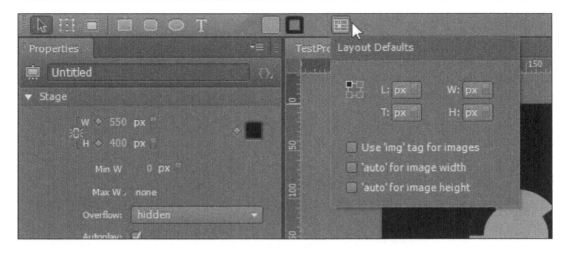

 These choices only affect anything new that is created in our composition or newly imported to it. Currently established elements retain their settings.

The following table details the choices we have when determining layout preferences for an Edge Animate composition. The units for horizontal, vertical, width, and height, though they appear to have the same description, are distinct values; this is clear when you adjust these parameters on the Stage.

Preference	Description
Corner Alignment	This selects which corner to align to by default.
Horizontal Position Units	These toggle between pixels and percentage for new elements.
Vertical Position Units	These toggle between pixels and percentage for new elements.
Width Units	These toggle between pixels and percentage for new elements.
Height Units	These toggle between pixels and percentage for new elements.
Use 'img' tag for images	When importing images, use the img tag type.
'auto' for image width	When importing images, set width to auto.
'auto' for image height	When importing images, set height to auto.

Rulers

When **Rulers** enabled, rulers are set along the top and left-hand side axis of project stage in a similar fashion to other Adobe creative applications. They assist in visualizing the measurements between elements, the relation to the Stage registration point, element alignment, and more.

Rulers also serve with the generation and positioning of manual **Guides**, which we will examine in the next section.

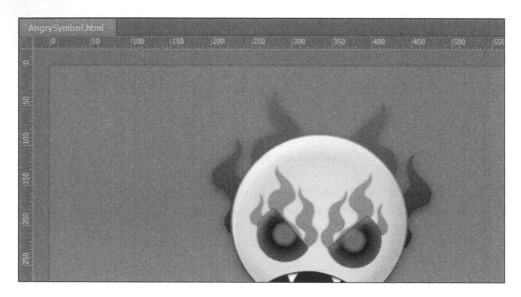

 To toggle rulers on and off, choose the **Rulers** option from the **View** menu in the application, or use the keyboard shortcuts: *Ctrl + R* (for Windows) and *Command + R* (for Mac).

Guides

Guides are used alongside **Rulers** in order to more precisely plot out and position elements on the Stage. They can also be used to scope out areas in which we can draw elements using tools such as the **Rectangle** tool or the **Rounded Rectangle** tool:

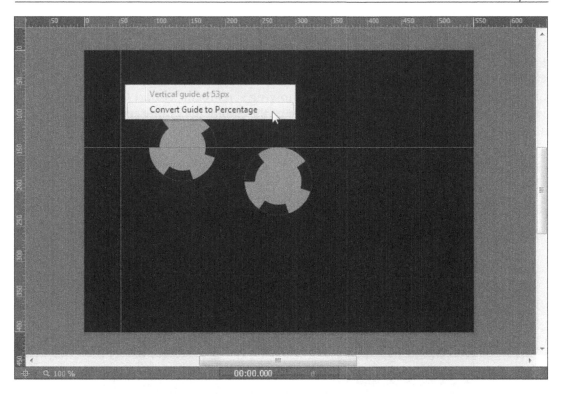

To create a new **Guide**, be sure that **Rulers** are activated and are visible within the Stage panel. Click upon a ruler and drag the new **Guide** out along that specific axis. Once the **Guide** is positioned exactly where we like, release the mouse to drop the **Guide** in place.

Once the **Guide** has been placed, it can remain a pixel-based **Guide** or be transformed into a percentage-based **Guide** to assist with responsive layout tools. To convert the **Guide** from pixel units to percentages, hover over the **Guide** and right-click. We now have the option **Convert Guide to Percentage**. The **Guide** will now appear in a more teal color than the normal violet to distinguish it from a pixel-based **Guide**. Resizing the Stage will shift the **Guide** as well—as it is now positioned based upon percentage and not absolute pixel units.

To remove the **Guide**, simply click upon it and drag it back into the **Ruler**. **Guides** can be locked from the **View** area of the application menu. Snapping can also be controlled from the **View** menu.

Smart Guides

When **Smart Guides** are enabled, dragging elements around the Stage will cause temporary guides to appear, which can assist with the placement of elements. These **Guides** will appear in alignment of other elements, or in order to align with aspects of the Stage itself. For instance, in the following screenshot, **Smart Guides** appear when an element is dragged to the center of the Stage, informing us that we will be able to center the object if dropped upon this location.

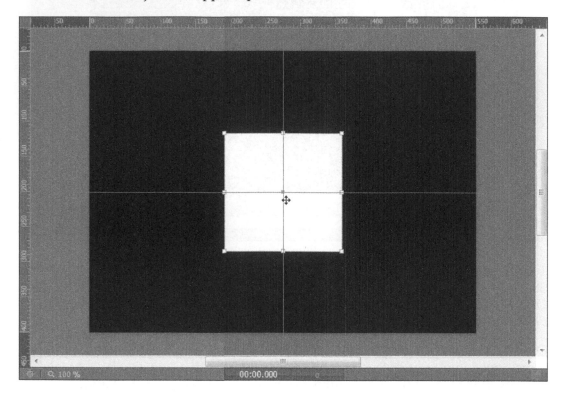

 Smart Guides can be disabled from the application menu under **View** | **Smart Guides**. Keyboard shortcut: *Ctrl + U* (for Windows) and *Command + U* (for Mac).

Adobe Edge Animate menu items

We'll now have a look at some of the Edge Animate menu items, which can be used along with content produced by the drawing tools.

Edit

The **Edit** menu allows for direct object manipulation through cut, copy, and paste commands, along with selection options and access to an undo/redo history.

Command	Description
Undo	This reverts the previous action. This command will change based upon context, letting the user know precisely which action will be affected.
Redo	This reverts the previous **Undo** command. This command will change based upon context, letting the user know precisely which action will be affected.
Cut	This removes the selected element. The user may decide to paste this element elsewhere.
Copy	This copies the selected element. The user may decide to paste this element elsewhere.
Paste	This pastes the previously cut or copied element onto the Stage while preserving element properties such as position, opacity, rotation, and so forth.
Paste Special	This is actually a series of commands which allow pasting specific attributes. We'll have a deeper look at this item in *Chapter 6, Creating Motion Through the Timeline*.
Duplicate	This makes a perfect one to one copy of the selected element. All properties and attributes are preserved and the original object is left intact.
Select All	This selects everything on the Stage.
Transform	This activates the **Transform** tool.
Delete	This removes the selected element from the Stage without preserving the object for a paste command in the future.
Keyboard Shortcuts...	This opens the **Keyboard Shortcuts** dialog.

View

Commands from the **View** menu determine how the Stage appears within the application window. We will be looking specifically at those items in the **View** menu which pertain to **Rulers** and **Guides**.

Command	Description
Rulers	This enables rulers to appear along the upper and left planes of the Stage.
Guides	This toggles manually created **Guides** on and off from view.
Snap to Guides	This will allow dragged elements to snap to manually created **Guides** for simpler repositioning and alignment.
Lock Guides	This will lock any previously existing **Guides** so that they cannot be accidentally moved or deleted.
Smart Guides	This will enable smart guides to appear when dragging elements around the Stage. **Smart Guides** assist in the alignment of items in relation to one another.

Modify

The **Modify** menu includes commands which pertain to elements on the Stage and how the Stage interacts with these elements. Most of these commands pertain to layout and distribution options, but also particular commands which deal with the management of symbols.

Command	Description
Arrange	The **Arrange** commands modify the z-index of visual elements on the Stage.
**Arrange	Bring To Front**	This command switches the selected element z-index position to the very top of the viewing stack.
**Arrange	Bring Forward**	This switches the selected element z-index position to the spot above its current position within the viewing stack.
**Arrange	Send Backward**	This switches the selected element z-index position to the spot below its current position within the viewing stack.
**Arrange	Send To Back**	This switches the selected element z-index position to the very bottom of the viewing stack.
Align	The **Align** commands adjust the x or y positions of selected elements to one another.
**Align	Left**	This aligns selected elements to the left-most element.
**Align	Horizontal Center**	This aligns selected elements to their horizontal center.

Command	Description
**Align	Right**	This aligns selected elements to the right-most element.
**Align	Top**	This aligns selected elements to the top-most element.
**Align	Vertical Center**	This aligns selected elements to their vertical center.
**Align	Bottom**	This aligns selected elements to the bottom-most element.
Distribute	The **Distribute** command adjusts the x or y positions of selected elements to one another. It requires that three or more elements be selected in order to function properly.
**Distribute	Left**	This distributes selected items along the left-hand side edge.
**Distribute	Horizontal Center**	This distributes selected items along the horizontal center.
**Distribute	Right**	This distributes selected items along the right-hand side edge.
**Distribute	Top**	This distributes selected items along top edge.
**Distribute	Vertical Center**	This distributes selected items along vertical center.
**Distribute	Bottom**	This distributes selected items along the bottom edge.
Convert to Symbol...	This will convert the selected elements on the Stage into a new symbol, allowing us to provide a name for it before doing so through a simple dialog.
Edit Symbol	As this command pertains to **Symbols**, we'll examine this particular menu item in *Chapter 8, Making use of Symbols, Nested Elements, and Grouping*.

Summary

In this chapter, we've examined how to use the drawing tools within Edge Animate to add simple shapes and text areas to our project. Additionally, we've demonstrated a variety of ways to work with these elements within a composition. Generally, no matter how different the properties of each of these assets, they can all be employed within an Edge Animate composition in very similar ways.

In this next chapter, we'll have a look at how to use the **Selection** and **Transform** tools to perform further manipulation of elements upon the Stage.

3
Selecting and Transforming Elements

Now that we've created a number of elements in the Stage using the internal drawing tools available in Adobe Edge Animate, we can begin to discuss the Selection and Transform tools and explore their usage with created elements.

This chapter will explore:

- The Selection tool
- The Transform tool
- The Edge Animate Stage
- The Elements panel
- Grouping elements

We will also look over the various properties available through element selections, and examine the menu items which pertain to these particular aspects of the application.

Locating the Selection and Transform tools

Both the Selection and Transform tools are located at the far-left side of the Edge Animate toolbar. The toolbar itself, by default, is located directly underneath the application menu at the very top-left of the application window. We can see them grouped alongside other Edge Animate tools:

The Selection tool

Selection Tool (V) is used (as its name suggests) to select one or more elements in the Stage and modify their properties through the mouse, menu commands, keyboard commands, or the **Properties** panel.

The Selection tool appears as a little cursor arrow and is used to make selections in the project's Stage. Any elements added to the Stage can be selected using this tool and by holding down the *Shift* key, a user can add additional elements to the selection.

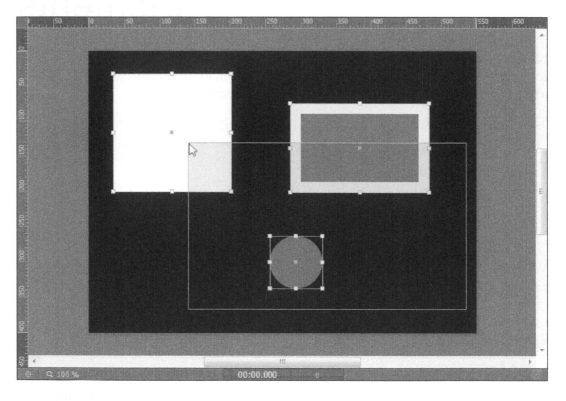

To select many elements in the Stage at once, we can also click-and-drag across all of the elements we wish to select. This will draw a selection rectangle during the selection process, which will go away once a selection has been completed.

Ctrl+ Click (Windows) or *Command + Click* (Mac) on elements to toggle select incongruous elements.

Shift + Click on elements to toggle select congruous elements.

When multiple elements have been selected in this manner, the **Properties** panel will display only those properties which are shared between object types. For example, if we were to select both a rectangle and text element at once, we would be able to modify **Position and Size** of both objects at once, but could not edit the Font Size or Border Radius, as these properties are specific to each object type.

 We may also click on multiple elements while holding the *Shift* key in order to select/deselect multiple objects in the Stage. Once objects are selected, they can be modified in many different ways through use of the panels and menu systems within the Edge Animate application window.

Using the Selection tool

To select an element in the Stage using the Selection tool, all we need to do is choose **Selection Tool (V)** from the toolbar and then use it to click on the element we wish to select. This will allow us to modify the properties of this element through either movements with the mouse, through keyboard shortcuts, or most extensively by using the **Properties** panel.

Let's perform a quick exercise to demonstrate direct interaction on visible elements with the Selection tool:

1. Create a new Edge Animate project and draw out a rectangle element in the Stage. The property choices do not matter much in this instance, so use whatever you like.

2. After creating the element, the Selection tool will automatically be selected. We can now perform a variety of modifications on our selected element through use of this tool.

3. Click-and-drag with the mouse to change the **X** and **Y** Position properties of the selected element.

4. Click-and-drag any of the eight small, white size handles to adjust the width and height Size properties of the selected element.

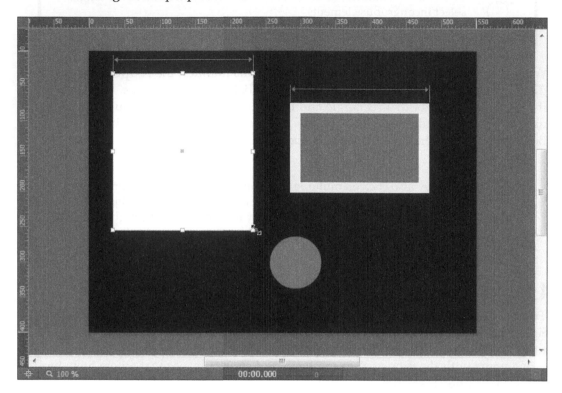

The Transform tool

Transform Tool (Q) allows us to modify certain transform properties through direct manipulation of the object in the Stage. There is a subtle difference here, between the Transform and Selection tools, but it is a very important one.

When using the Transform tool to modify an element, we are modifying transform properties in relation to the Transform Point, while the Selection tool can modify only properties such as width, height, and location.

 The tool appears as a transform box complete with modification handles.

Using the Transform tool

Let's perform a quick demonstration to get acquainted with this tool:

1. Create a new Edge Animate project and draw out a rectangle element in the Stage. The property choices do not matter much in this instance, so use whatever you like.

2. After creating the element, the Selection tool will automatically be selected. Since we want to use the Transform tool, select **Transform Tool (Q)** from the toolbar.

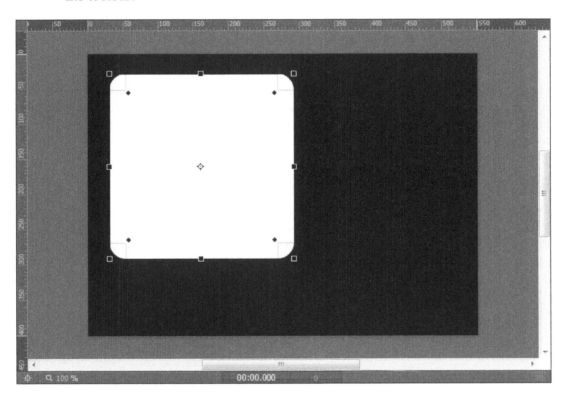

3. The selected element will still be selected but will look different (this is illustrated in the next diagram) as we are now using the Transform tool.

4. Click on any of the black squares along the element edges and drag it to perform a basic transform upon the element. Notice that as we do this, the Scale properties within the **Properties** panel shift along with our movements. Recall that when doing something similar with the Selection tool, it was the Size property that adjusted. This is an important distinction!

5. Click-and-drag any of the four small black diamonds to adjust the corner radii properties of the selected element:

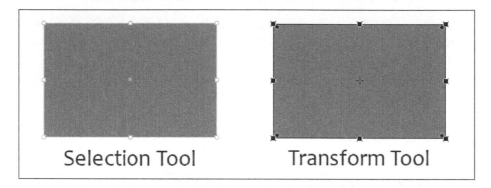

Selection Tool   Transform Tool

Here we can see that there are distinct visual differences between an element's selected appearances when comparing the Selection tool to the Transform tool. For instance, the black diamonds which control corner radii and the little crosshair representing a Transform Point will only appear in the transform mode.

Manipulating the Transform Point

One of the most powerful (and useful) concepts to remember when working with the Transform tool is the Transform Origin property and the corresponding Transform Point. The Transform Origin determines how any transform is calculated upon the element, no matter if it has to do with scale, rotation, or skew.

 Moving the Transform Origin point by clicking on it and dragging it to a new location with the mouse will allow the rectangle element to be transformed as though pinned to this point instead of the element center.

Let's perform a series of manipulations within Edge Animate to demonstrate this:

1. Create a new Edge Animate project and draw out a rectangle element in the Stage. The property choices do not matter much in this instance, so use whatever you like.

2. After creating the element, the Selection tool will automatically be selected. Since we want to use the Transform tool, select **Transform Tool (Q)** from the toolbar.

3. Notice the Transform Point defaults to the center of the element we just created:

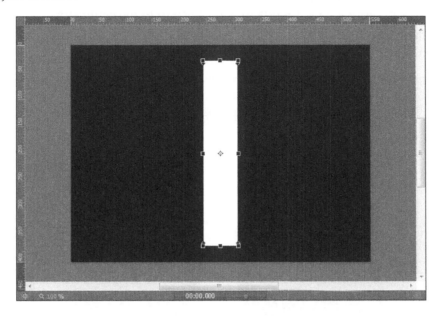

4. Enter the **Properties** panel and change the rotation to -25 degrees. We can see that the element rotates around the center, since this is where the Transform Point is located:

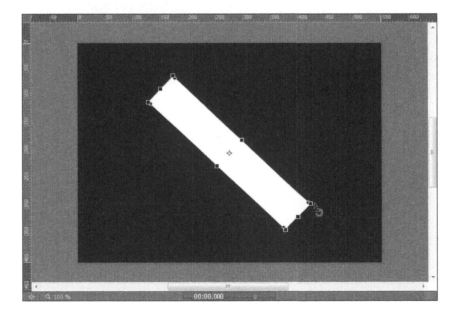

5. Set the rotation back to 0 degrees.

6. Using the mouse, click-and-drag the Transform Point to the top-center of the element. Notice how it tends to want to snap to the center-top.

7. Release the mouse and a take note of how the Transform Origin has changed within the **Properties** panel:

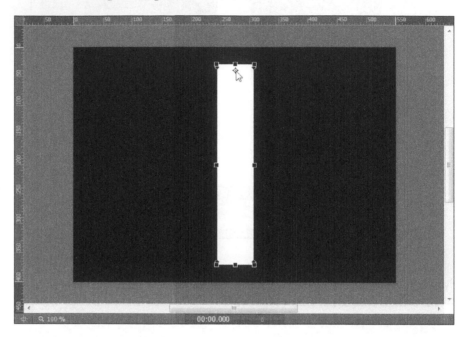

8. Now when we make adjustments to the rotation property of this element, we can see that it rotates from the top-center. This is where we have relocated the Transform Point.

9. Set the rotation to -25 degrees once again to see differences in how the same transform effect is applied:

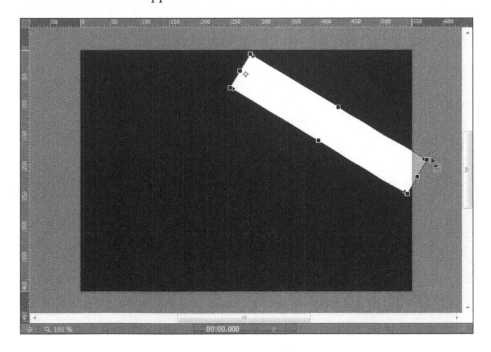

 The Transform Point can be moved anywhere within the element or even outside of the element to create a number of interesting motion effects.

The Edge Animate Stage

The **Stage** in an Edge Animate project is the main visual element within the eventual published composition. All visual elements are displayed within this defined area and any interactions are executed through this window:

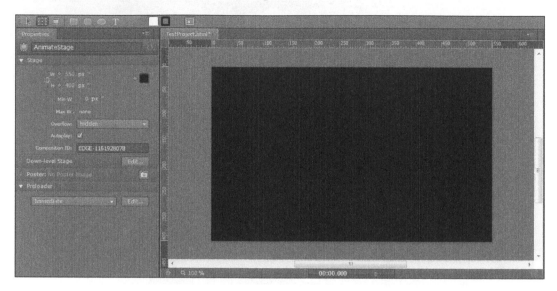

To select the Stage in order to manipulate its properties, simply deselect any elements that may exist and edit properties exposed within the **Properties** panel. These properties will be examined one by one in the next section.

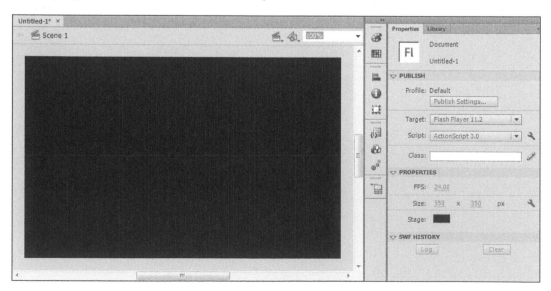

When comparing Edge Animate with Flash Professional, we can see a number of differences between each stage implementation. For instance, in Edge Animate we can adjust and even animate the Stage size and color, while in Flash Professional we can perform no such action.

Manipulating the Stage

One of the interesting things about working with the Stage in an Edge Animate project is that many of the Stage properties can be changed, and even animated, while the composition is playing. Properties such as Background Color, Width, and Height can all be adjusted whenever we like through the Timeline or by defining Actions. This flexibility opens up some interesting possibilities.

Rulers and Guides

As mentioned in the previous chapter, the Edge Animate Stage includes the option of enabling **Rulers** and **Guides**, both of which are intended to assist with object arrangement and layout within our compositions. These options are both enabled from the **View** option in the application menu:

As indicated by the previous screenshot, we also have two additional stages available to us from within an Edge Animate project, **Preloader Stage** and **Down-level Stage**. To learn more about both of these options, refer to *Chapter 10, Publishing Edge Animate Compositions*.

Center the Stage

Immediately beneath the Stage we can see a small icon which looks like crosshairs. This is the **Center the Stage** control and is used to recenter the Stage if we have scrolled too far along the vertical or horizontal axis and need to refocus. This is especially useful when the view is zoomed in.

Zoom controls

To the right of the **Center the Stage** control, we also have access to some zoom controls. These controls function in two ways; we can click on the percentage value and type in a new value, or we can hover the cursor over the displayed value and shift it by clicking and dragging to the left or right.

Building responsive compositions

One of the goals of Adobe Edge Animate is to enable designers to build content for all manner of screens. Some of these screens are very high resolution, while others can be quite small. We have the ability to build our compositions in two ways, as a pixel-constrained composition or as a percentage-based composition. If we choose to build on a percentage-based Stage, we can then mix elements with both pixel- and percentage-based units to create a more responsive design.

Making a document responsive

For certain compositions that will need to adapt to a variety of screen sizes or page layouts, we can use percentages in place of a set pixel size when defining our composition resolution. This will enable the composition Stage to fill a certain percentage of its container element when published, as defined by the **Document Object Model (DOM)**.

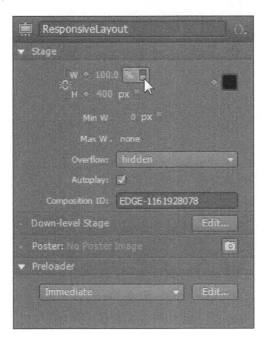

 One of the really neat things about making the Stage responsive in this way is that we can actually combine both percentage and pixel definitions on the same object, or even differ these unit types across all of the elements within a composition.

Making elements responsive

We can also set the units of individual elements to be measured in either pixels or percentages. In this way, we can for example define the width of a certain element to be 25 percent of the Stage or some other containing element. In this case, if the Stage were resized to 400 pixels in width, the element in question would be 100 pixels in width. As demonstrated in the following screenshot, the units of various properties can be mixed and need not conform to one or the other:

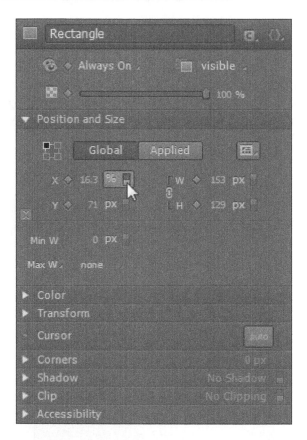

Global versus Applied

Apart from configuring many of the properties of Edge Animate elements to accept either percentage or pixel values, we can also specify whether we want **Position and Size** of an element to represent values relative to either the **Global** container (the Stage) or an **Applied** container (the immediate parent element).

To switch between each coordinate system, we simply click on the **Global/Applied** toggle set control within the **Properties** panel with an element selected, as seen in the following screenshot:

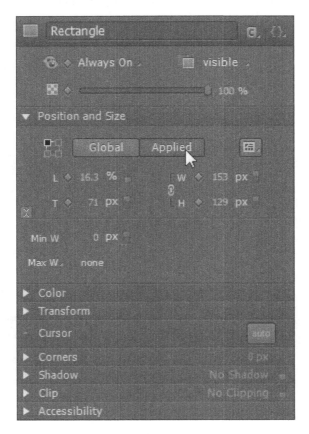

Not only can we choose between **Global** and **Applied** coordinates, but Edge Animate also provides a mechanism to determine how elements are pinned relative to the four corners of the chosen coordinate system. This functionality is enabled through the small grid of selectable pin points to the left of the coordinate system toggle.

Responsive presets

Adobe Edge Animate also comes equipped with a number of responsive presets, which can be applied to elements through the **Properties** panel once they have been selected. In the case of rectangles and ellipses we have two choices: **Scale Position** and **Scale Size**.

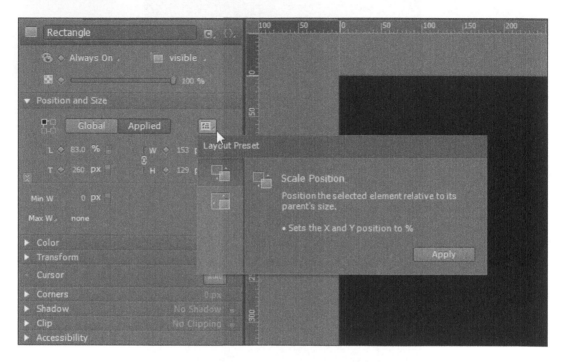

Scale Position

This positions the selected element relative to its parent's size and sets the X and Y position to percent.

Scale Size

This scales the selected element relative to its parent and sets the width and height to percent.

 Note that these are the presets for drawing objects. Other element types include more specific and varied presets aligned with the element type. We will address other presets as we discuss different object types in forthcoming chapters.

Simulating various screen sizes

When testing our responsive design settings, we can actually simulate various screen sizes directly within Edge Animate through the use of resizable Stage handles along both the X and Y axis. These appear as small white marks along the Ruler and can be dragged across to resize the Stage. This mechanism provides a nice method of resizing the Stage to test how various elements react.

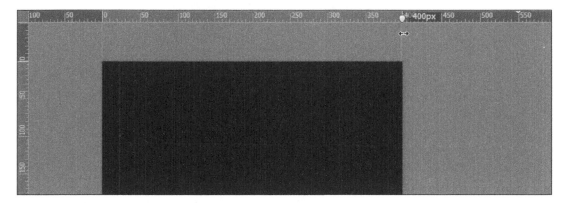

 You will notice in the previous screenshot that the previously set Stage size remains marked at **550**px, even when we shift the Stage resize handle to **400px**.

The Elements panel

The **Elements** panel is a representation of all the HTML elements included as part of our Edge Animate project. Every element is always nested within the Stage, and elements such as this, which contain subelements, can be twirled down to expose those elements.

We may also toggle visibility of particular elements by toggling the eye icon on and off, as well as the lock icon. When an element is locked, Edge Animate will prevent us from modifying the properties of that particular element.

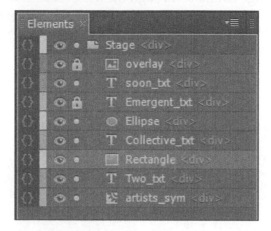

We can easily determine the type of element selected, by the icon that appears directly to the left of the element name. For instance, rectangle elements will have a little rectangular icon while ellipse elements will have an icon resembling an ellipse.

Element visibility

As mentioned earlier, the small eye icons within the **Elements** panel are used to toggle visibility on and off. We can also toggle the visibility of any element by clicking on the eye icon to the left of the element name. Note that this only toggles visibility of an element within the Edge Animate interface; it has no effect on a published composition.

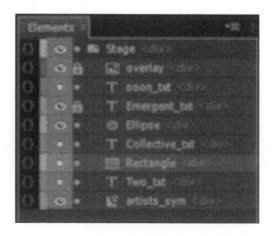

We are able to click-and-drag across the visibility column in order to toggle multiple elements visibility with one swipe. Element visibility can also be toggled from the Timeline.

Locking elements

Clicking on the small dot next to the eye will lock a particular element and thus disable editing for that element. As expected, clicking on the resulting lock icon will enable editing once again.

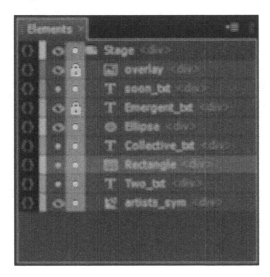

 We are able to click-and-drag across the lock column in order to lock multiple elements with one swipe. Elements can also be locked and unlocked from the Timeline or from a right- or option-click within the **Elements** panel, or even from an element directly on the Stage.

Managed versus unmanaged elements

Edge Animate has the concept of certain elements being "managed", while others are "static". This is illustrated by the icons within the **Elements** panel—a bright white **</>** indicates an unmanaged element. Any other icon type is for a managed element.

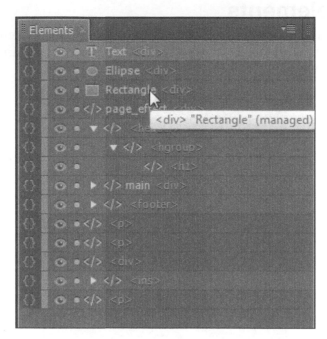

Managed

These are elements which were created by Edge Animate tooling. We have full control over these specific elements. If working within an Edge Animate project that has never included external documents, chances are that all elements will be managed.

Static

These are elements that have either been added through external tooling, or are present within an HTML document that has been opened within Edge Animate. The Edge Animate tooling only has limited control over such elements.

 Hovering the mouse cursor over an element in the **Elements** panel will also reveal a tooltip stating whether the element is "managed" or "static".

Reordering elements

To reorder elements, we can drag-and-drop individual elements within the **Elements** panel. The new location of the dragged element will appear as a thick black line between elements. This will effectively modify each element's z-index accordingly, and works very similar in concept to the Photoshop Layers panel.

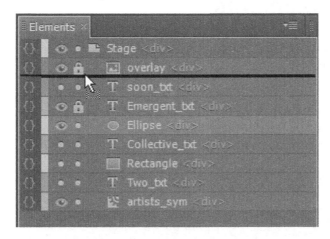

Renaming elements

There are a number of places within which we are able to rename elements. The **Elements** panel is just one of these. Simply double-click on the element name to rename it:

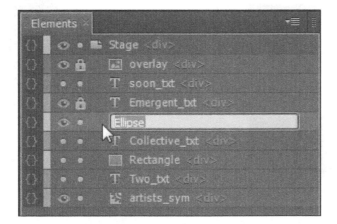

Elements can be renamed using the same method from the Timeline and can always be renamed from within the **Properties** panel.

Grouping elements

Grouping is a method of defining a set of multiple elements in order to manipulate certain properties all at once. Most often, this technique is used to move a set of elements around easily, without having to worry whether their position in relation to one another may change.

Edge Animate provides a number of methods for grouping elements. The simplest of these is to select multiple elements in the Stage, perform a right-click on the selected set, and choose **Group Elements in DIV** from the context menu that appears.

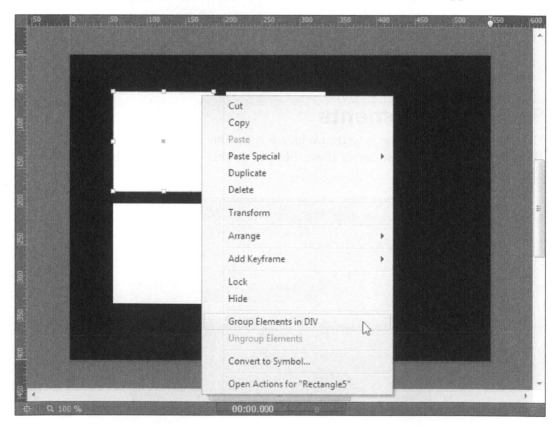

We can also group selected elements from the application menu. Choose **Modify | Group Elements in DIV**. Keyboard shortcut: *Ctrl + G* (Windows) or *Command + G* (Mac).

The grouped elements now can be moved about as one and appear within the **Elements** panel as nested within a parent DIV, as seen in the following screenshot:

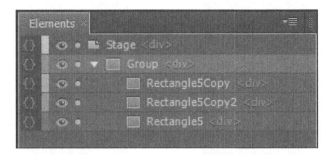

To ungroup individual elements, we can drag them outside of the group container elements within the **Elements** panel. The option to ungroup is also available from the application menu or through the right-click context menu.

 Grouping is a very similar concept to nesting, though a group will lose many of the properties normally adjustable within an Edge Animate element. To read more about both nesting and grouping, we can refer to *Chapter 8, Making Use of Symbols, Nested Elements, and Grouping*.

Properties shared by all element types

The following properties are shared between all Edge Animate elements. No matter if we are working with drawing tool elements, imported assets, or even complex Symbol objects, we will be able to adjust these properties through the Selection tool and the **Properties** panel.

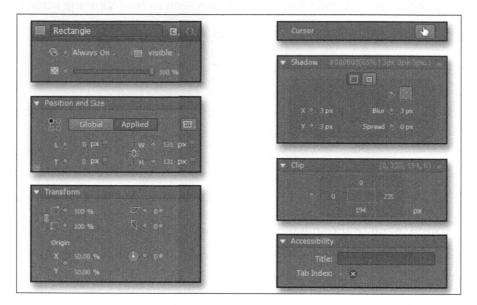

 The previous screenshot illustrates the different properties available to us through the various element types in Edge Animate. Notice how many properties are shared between types.

Element properties

This is the main properties panel segment for an element and is the only segment which cannot be collapsed. It contains some basic settings such as the element ID, class and action attributes, visibility, overflow, and opacity settings:

ID

ID is used throughout Edge Animate to identify a particular element in the Elements panel, the Timeline, and also via various Actions through the use of JavaScript code. Note that IDs are unique—we cannot use a single ID more than once within an Edge Animate project.

Class

This is a class definition that can be assigned to our elements in order to target them specifically through a custom CSS file external to our composition.

Actions

This enables us to bind Actions to the selected element.

Visibility

This setting is accessed from the **Properties** panel and determines whether an element is actually displayed upon playback or not. There are three distinct settings for this property:

Command	Description
Always On	This is the default and simply means that the element is visible over the course of the animation. Selecting **Always On** when previously using either of the other two settings will remove all keyframes that have to do with element display from the Timeline.
On	The element is visible from the start. The idea is to handle visibility through Timeline Triggers or other Actions.
Off	The element is hidden from the start. The idea is to handle visibility through Timeline Triggers or other Actions.

Overflow

This property determines how an element behaves when nested elements extend past its borders. There are four choices:

Command	Description
visible	Elements which extend past the borders will remain visible
hidden	Elements which extend past the borders will be rendered invisible
scroll	The element will present scrollbars to the user, even if not necessarily needed
auto	Elements which extend past the borders will cause scrollbars to appear automatically, as needed

Opacity

The degree of transparency exhibited by a particular element. This can range from **0** % to **100** % with **100** %, being fully opaque.

Position and Size properties

This panel section contains all of the properties necessary when tweaking the position and size of a particular element. We can also switch between global and local relative coordinates, apply certain presets based upon the element type, and specify a minimum and maximum width:

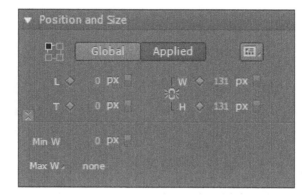

Position

The **X** and **Y** coordinates (or **L** and **T** coordinates when **Applied** is selected) that an element will be positioned at in the Stage, in pixels.

> Unlike Flash Professional content, Edge Animate is not capable of subpixel rendering.

Size

This property determines the width and height of an element, specified in pixels. These values can be locked together through use of the link icon between them.

Transform properties

This section exposes the properties related to an element's transform. These properties include scale, skew, and rotation settings:

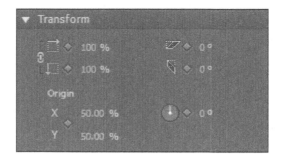

Scale

The scale property is based on percentage. Both the X and Y scale can be linked or changed independently. These values can be locked together through use of the link icon between them.

Skew

The skew of an element can be performed along either the X or Y axis.

Transform Origin

This is the point from which any transformations such as rotation or scale will be applied, and is determined by the **X** and **Y** percentage values.

 Note that this can actually be located beyond the bounds of a particular element.

Rotate

This property determines the degrees of rotation relative to the Transform Point of the specified element, with **0** degrees being original rotation.

Cursor properties

This property allows us to select a cursor to use when the mouse hovers over the selected object:

Cursor

This property allows us to trigger a cursor change upon hover.

Shadow properties

This panel section exposes shadow properties for a selected element. These include the shadow color, offset, and blur. The small switch on the upper-right allows us to quickly toggle the shadow on and off.

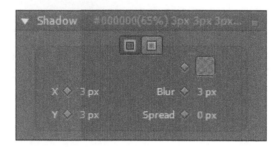

Shadow type

This property determines whether the shadow should be inset or not. This is not available on text elements.

 In the case of text elements, we do not have the option to choose to inset our shadow.

Shadow color

The color of a box or text shadow.

Shadow horizontal offset

The horizontal offset of our shadow in pixels.

Shadow vertical offset

The vertical offset of our shadow in pixels.

Blur radius

This property defines the shadow blur radius in pixels.

Spread

The spread of our shadow in pixels.

Clip properties

This panel section contains the properties related to an element's clipping behavior. The small switch on the upper-right allows us to quickly toggle the clipping on and off:

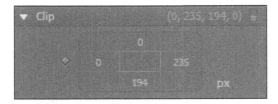

Clip

Clipping an element from the top, bottom, left, or right will render a portion of the selected element invisible from the specified side based upon specified pixels.

Accessibility properties

This panel section exposes properties which can help improve accessibility, including a **Title** attribute and **Tab Index**:

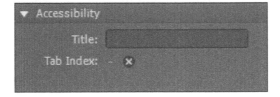

Title

This property assigns a title attribute to HTML elements.

Tab Index

The specific tab index for accessibility purposes.

Stage properties

The Edge Animate Stage itself also has a number of properties which can be controlled through the **Properties** panel. In order to access the **Stage** properties, simply click anywhere in the Stage where another element is not present, or select **Stage <div>** in the **Elements** panel.

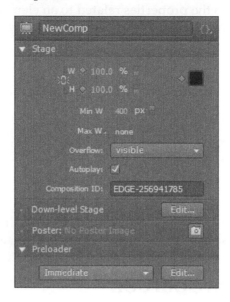

Document title

This property sets the <title> tag value in the <head> section of our HTML document.

Width

This property sets the width of the Stage in pixels.

Height

This property sets the height of the Stage in pixels.

Background color

The color to apply to our Stage background in RGBA format: red, green, blue, alpha.

Unlike Flash (SWF) content, Edge Animate animations can have semitransparent background colors.

Overflow

This property determines how the Stage behaves when elements extend past its borders. There are four choices:

Command	Description
visible	Elements which extend past the Stage borders will remain visible
hidden	Elements which extend past the Stage borders will be rendered invisible
scroll	The Stage will present scrollbars to the user, even if not necessarily needed
auto	Elements which extend past the Stage borders will cause scrollbars to appear automatically, as needed

Autoplay

This determines whether the main Stage timeline should begin playing automatically, or pause until a command is given for explicit playback.

Composition ID

This is the unique identifier used by the Edge Animate Runtime API to target a specific composition. It can be changed if necessary.

Poster

Allows creation of a poster frame from the current playhead position.

Down-level Stage

This property allows quick access to the Down-level Stage.

Preloader

This property allows quick access to the Preloader Stage.

Adobe Edge Animate menu items

In this section, we'll have a look at some of the Edge Animate menu items that can be used when dealing with the Stage.

View

Commands from the **View** menu determine how the Stage appears within the application window. This is especially useful when performing fine-tuned tweaks to elements in the Stage.

Command	Description
Zoom In	Zooms in the entire Stage for fine adjustments when placing objects or modifying their properties. If the Stage appears larger than its panel, scrollbars will be present.
Zoom Out	Zooms the Stage out further. Useful for when working on smaller, cramped screens.
Actual Size	Resets the Stage to 100 percent its actual size as determined in the **Properties** panel.
Rulers	Toggles rulers on and off.
Guides	Toggles guides on and off.
Snap to Guides	Allows elements to snap to guides when dragged in close proximity.
Lock Guides	Locks all current guides so that they cannot be moved or deleted mistakenly.
Smart Guides	Enables smart guides for temporary assistive help in aligning elements.
Preloader Stage	Access the composition Preloader Stage.
Down-level Stage	Access the composition Down-level Stage for older browsers.

Summary

In this chapter, we had a good look at two very important tools when working on an Edge Animate project: the Selection and Transform tools. Much of what we will discuss in upcoming chapters will depend upon the successful use of these two tools. We had a good overview of some assistive tooling for authoring more adaptable, responsive compositions. We then explored the Stage in greater detail and had a good look at the **Elements** and **Properties** panels.

In the next chapter, we're going to examine the use of text elements through the Text tool and how to integrate web fonts into our Edge Animate projects.

4

Using Text and Web Fonts

While it is possible to create text in another program such as Adobe Photoshop or Fireworks, render a bitmap image, and bring that into Edge Animate for use in a composition, it is often preferable to work directly with actual text elements in a project. In this chapter, we'll have a look at the Text tool in Edge Animate and how it can be used to easily create such text elements. We'll also look at:

- Possible text element types
- Text element properties
- Using web fonts in a project

Finally, we'll explore the Library panel through the inclusion of external web fonts and how to manage these fonts within a project.

Locating the Text tool

Text Tool (T) can be found within the Edge Animate toolbar. The toolbar itself, by default, is located directly underneath the application menu at the very top-left of the application window. We can see it grouped alongside other Edge Animate tools:

The Text tool

The Edge Animate Text tool allows us to create text elements on the Stage, which can be animated through the Timeline or have interactivity applied to them through the Actions panel. We can also perform advanced functions such as modifying the textual contents through the application of various Actions, which we will see later on in this book.

 The Text tool appears as an iconic **T** in the Edge Animate Toolbar.

Using the Text tool, we are able to define text elements within an Edge Animate project and modify certain visual properties of those elements. We can click directly in the Stage to create text at the insertion point location, or click-and-drag a textbox into whatever size is needed.

 Like any of these tools, all of the specific element properties can be adjusted and changed through the **Properties** panel.

Text element types

Elements created with the Text tool will default to a `<div>` HTML element, but can actually be changed to employ any of the HTML elements shown in the following screenshot:

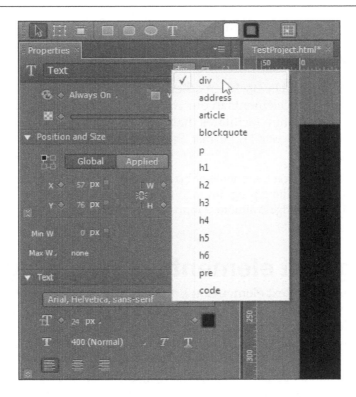

The following table describes the possible text element types:

Category	Description
`<div>`	Defines a division element within an HTML document and is often used for generic block-level elements.
`<address>`	Normally added to the header or footer of an HTML document. The address tag defines contact information for the document owner.
`<article>`	Defines a block of self-contained content. Commonly used for an article or blog post.
`<blockquote>`	An element which defines a section of text which has been taken from a source other than the current document.
`<p>`	Denotes a block element which signifies a paragraph of text.
`<h1>` to `<h6>`	h1 to h6 are basic HTML heading tags. They can be used to denote a hierarchical set of headings within a parent element.
`<pre>`	Denotes preformatted text. Normally, the pre tag will preserve whitespace and line breaks.
`<code>`	Ideal for displaying blocks of code within HTML.

As we can see though these element definitions, most of the differences here are simply *semantic*, though semantic meaning is a core consideration when dealing with HTML-based content.

These type definitions can be useful in other ways too. Perhaps we want to apply a CSS text-shadow to *all* h1 elements in our composition or apply a gradient to certain drawn elements. This feature facilitates that workflow. To see an example of how to do this, have a look at *Chapter 11, Further Explorations with Adobe Edge Animate*.

[Advanced text treatments or bizarre fonts can also be rendered from an image editing program as SVG or bitmap images and included within an Edge Animate composition in that way.]

Creating text elements on the Stage

It's very simple to create text elements in Edge Animate with the tools provided. While these elements are formed in much the same way as rectangle or ellipse elements, they do provide a number of unique attributes—especially in terms of custom typefaces and dynamic alterations through the Edge Animate Runtime APIs.

[For more information about changing the values associated with text elements dynamically, refer to *Chapter 7, Interactivity with Actions, Triggers, and Labels*.]

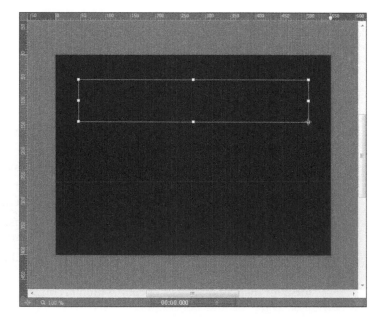

Creating text elements

Following are the steps to create a new text element using the Text tool:

1. Create a new Edge Animate project and name it `TextTool.html`.

2. Select **Text Tool (T)** from the Edge Animate toolbar.

3. Hover over the Stage. Notice that the cursor now appears as a crosshair.

4. Click anywhere on the Stage and drag. Notice that as you do so, the text element outline will grow or shrink, depending upon how far you drag from your original point. When you are happy with the size of your text element, release the mouse button to complete this task.

 Alternatively, we can simply click on the Stage and begin typing using this tool. The text element will expand to accommodate the characters that are input.

5. The Selection tool will automatically be activated for us and the text element just created will be in a selected state. A small input box will appear aside the newly-formed text element, allowing us to type whichever text we want to be displayed.

6. Once we have finished typing our text, we can press the *Esc* key or click off of the text element to finish. We will now be able to modify that element through the **Properties** panel.

We now have a complete text element on the Stage, which displays the text that was entered upon its creation:

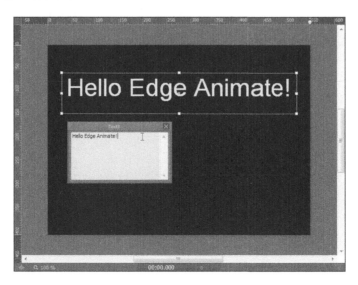

Double-clicking on any text element will allow us to edit the text that is displayed within that element. Text elements in Edge Animate can support multiline text, if desired.

Point text versus Paragraph text

As mentioned earlier, there are two ways of creating a text element on the Stage. These are referred to as **Point** text and **Paragraph** text:

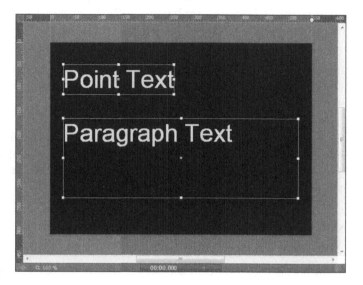

Point text

The div created does not wrap text to the next line. The flow of text entered will be from left to right, on a single line.

Paragraph text

The div created wraps text to the next line as defined by the bounds created from click-and-drag.

Text property retention

Similar to the behavior of the Rounded Rectangle tool, the Text tool will retain any of the properties from its previous use. To see this behavior in action, perform the following steps:

1. With the text element we just created selected, look over at the **Properties** panel.

2. Modify the Font Size and Text Color to be something other than the default.

3. Now select **Text Tool (T)** from the Edge Animate toolbar.

4. Draw out another text element on the Stage using whichever method that suits you:

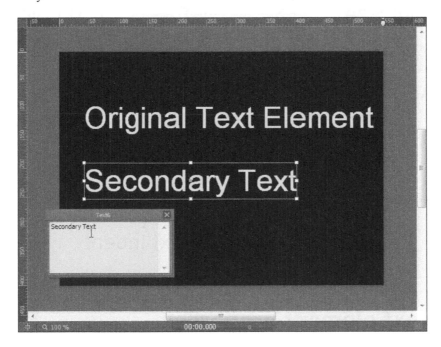

Notice that this new element retains all of the properties which were adjusted upon the previous text element.

Properties unique to text elements

Text elements in Edge Animate have a number of unique properties exposed through and made available for manipulation by the **Properties** panel. We will have a look at each of these properties now.

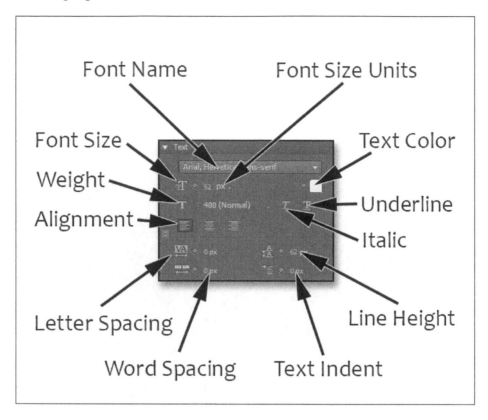

Main text element properties

Within the main text element properties area, we find options such as font family, size, color, alignment, and so on. These are the basic attributes of any text element.

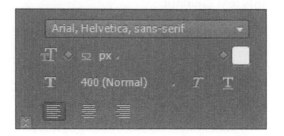

Category	Description
Font Name	These are core fonts that almost every computer is expected to be able to display. They are arranged here in groups, to allow for fallback in case the primary font is not available on a user's system.
	This is often expressed in CSS, such as follows:
	`font-family: 'Lusitana' , serif;`
Font Size	Normally a numeric size attributed to the chosen font. This setting functions along with Font Size Units.
Font Size Units	The unit of measurement to attribute to a chosen Font Size. Choices include px, %, or em.
Text Color	The color to apply to our text in RGBA format: Red, Green, Blue, Alpha.
Bold	A toggle for the chosen font's bold property. Emboldens the text.
Italic	A toggle for the chosen font's italic property. Italicizes the text.
Underline	A toggle for the chosen font's underline property. Applies a visual line beneath the text.
Align Left	Only usable in text elements that are given a certain width which is greater than the space occupied by the provided text. Aligns given text to the left.
Align Center	Only usable in text elements that are given a certain width which is greater than the space occupied by the provided text. Aligns given text to the center.
Align Right	Only usable with text elements that are given a certain width which is greater than the space occupied by the provided text. Aligns given text to the right.

Secondary text element properties

To reveal the secondary text element properties, we can click on the little expander at the bottom of the main text properties to reveal these options. These include spacing and paragraph options.

Category	Description
Text Indent	Indents the first line of a text element by a certain number of pixels.
Line Height	Adjusts the spacing between lines of text.
Letter Spacing	Adjusts the spacing between letters of text.
Word Spacing	Adjusts the spacing between each word.

Text shadows

Similar to other elements within Edge Animate, text elements can have shadows applied to them through the `text-shadow` CSS definition. The **Shadow** panel section exposes shadow properties for a selected element. This includes the shadow color, offset, and blur. The small switch on the upper-right allows us to quickly toggle the shadow on and off.

 Notice in the previous screenshot that certain properties available to us with `box-shadow` are not available when using `text-shadow`.

Category	Description
Shadow Color	The color of a text shadow
Shadow Horizontal Offset	The horizontal offset of our shadow in pixels
Shadow Vertical Offset	The vertical offset of our shadow in pixels
Blur Radius	Defines the shadow blur radius in pixels

Using web fonts in Adobe Edge Animate

Web fonts are externally hosted font definitions that can be defined and stored within the **Library** panel for use upon text elements. For this example, we will be using Google Web Fonts (`http://www.google.com/webfonts`), but a service such as Adobe Edge Web Fonts (`http://html.adobe.com/edge/webfonts/`) or TypeKit (`http://typekit.com/`) can also be employed.

About web fonts

The idea of using web fonts is not a new concept, but it wasn't until recently that it became a viable model of font usage in web design, due to traditional copyright issues being either subdued by fee-based commercial font services, or by the emergence of services which only use freely usable, open fonts.

 In actuality, Edge Animate can use many different types of fonts and font services. It all depends upon what is supported by our target browsers.

Generic font definitions

These are nonspecific font categories that do not specify any specific typeface. Rather, it is left to the client operating system to use the default font within any category to render text.

These category definitions include:

Category	Description
Serif	Designs which contain many barbs and appendages
Sans-Serif	Straight, clean designs
Monospace	Often used in code editors as whitespace and characters take up the same amount of space no matter the count
Cursive	Resembling handwriting, often having interconnected letters
Fantasy	Somewhat wild fonts… these designs are all over the place

Serif	-	Georgia
San-Serif	-	Arial
Monospace	-	Consolas
Cursive	–	*Segoe Script*
Fantasy	–	**Broken Ghost**

Microsoft's core fonts for the Web

This widely distributed set of fonts includes Arial, Courier New, Times New Roman, Comic Sans, Impact, Georgia, Trebuchet, and Verdana. It was distributed by Microsoft from 1996–2002, and was adopted as the set of fonts that web designers could feel confident using on a web page due to widespread distribution across Windows and Mac OS. For years, these were the only choices that were acceptable for use on the Web. As of the writing of this book—they are still, by far, the most heavily used fonts in web design.

A number of techniques have arisen to break free of these typeface restrictions. These include creating images of characters using the font of choice, though this method is bad for both the sight-impaired and for search engine optimization. Another alternative is to use a rendering mechanism such as sIFR (`http://wiki.novemberborn.net/sifr/`) to employ a combination of technologies in rendering small bits of text from HTML through JavaScript, for rendering in the typeface of one's choice in Flash. This is better than using images since it can be read by search engines and screen readers, but is still not ideal.

Note that while it is now possible to use a variety of fonts within modern browsers, many older implementations will not support any typeface beyond the set of fonts which has been established as a standard set. A number of these font sets are included in the Edge Animate **Properties** panel when dealing with text elements.

Hosted web font services

Web fonts have begun to make an impression upon the current web design landscape. A variety of font hosting services from Google, Adobe, and others have emerged in the past couple of years to make utilizing these fonts easy and legal. This has made using web fonts far more accessible for use since web designers no longer have to worry about implementation, hosting, or legal issues.

Web fonts employ the `@font-face` CSS declaration, which allows both a `font-family` property for identification and a `src` property pointing to the actual font file.

Those familiar with the Apache Flex framework will already be familiar with embedding fonts in this manner.

Some of these hosted services include:

- Google Web Fonts (`http://www.google.com/webfonts`)
- Adobe Edge Web Fonts (`http://html.adobe.com/edge/webfonts/`)
- Adobe TypeKit (`https://typekit.com/`)
- Typotheque (`http://www.typotheque.com/webfonts`)
- MyFonts (`http://webfonts.myfonts.com/`)
- WebType (`http://www.webtype.com/`)
- FontsLive (`http://www.fontslive.com/`)
- Fontdeck (`http://fontdeck.com/`)
- Font Squirrel (`http://www.fontsquirrel.com/`)
- Fonts.com (`http://webfonts.fonts.com/`)

Applying web fonts to an Edge Animate project

In order to use a custom font within our Edge Animate project, there are some steps we must take to register and configure our font definitions within Edge Animate.

To define a Font asset within the Library, perform the following steps:

1. Go to Google Web Fonts and choose a font to use within an Edge Animate composition:

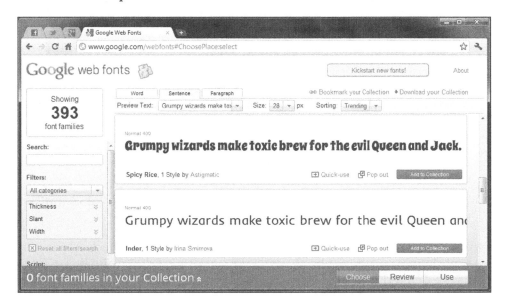

2. Grab the linkage tag. It will look something like the following:

```
<link href='http://fonts.googleapis.com/css?family=Flavors'
rel='stylesheet' type='text/css'>
```

3. Also note the given name of the font. In this case, `Flavors`. We will need this as well.

4. Within Edge Animate, go to the **Library** panel and click on the **+** icon next to **Fonts**.

5. In the **Add Web Font** dialog that appears, paste in the full linkage tag copied from the font service into the **Embed Code** field.

6. Within the **Font Fallback List** input, paste the name of the font being included. We can also provide a comma-separated list of additional fonts in case there is a problem.

7. When finished, click on **Add Font** to close the dialog. This font will now appear within the **Library** panel and become accessible from the internal font list when dealing with text elements.

To test our new font in an Edge Animate composition, perform the following steps:

1. With **Text Tool (T)** selected, click on the Stage.

2. Type `Custom Web Fonts ROCK!` and press the *Esc* key.

3. In the **Properties** panel, use the Font Name drop-down to select the web font we created earlier.

4. We can now adjust additional element properties (such as color) until we are happy with the outcome.

Now we have a custom web font that can be used within this project. At this time, custom font definitions cannot be shared across multiple Edge Animate projects. They must be defined for each and every project (although they can be shared within Edge Animate Symbol Files).

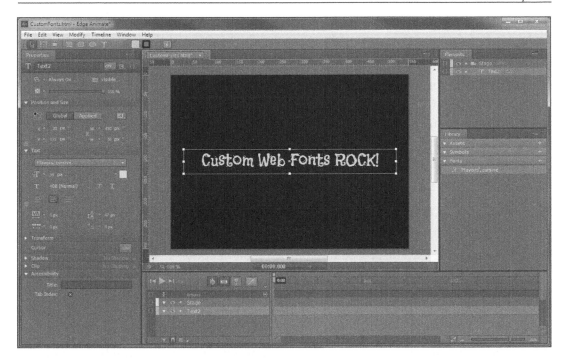

To see this project in action, have a look within the CustomFonts directory included in this book's sample files.

Of course, text elements using web fonts can also be animated just like any other text element! For more on animating content, refer to *Chapter 6, Creating Motion Through the Timeline*.

Using local fonts from your collection

Web font services are a great choice when they have the typeface needed for a project, but what if none of these services has the desired font? Well, it is totally possible to use our own fonts in Edge Animate projects as well.

 This assumes that we have the rights to use and distribute the desired font files. Do this without permission and we could be served with a takedown notice or lawsuit by the copyright holder!

To do this locally, we will first need to define a CSS file which uses `@font-face` in order to declare both the name of the font and the location of the font file itself. This CSS file is what will be linked within the Edge Animate **Library** panel.

1. Create a directory called `LocalFont`. All of the files we create manually as well as our Edge Animate project files will reside in this directory.

2. Move the fonts we wish to use into the directory just created. In this case, we are using the following files:
   - `BBrick.otf`: The font file itself in OpenType format
   - `OFL.txt`: The **SIL Open Font License (OFL)**

3. Create a new CSS file in your editor of choice. We'll be using a font called `Banana Brick` for this example and will name the CSS file `BBrick.css`.

4. Within the CSS file, place the following bit of code:
   ```
   @font-face {
     font-family: 'Banana Brick';
     src: url('BBrick.otf');
   }
   ```

5. Save the file. This now provides our font with a name that can be used in Edge Animate through the `font-family` property, and makes reference to the font file itself through the `src` property.

Now that we have a CSS file pointing to our font file, we'll need to create our project in Edge Animate and declare our web font within the **Library** panel for use.

1. First, create a new Edge Animate project and save it as `LocalFont.html` within the same `LocalFont` directory we created earlier. Project specifics do not matter.

2. Now, go to the **Library** panel and click on the **+** icon next to **Fonts**.

3. In the **Add Web Font** dialog that appears, paste in the following linkage tag, which refers to the CSS file we had created previously:
   ```
   <link href='BBrick.css' rel='stylesheet' type='text/css'>
   ```

4. Within the **Font Fallback List** input, paste the name of the font being included. In this case, `'Banana Brick'`. Since this font name is more than one word long, we must enclose the name in single quotes. We may also provide a comma-separated list of additional fonts in case there is a problem.

5. When finished, click on **Add Font** to close the dialog. This font will now appear within the **Library** panel and become accessible from the internal font list when dealing with text elements.

6. To complete the exercise, select **Text Tool (T)** and draw out a text element on the Stage.

7. Type in whatever you like for text. In this case, we typed in Local Font Declaration.

8. With the text element selected, change the Font Family within the **Properties** panel to **Banana Brick**. The text element on the Stage will immediately change based on this action.

   Now, we can see the Edge Animate project using a local font definition.

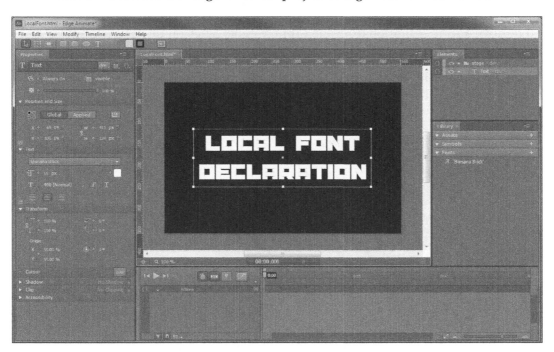

For an example of using local fonts within an Edge Animate project, have a look at the `LocalFont` directory included in this book's sample files.

> Note that even though we are using the term "local font" here, this will work just as well after being uploaded onto a remote server. We simply must be sure that the CSS rules refer to the correct path once on the server.

Managing fonts in the Edge Animate Library

We've seen how to add font definitions to the **Library** panel, but what if we want to either remove or change these definitions somewhat? Thankfully, Edge Animate makes either task quite simple.

> To use a set of custom fonts across projects, we can employ the `.ansym` file format. To learn more about this, refer to *Chapter 8, Making Use of Symbols, Nested Elements, and Grouping*.

To remove a font definition from the **Library** panel, click on the font definition to remove and then press the *Delete* key on the computer keyboard.

To modify a font definition, simply double-click on it within the **Library** panel to bring the **Edit Web Font** dialog box back up. From here, we can add or remove fallback fonts or even change the font definition all together.

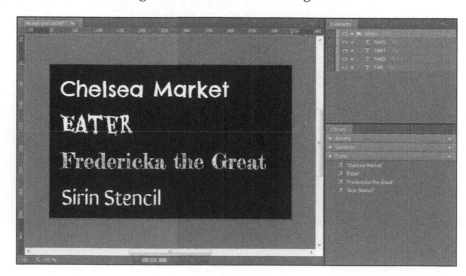

Have a look at the project within the `ManyFonts` directory included in this book's sample files to see a good example of managing fonts within a project.

 Unfortunately, there is no mechanism available to specify the range of characters to include (as when embedding fonts in Flash), since we require the entire font file. Keep this in mind when considering overall page load time.

Viewing fonts within {projectname}_edge.js

If we want to see how Edge Animate defines our custom font definitions, or need to make some adjustments to these fonts by hand; we can do so through manipulation of the `{projectname}_edge.js` file.

Close to the top of the file will be a `fonts` variable declared, which list the particulars of each font we have declared within Edge Animate:

```
var fonts = {};
    fonts['\'Flavors\', cursive']='<link
href=\'http://fonts.googleapis.com/css?family=Flavors\'
rel=\'stylesheet\' type=\'text/css\'>';
```

The structure is arranged so that the first string is the font name, followed by a colon, and completed by the CSS linkage string.

If we have multiple fonts defined within a project, the font definitions are all added one after the other, shown as follows:

```
var fonts = {};
    fonts['\'Flavors\', cursive']='<link
href=\'http://fonts.googleapis.com/css?family=Flavors\'
rel=\'stylesheet\' type=\'text/css\'>';
    fonts['\'Sirin Stencil\'']='<link
href=\'http://fonts.googleapis.com/css?family=Sirin+Stencil\'
rel=\'stylesheet\' type=\'text/css\'>';
    fonts['\'Fredericka the Great\'']='<link  href=\'http://fonts.
googleapis.com/css?family=Fredericka+the+Great\' rel=\'stylesheet\'
type=\'text/css\'>';
    fonts['\'Chelsea Market\'']='<link href=\'http://fonts.googleapis.
com/css?family=Chelsea+Market\' rel=\'stylesheet\' type=\'text/
css\'>';
    fonts['\'Eater\'']='<link href=\'http://fonts.googleapis.com/
css?family=Eater\'
rel=\'stylesheet\' type=\'text/css\'>';
```

It is entirely possible to have multiple web fonts defined in an Edge Animate project, but keep in mind that the font files must be downloaded to the user's browser cache in order to render. This could take some time and may extend the time it takes our composition to fully load.

Summary

In this chapter, we've had a good overview of the Text tool and the creation and management of text elements within Adobe Edge Animate. We were also able to demonstrate the inclusion of external web fonts through services such as Typekit and Google Web Fonts, allowing our compositions to use many fonts beyond the standard "web-friendly" type sets. This chapter has also marked our first real introduction to the Edge Animate Library.

In the next chapter, we'll have a look at how to import external image assets into an Edge Animate project that can be used in many of the same ways as element types we've already explored.

5
Importing External Assets

So far in this book, we've seen a number of ways in which we can create elements within an Edge Animate project using the tools available within the application itself. While rectangles, ellipses, and text are certainly useful, the inclusion of external image assets within a project can really take a composition to the next level.

In this chapter, we'll have a look at how to:

- Import Scalable Vector Graphics
- Import bitmap file types
- Adjust the properties of imported elements

We will also examine methods of exporting assets from a variety of other Creative Suite applications for use within Adobe Edge Animate.

Importing external assets

Apart from the creation of basic vector and text elements within an Edge Animate composition, we also have the ability to import external assets for use in a project. These assets may have been prepared in another application such as Adobe Photoshop, Illustrator, or Fireworks. Generally, we would want to use these imported assets more than the simple shapes generated by Edge Animate, but this will depend upon the project.

File types which can be imported into Edge Animate include:

- **SVG**: Scalable Vector Graphics
- **PNG**: Portable Network Graphics
- **JPEG**: Joint Photographic Experts Group
- **GIF**: Graphics Interchange Format

We'll have a look at each of these formats and then go through a brief usage example.

> Note that unlike other element types, there are no tools to create images within the Edge Animate application itself. Adobe Edge Animate relies upon other applications such as Photoshop or Illustrator for the creation of external image assets.

Image element types

Elements imported into an Edge Animate project will default to a `<div>` HTML element, but can actually be changed to alternatively employ an `<img>` element.

The possible imported image element types are as follows:

- `<div>`: Defines a division element within an HTML document and is often used for generic block-level elements
- `<img>`: Allows the embedding of an image file within HTML and includes a number of properties specific to these elements

As we can see from these element definitions, most of the differences here are simply *semantic*, though semantic meaning is a core consideration when dealing with HTML-based content.

These image element definitions can be useful in other ways too. Perhaps we want to apply an advanced CSS3 property to any `<img>` elements in our composition. This feature facilitates that workflow. To see an example of how to do this, have a look at *Chapter 11, Further Explorations with Adobe Edge Animate*.

> Like other elements, advanced image treatments can also be simply rendered from an image editing program as SVG or bitmap images and included within an Edge Animate composition in that way.

Properties unique to image elements

There are certain properties which are unique to imported images assets. These properties are identical no matter what file type has been imported.

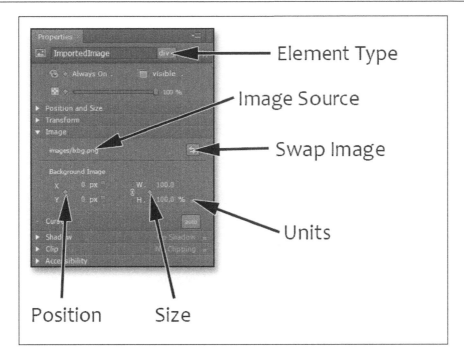

Image Source

This isn't actually a property that can be adjusted through the **Properties** panel, but it does display the location of the imported image asset for reference.

Swap Image

This button will bring up a list of images within the project **Library**. Choosing an image from this dialog replaces the selected image source.

Background Position Offset X

A setting used for offsetting the image asset along the **X** axis within the element definition.

Background Position Offset Y

A setting used for offsetting the image asset along the **Y** axis within the element definition.

Background Position Units

We can choose to define **X** and **Y** source offset based upon pixel units or percentages. This is useful for a more responsive layout of elements.

Background Size Width

This is used for setting the image asset Width within the element definition.

Background Size Height

This is used for setting the image asset Height within the element definition.

Background Size Units

We can choose to define Width and Height based upon pixel units or percentages. This is useful for a more responsive layout of elements.

More about image elements

There are a few other items of note when it comes to image assets and their associated properties, which we will now address.

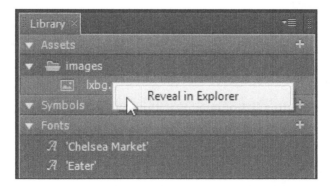

Reveal in Finder/Explorer

Right-clicking upon an image within the **Library** panel will allow us to open the operating system file browser to the exact location of the background asset being used in the selected element.

The alt attribute

This value populates the `alt` attribute upon the image in HTML—providing alternative text for accessibility purposes. It is accessible through the **Accessibility** area of the **Properties** panel.

Scalable Vector Graphics

Scalable Vector Graphics (**SVG**) is an XML-based file format that describes how to draw vector objects through polygon, path, and fill definitions. These objects are described in a way which informs SVG-capable clients of the structure and informs the clients how everything should be visually rendered.

SVG differs from bitmap formats such as JPG or PNG in that the image data is processed as needed based upon the mathematic information contained within the SVG file. Because of this, these vector objects are easily scalable and can be represented at many different sizes with no apparent distortion while using the same base data.

In the next example, we see the SVG code for an object generated through Adobe Illustrator. This code is derived from the `star.svg` file, which is included in this book's assets. To view the vector object, simply drag this file into an SVG-capable browser and it will be rendered on screen.

 An excerpt of the file structure is shown next; if we want to view the entire structure, the file may be opened in a text editor such as Microsoft Notepad or Adobe Dreamweaver.

To become more familiar with the SVG file format, a sample named `star.svg` has been included. A portion of this file is displayed as follows:

```
<?xml version="1.0" encoding="utf-8"?>
<!-- Generator: Adobe Illustrator 15.1.0, SVG Export Plug-In . SVG
Version: 6.00 Build 0)  -->

<!DOCTYPE svg PUBLIC "-//W3C//DTD SVG 1.1//EN" "http://www.w3.org/
Graphics/SVG/1.1/DTD/svg11.dtd">

<svg version="1.1" id="Layer_1" xmlns="http://www.w3.org/2000/
svg" xmlns:xlink="http://www.w3.org/1999/xlink" x="0px" y="0px"
width="640px" height="480px" viewBox="0 0 640 480" enable-
background="new 0 0 640 480" xml:space="preserve">

    <g>
        <polygon fill="#414042" points="303,67.781 357.435,178.078
```

```
        479.153,195.764 391.076,281.617 411.869,402.845 303,345.609
        194.131,402.845 214.923,281.617 126.847,195.764 248.565,178.078      "/>
            <g>
                <g>
                    <polygon fill="none" points="263.211,48.892
        219.32,137.825 32.207,165.014 167.604,296.992 135.641,483.35
        303,395.364           470.36,483.35 438.396,296.992 573.793,165.014
        386.68,137.825 342.492,48.291 263.714,87.17 328.342,218.121
        385.007,226.354           344.003,266.322 353.683,322.76 303,296.114
        252.316,322.76 261.997,266.322 220.993,226.354 277.658,218.121
        341.988,87.773                    "/>


        <!--BULK OF SVG CODE REMOVED FOR BREVITY -->


                    <path fill-rule="evenodd" clip-rule="evenodd" d="M
        84.896,167.553c0.984,0.127-2.648,0.475-1.372,0.811           c-1.828-
        0.145-6.564,0.724-7.481,0.252c-4.083,0.807-6.354,1.543-
        3.53,2.104c-3.976,1.05-9.76,1.867-15.31,2.416           c2.303,2.512,4.02
        7,4.641,4.871,5.939c-0.943,1.146-5.629-1.925-11.134-6.977l-1.625-1.525
        c4.788-0.735,10.509-1.232,15.706-1.723c5.208-0.492,9.901-0.978,12.924-
        1.731c3.188-0.285,11.81-1.521,16.417-1.814           c-0.303,0.429,0.396,
        0.217,1.244,0.547c-3.009,0.549-8.856,1.191-7.529,1.597C86.752,167.576,
        85.693,167.61,84.896,167.553z"/>
                </g>
            </g>
        </g>
    </svg>
```

 We probably wouldn't ever want to write an SVG code by hand.

Importing SVG images

Once an image file is imported into an Edge Animate project, it can be manipulated, animated, and scripted just as any other element. To import an SVG file into Edge Animate, we perform the following actions:

1. Navigate to the Edge Animate application menu.
2. Select **File | Import...**.
3. A system file browser dialog will appear. Navigate to the .svg file you wish to import.
4. Select the file and click on **Open**.

5. The file will now be placed on the Stage and also added to the project **Library** under **Assets**. From here, we can add multiple instances of this asset to the Stage.

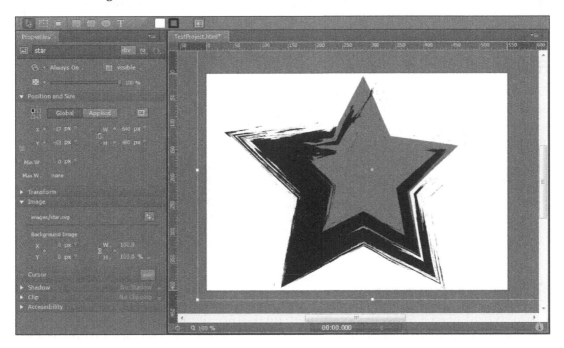

 Note that the file instance placed upon the Stage will be using the exact dimensions of the imported file itself, so it may overlap the boundaries of the Stage. This can be remedied through element manipulation by using the **Properties** panel. It is the same case in regard to bitmap images and is not unique to SVG.

Now that the SVG image asset has been imported and an instance of this asset resides upon the Stage, we can use the Selection and Transform tools to perform manipulations such as resize, scale, and skew, just as we can with text or rectangle elements.

Since animation is possible within SVG files and Edge Animate compositions are built upon HTML, animated SVG files are fully supported within an Edge Animate composition so long as the target browsers support animated SVG files. The animation within an SVG file is not something that can be controlled through Edge Animate itself, as it is a part of the SVG file and so will act independently of the Edge Animate Timeline.

It is also possible to simply drag-and-drop a `.svg` file from our operating system file explorer onto the Stage. This action will have the same effect as described earlier when working through the application's **Import...** command.

SVG notifications

Certain actions taken within an Edge Animate composition will trigger the internal notification system. For instance, when employing SVG files within a project, we can see the small blue notifications icon appear at the bottom-right of the Stage. This lets us know of known browser incompatibilities or other points to take into account.

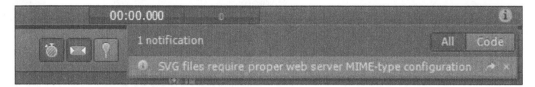

Bitmap images

Also referred to as a **raster** image, **bitmap** images are those which are composed of a rectangular grid of individual pixels. Each pixel in this grid can include both color values and optionally transparency values (depending upon the image format).

Bitmap images are great for highly detailed images such as photographs, since they define detail at a pixel level. They also do not require the client to perform any heavy calculations upon the image data in order to render it to a viewable state, since that information is already present within the pixel grid. The client simply has to read the data in properly.

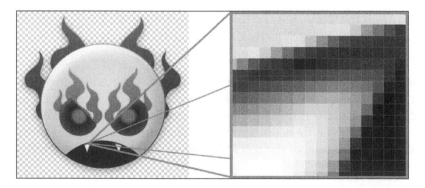

Unlike SVG and other vector graphics formats, bitmap images are resolution-dependant. This means that they cannot be scaled or otherwise manipulated without significant visual artifacting.

Types of bitmap images

Adobe Edge Animate can import any image file type that can be used within general web design workflows. These are the same PNG, JPG, and GIF image files that are considered universally usable in all modern browsers.

There are a number of differences to note between these file types. They each have aspects which lend them toward a particular use and it would serve us well to understand some basic differences.

Portable Network Graphics

Portable Network Graphics (PNG) is the most versatile of bitmap image formats due to the control present over image quality and transparency. Of all the formats presented here, PNG is the only one that includes a full channel of transparency for a full range of opacity values per pixel. The compression used in PNG is also *lossless*—meaning that while the information present in the file is compressed, no data is actually removed.

 PNG image files do tend to be larger than their counterparts—so best be wary of this when considering overall page load.

Joint Photographic Experts Group

The Joint Photographic Experts Group (JPEG, or JPG) file format is traditionally used for complex images such as photographs. The quality is variable, and deciding upon a quality setting when creating a JPG involves a balance between file size and the prominence of any image artifacting, which can result in rendering the image poorly.

The compression used in JPG differs from PNG in that it is a *lossy* format—meaning that data is actually removed upon compression. JPG files are often much smaller than a comparable PNG, but quality can suffer. JPG includes no option for transparency whatsoever.

Graphics Interchange Format

The **Graphics Interchange Format (GIF)** file type is useful for solid colors and simple shapes due to limitations in the associated color pallet. A GIF file is limited to 256 colors—a drastic drop from the millions of colors available in PNG or JPG.

GIF files are also compressed using a *lossy* file compression algorithm, but do include a simple type of transparency. GIF transparency differs greatly from that used in PNG because when using GIF, pixels are either fully opaque or fully transparent—there is no ranged transparency value whatsoever.

A unique aspect of the GIF file type is that GIF files can be animated in a very basic way.

Adobe Edge Animate has no problem incorporating animated GIF images into a composition since we are dealing with HTML, within which animated GIF images are fully supported.

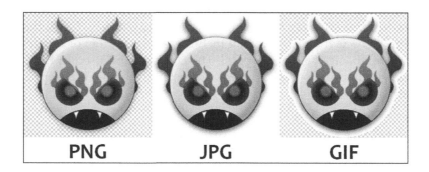

In the previous image, we can see the differences in transparency options between the PNG, JPG, and GIF file formats. A checkered background indicates areas of the image which are transparent.

Importing bitmap images

Once an image file is imported into an Edge Animate project, it can be manipulated, animated, and scripted just as any other element. To import a bitmap image file into Edge Animate, we perform the following actions:

1. Navigate to the Edge Animate application menu.
2. Select **File | Import...**.

3. A system file browser dialog will appear. Navigate to the `.png`, `.gif`, or `.jpg` file you wish to import.

4. Select the file and click on **Open**.

5. The file will now be placed onto the Stage and also added to the project **Library** under **Assets**. From here, we can add multiple instances of this asset to the Stage.

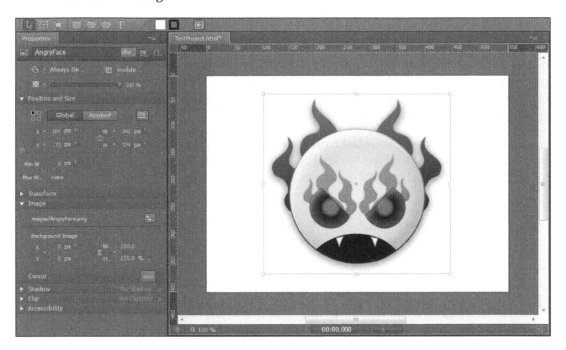

 Note that similar to SVG files, the bitmap file instance placed upon the Stage will be using the exact dimensions of the imported file itself, so it may overlap the boundaries of the Stage. This can be remedied through element manipulation by using the **Properties** panel.

Now that the bitmap image asset has been imported and an instance of this asset resides upon the Stage, we can use the Selection and Transform tools to perform manipulations such as resize, scale, and skew just as we can with text or rectangle elements. Unlike vector-based elements, however, visible artifacting, blockiness, and other distortions will occur with bitmap objects.

It is also possible to simply drag-and-drop a .jpg, .png, or .gif file from our operating system file explorer onto the Stage. This action will have the same effect as described above when working through the application's **Import...** command, but we will be able to precisely place the imported image onto the Stage when employing drag-and-drop.

Using animated GIFs

One of the great things about Edge Animate content being built upon web standards is that file types that *can* be supported for playback in a web browser, *will* be supported within an Edge Animate composition. This is the case with animated GIF files and provides an interesting dynamic of integrating different methods of animation within a composition.

Animated GIFs can be generated from any application which supports these simple, frame-based animations. Fireworks, Flash Professional, and many freely available tools support the creation and export of animated GIF files.

 Note that in Edge Animate, we have no control over how the GIF animation plays back. This behavior is set at the time of GIF authoring.

Working with imported assets

Any imported assets will always be available in the **Library** panel under **Assets**. From here, we can drag-and-drop instances onto the Stage in order to create instances of these assets for further manipulation.

The **Assets** group within a project **Library** panel helps to keep things organized and preserves imported files, even when all instances are removed from the Stage.

Considerations when working with imported assets

If using imported assets within an Edge Animate project, these assets are automatically moved into their own directory upon import. This directory is labeled `images` and resides at the root of our project. We must be sure, when uploading output files to a server, that we include this directory.

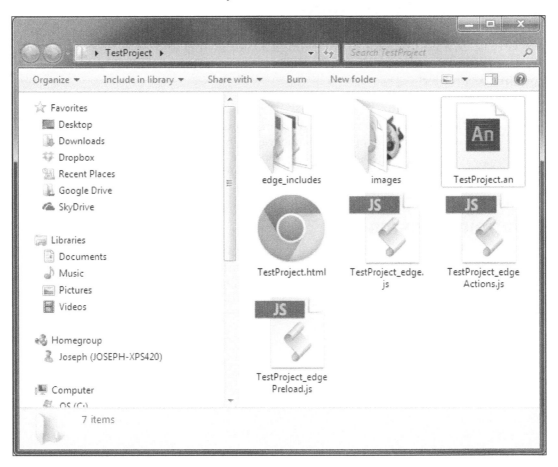

This actually makes it pretty simple to replace any image assets by overwriting them within the `images` directory. So long as the dimensions of each image file are the same, there should be no problems with this.

Managing assets within the Library

Once we have image assets within a project **Library**, there are a number of interesting things we can do with them. Let's have a look at some neat things we can do through the **Library** panel.

Asset instance creation

The presence of asset instance creation within the Library allows instances of these assets to be created upon the Stage through a simple drag-and-drop process. Simply click on the asset and drag it onto the Stage from the **Library** panel. The process couldn't be simpler!

 Remember that we can also drag image assets from the file system directly onto the Stage in much the same way, but if the image already exists within our project, it will create duplicate entries within the **Library** panel. We want to avoid this as it can cause confusion and project bloat.

Swapping assets

Clicking on the swap assets button in the **Properties** panel allows us to swap out the image asset used as the source of an image element. When we swap out an image source, this is the only property that changes; position, scale, x and y location, width and height—these properties all remain as they were.

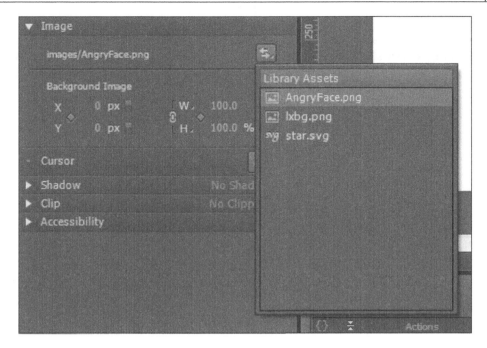

Importing Symbol Libraries

We are also able to import Edge Animate Symbol files into our projects through the use of Edge Animate Symbol files. These files have the extension `.ansym` (older preview versions of Animate used the extension `.eglib`, which actually still works in Animate 1.0) and can be imported through a mechanism within the project **Library**:

 We'll examine the creation of symbols and how to export Edge Animate Library files in *Chapter 8, Making Use of Symbols, Nested Elements, and Grouping*.

The **Edge Animate Symbol** file format is actually a specialized archive file that Edge Animate understands. It can be opened within any archive extraction program. In the following screenshot, we've opened the `.ansym` file with the open source 7-Zip (`http://www.7-zip.org/`) application:

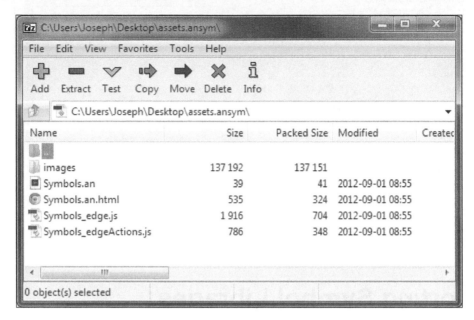

 This file system should look familiar if we already understand how Edge Animate projects are structured. Notice how everything within an Edge Animate Library file is set up like a mini composition.

Exporting assets from other Creative Suite applications

The chances are that if we use Adobe Edge Animate, we are familiar with and use a number of other Adobe Creative Suite applications. This part of the chapter will detail the primary methods of getting assets from certain applications such as Photoshop or Illustrator into Edge Animate as external image assets—no matter what the file type.

Exporting from Illustrator

Adobe Illustrator is an excellent choice for vector art creation and manipulation as part of the Creative Suite. Exporting image assets from Illustrator for use in Edge Animate can be accomplished in a number of ways depending upon whether we require bitmap renderings or an SVG file to retain all the vector information.

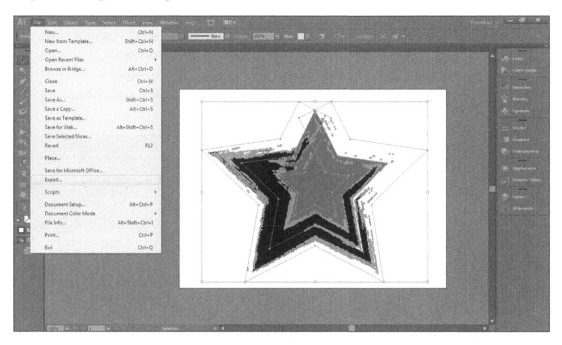

To export a bitmap image asset from Illustrator, perform the following steps:

1. Assuming your Illustrator project is open within the application; in the application menu, choose **File | Save for Web...**.

2. The **Save for Web...** dialog will appear, allowing us to make some decisions around the file format to export.

3. Make the necessary adjustments to our image export options, including file type, quality, palette, and transparency depending upon whether we are exporting as JPG, PNG, or GIF.

4. Once the export settings have been confirmed, click on **Save...**.

5. This will open a file explorer through which we can rename the exported file and decide upon its destination directory. When ready, click on **Save** to complete the file export process.

To export a SVG image asset from Illustrator, perform the following steps:

1. Assuming your Illustrator project is open within the application; in the application menu, choose **File | Save As...**.

2. The **Save As** dialog will appear, allowing us to make some decisions around the file format to export.

3. This will open a file explorer through which we can rename the exported file and decide upon its destination directory. Choose **SVG (*.SVG)** as the format and click on **Save** to complete the file export process.

   Once the asset has been saved to the file system, we only need to drag-and-drop it into our Edge Animate project or go through the import process.

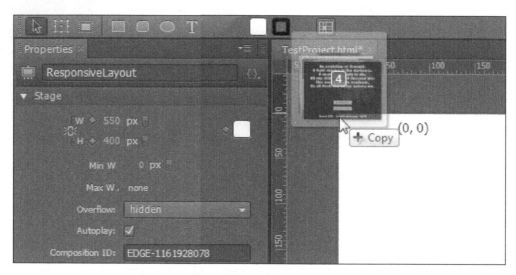

 Note that to retain all positioning aspects of single or even multiple assets exported from Illustrator, we simply need to retain the same document size across all of our image assets—exporting them one at as time as single layers. This allows us to select all the images in our operating system file browser and drag them all onto the Edge Animate Stage, aligning with its (0, 0) position using guides as shown in the previous screenshot.

Exporting from Adobe Photoshop

Adobe Photoshop is the premiere bitmap image compositing and adjustment application in the Creative Suite. Exporting image assets from Photoshop for use in Edge Animate is fairly straightforward thanks to the **Save for Web...** option.

To export an image asset from Photoshop, perform the following steps:

1. Assuming your Photoshop project is open within the application, in the application menu, choose **File | Save for Web...**.

2. The **Save for Web...** dialog will appear, allowing us to make some decisions around the file format to export.

3. Make the necessary adjustments to our image export options, including file type, quality, palette, and transparency depending upon whether we are exporting as JPG, PNG, or GIF.

4. Once the export settings have been confirmed, click on **Save...**.

5. This will open a file explorer through which we can rename the exported file and decide upon its destination directory. When ready, click on **Save** to complete the file export process.

    Once the asset has been saved to the file system, we only need to drag-and-drop it into our Edge Animate project or go through the import process.

Exporting from Fireworks

Adobe Fireworks is an excellent choice for web image asset design and blends both vector and bitmap assets in a really unique way. Exporting assets is a bit different in Fireworks than in our previous two examples, simply because there are so many options to be considered. We'll demonstrate the most straightforward one here.

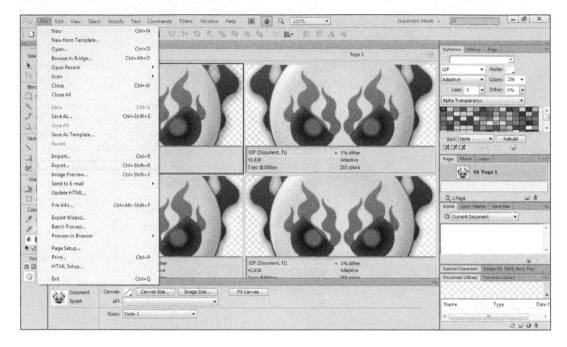

The simply export a Fireworks document as an image for the Web, perform the following steps:

1. Assuming the document is open, have a look at the **Properties** panel, which by default resides at the bottom of the application window.

2. Within this panel, choose the file format we wish to export as:

3. If desired, we can visit the **Window | Optimize** panel to make further adjustments.

4. In the application menu, choose the **File | Export... | Images Only** command. This will open the export dialog and will export only the images and not any accompanying HTML.

5. Browse to the location we wish to save the file in, optionally rename the file, and click on **Save** to complete the export process.

   Just like any asset, once the asset has been saved to the file system, we only need to drag-and-drop it into our Edge Animate project or go through the import process.

Using the Edge Animate extension for Fireworks

One of the great things about Adobe Fireworks is the vast array of extensions which the community has built up over the years. The application truly has the greatest library of extensions out there and with new ones being released all the time, there is much to like.

John Dunning has created an extension for Fireworks that explicitly ties into Edge Animate for a simplified workflow across products. Since this is an extension, it needs to be downloaded and installed separately from Fireworks CS6.

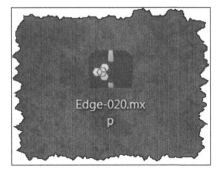

The download can be found by visiting `http://johndunning.com/fireworks/about/EdgeAnimate`. Download the `.mxp` file to a local disk and then run it to automatically open the Adobe Extension Manager.

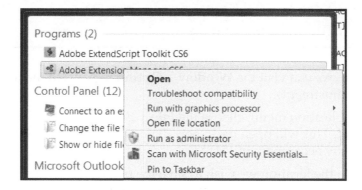

 Note that if using Windows, we may need to first run Adobe Extension Manager CS6 as administrator. To do so, right-click on the Adobe Extension Manager CS6 shortcut and choose **Run as administrator**. Then we can click on install as normal.

As an alternative to executing the `.mxp` file itself, we can open the Adobe Extension Manager and choose **File | Install Extension** and then browse for the `.mxp` to install.

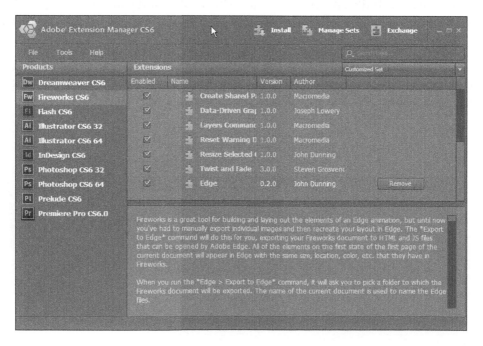

Once the extension is installed, we can click on **Fireworks CS6** in the left-hand **Products** sidebar and see the list of installed extensions, including the extension for Edge Animate we just installed. We are now finished with Adobe Extension Manager CS6 — it can be closed.

Using the extension

The first step in using the Fireworks Edge Animate extension is to actually create a layout in Fireworks. There is an example banner layout included in the files for this book under the `FireworksBanner` directory.

Once a layout is ready to export to Edge Animate, we choose **Commands** from the Fireworks application menu and select **Edge | Export to Edge**. This will open a file dialog which can be used to browse to the folder where we want to generate the Edge Animate project files.

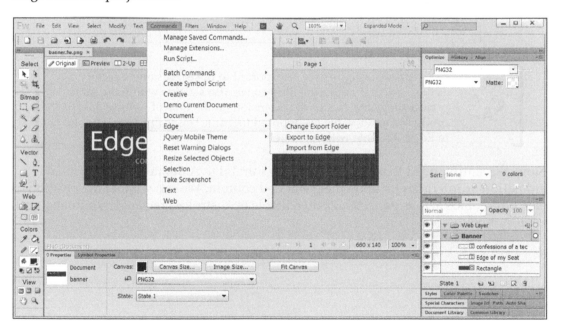

 We can also import an Edge Animate composition into Fireworks through this same menu. The example in this book used the Edge Animate extension version 0.2.0 — it is very possible things will improve or otherwise change in newer releases of the extension.

Once the Fireworks layout has been exported, we can browse to the location chosen to see what the extension has built for us. Interestingly enough, we will find an entire Edge Animate project directory structure and complete set of project and asset files waiting for us!

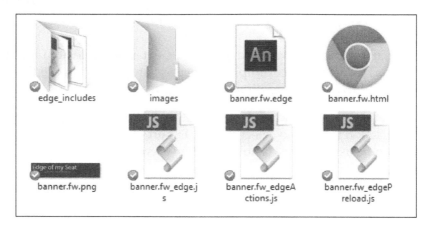

 In the previous figure, we've exported to the exact same directory as the .fw.png authoring file—so we also see that within the same project directory. Notice the extension (at the time of writing this) produces a .edge file (as opposed to .an). This is fine—it will open in Edge Animate without issue!

Now, we simply need to open the .edge file into Edge Animate and perform any animation or interactivity upon the generated content. We can see that the position of elements comes across perfectly, as do editable text, strokes, rectangles, bitmaps, and even symbols.

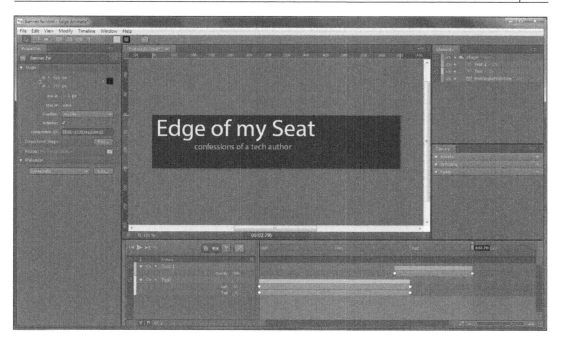

Notice that while we had a pattern applied to our background rectangle in Fireworks, this did not come across to Edge Animate. The export tool does have certain limitations, which we can most often get around by rendering such things as bitmap images before exporting.

Exporting from Flash Professional

Most people probably don't immediately think of Flash Professional as an image asset production tool—but considering all of the content that has been built using Flash Professional over the past decade or so, there is a wealth of assets contained in many a designer's collection of Flash Professional, content that could be repurposed for use in Edge Animate.

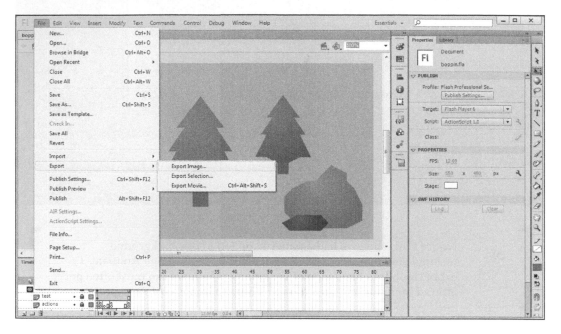

To export assets from Flash Professional, we must first arrange them onto the Stage in the way they should appear within our Edge Animate project:

1. Assuming we have opened a Flash Professional project and have brought the elements we wish to export as an image onto the Stage, choose **File** | **Export** | **Export Image…** from the application menu.

2. The **Export Image** dialog will appear, along with a choice of file type. Valid file types for Edge Animate are PNG, JPG, and GIF.

3. We may now browse to the location we wish to save the file in, optionally rename the file, and click on **Save** to complete the export process.

Flash Professional CS6 also has the ability to export sprite sheets and entire image sequences, which can be used in Edge Animate. We'll return to this application and the subject of sprite sheets and PNG sequences in *Chapter 9, Advanced Animation Techniques*.

Summary

In this chapter, we've examined how to import assets created by other applications to be brought into an Edge Animate project and used within a composition. We also had an overview of the differences between SVG and bitmap imports and use of the Edge Animate Library once assets have been imported to a project. Finally, we had a look at how to manage and nest elements within a composition and several workflow options from other Creative Suite applications. Generally, no matter how each of these assets is created, they can all be employed within an Edge Animate composition in very similar ways.

In the next chapter, we'll have a look at how to create motion through animating these elements along the Edge Animate Timeline.

6

Creating Motion Through the Timeline

The goal of Adobe Edge Animate is to allow users to easily create standards-based motion and interaction without having to deal with a lot of code by hand. This chapter explores the motion side of the equation through animated content and the Timeline.

This chapter covers the following topics:

- The Timeline
- The Playhead
- The Pin
- Transitions
- Keyframes
- Easing

We'll first examine the Timeline itself, along with a variety of the controls that are built into this integral panel. We'll then move through some demos in which we'll become familiar with both the Playhead and the Pin, along with a bit on element Transitions.

Animation within Edge Animate

There are many applications that enable the user to compose animated sequences. Users of Adobe Edge Animate may have experience in other programs such as Director, Flash Professional, After Effects, or even Photoshop. All of these applications handle animation in slightly different ways, but they do all share some aspects of animation techniques and tooling as well.

Like many digital animation programs, Edge Animate employs the concept of "tweening" between keyframes. In traditional cell-based animation, a master animator would draw out certain key frames for an animation sequence, and the frames in between these key frames would be created by apprentice or lower-ranked members of the animation team. The goal was always to create a smooth transition between each key frame created by the master animator, which would result in a completed animation sequence.

This process is performed programmatically within Edge Animate. As keyframes are placed along the Timeline, Edge Animate will record changes in property values as transitions at the position of the Playhead (moment in time). As authors, we have the additional ability to provide the tweening engine with instruction sets based upon a variety of easing equations. This allows a more natural flow between keyframes, and can also be used to achieved certain effects such as an elastic or bounce motion.

The Edge Animate Timeline

The **Timeline** is where all of the motion in an Edge Animate composition is orchestrated. The Timeline itself shares concepts and constructs from other Adobe applications, most notably Flash Professional and After Effects.

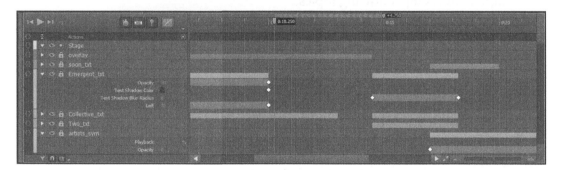

 Unlike the frame-based timeline in Flash Professional, the Edge Animate Timeline is purely time-based.

Playback controls

The playback controls in Edge Animate are all grouped together in the upper-left corner or the **Timeline** panel. These controls allow quick access to many of the playback options available through the Timeline.

Time

The time in Edge Animate is measured in standard decimal time code format (mm:ss.ddd), and this is how it is displayed in the Time control. As the Playhead moves along the Timeline, the information in this display is updated accordingly. A user can scrub the control to the left or right to adjust the current time, or simply click on it—making it editable.

Note that the time controls in Edge Animate are actually grouped along with the Stage and are accessible from directly beneath that panel. The controls are also broken up to allow separate modification of the Playhead time (yellow), and Pin time (blue), when enabled.

Timeline options

These options can be toggled on or off depending upon current needs, as they perform a variety of Timeline-related functions.

These options include the following:

- **Auto-Keyframe Mode (K)**: Selecting this option will enable Edge Animate to generate keyframes for various properties automatically as they are adjusted along the Timeline. When not selected, any keyframes must be inserted manually.

- **Auto-Transition Mode (X)**: When enabled, this informs Edge Animate to use immediate transitions between element property adjustments as they are animated across time.

- **Toggle Pin (P)**: Toggles the Pin on and off. We'll discuss the Pin in more detail shortly.

There are also a number of options present on the bottom of the Timeline:

- **Only Show Animated Elements**: When this option is selected, only those elements whose properties are animated will display within the Timeline. Static elements (such as a background image, perhaps) will be hidden.
- **Timeline Snapping**: Toggles Timeline snapping on or off.
- **Show Grid**: Toggles Timeline grid on or off and allows us to set the grid spacing units.

More about the Show Grid control

We are also able to set the grid spacing by clicking on the small arrow to the immediate right of this icon in order to access a small list of options. We can choose to display grid lines over a selection of measurements across the Timeline.

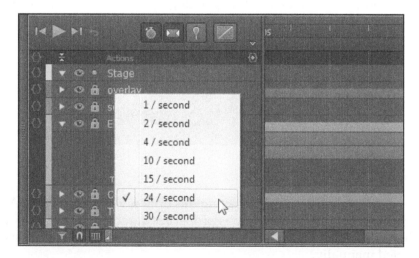

Timeline controls

There are basically only four controls within the Timeline that we need to be concerned with: the Playhead, the Pin, Zoom, and a set of Grid controls. The functionality between controls varies greatly here, as some are used for playback, some for animation, and others are simply there for the enhancement of our overall workflow. All, however, are very useful.

The Playhead

The **Playhead** is the larger of the two elements on the Timeline and is represented by a solid red line that indicates the current time. We can click on the Playhead and scrub back and forth to change the current time. When an animation is being played back through Edge Animate, the Playhead will move along with the current time.

> Normally, the Playhead and the Pin are both synced. If not, they can be resynced through the application menu: **Timeline | Toggle Pin**.

The Pin

The **Pin** is a unique control to Edge Animate. It is a way of pinning the current state of element properties to a certain time, while using the Playhead to determine at which time the animation should complete. The Pin can be positioned either before or after the time indicated by the Playhead—but it always indicates a starting point for the animation, with the Playhead indicating the end. Changing any element properties while the Pin is unsynced will create animation of those properties beginning at the Pin and ending at the Playhead position. In this way, we can quickly and freely create animation that is tightly controlled across the Timeline.

[To quickly sync or unsync the Pin from the Playhead, we can *double-click on the Playhead* to toggle between each state. We can also use the keyboard shortcut (*P*) to accomplish this same task—or even use the control in the Timeline which performs this action.]

When the Pin has been activated, the direction of animation is indicated through a colored strip of chevrons on the Timeline. The color will be yellow or blue, depending upon the direction of motion; blue indicates motion to the left of the Pin, while yellow indicates motion to the right of the Pin.

Zoom controls

There are two zoom controls in Edge Animate, which allow us to expand and contract the Timeline. One is the **Zoom Timeline to Fit** button that appears as dual arrows in the lower-right corner of the Timeline. This will expand or contract the entire span of the visible Timeline to the current width of the Timeline panel. It can provide a good overview of the entire animation. The second control is a slider which appears directly to the right and allows the user to manually control the zoom level of the Timeline to accommodate whatever we are specifically trying to accomplish at any particular time.

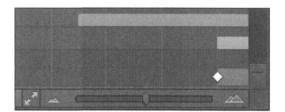

Keyframes

Similar to their representation in After Effects, keyframes in Edge Animate appear along the Timeline as small diamonds. Unlike keyframes in Flash Professional, Edge Animate keyframes are tied directly to the property that is being changed and not to the element itself. This allows for fine-grained property adjustments across the Timeline for any particular element. It is very flexible and a powerful way to animate selected element properties!

Keyframe navigation

There are a number of keyboard shortcuts in Edge Animate that assist with Timeline navigation—specifically when jumping across keyframes.

Command	Shortcut
Go to Previous Keyframe	*Ctrl + Left Arrow* (Windows), *Command + Left Arrow* (Mac)
Go to Next Keyframe	*Ctrl + Right Arrow* (Windows), *Command + Right Arrow* (Mac)

Creating motion

Animating element properties within Edge Animate is fairly straightforward. In this section, we're going to step through a number of basic ways to animate elements along the Edge Animate Timeline. Once using only the Playhead, and again using the Playhead in conjunction with the Pin. By performing the same animation in each way, we will get a feel for the different workflow styles Edge Animate makes available to us when animating element properties across time.

> Note that most elements will not appear within the Timeline until their properties are actually modified across time. The reasoning for this is if nothing is actually animated, there is no reason to clutter the Timeline.

Inserting keyframes

There are a number of mechanisms through which we can insert keyframes into our composition: using the Properties panel, the application menu, the Timeline Keyframe buttons, or through the right-click menu. Before we move on, let's have a quick look at each of these methods.

Adding keyframes through the Properties panel

With any element selected, we can position the Playhead upon the Timeline and look to the **Properties** panel to insert our keyframes. Notice how most of the property values have a small diamond next to them? By clicking on this keyframe control, we will manually insert a keyframe for that property into the current Playhead position for the selected element.

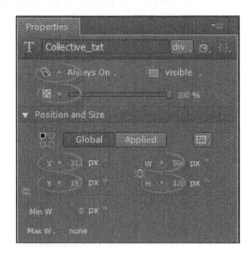

Adding keyframes through the application menu

With any element selected, we can position the Playhead upon the Timeline and look to the application menu to insert our keyframes. Simply navigate to the menu and choose **Timeline | Add Keyframe** and then select the type of keyframe to add, based upon the property we wish to set a keyframe for:

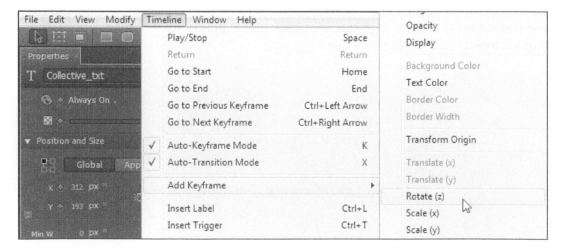

Not all properties have keyboard shortcuts assigned to them by default, though we can easily assign them for commonly used properties, if we wish. This is accomplished through the application menu: **Edit | Keyboard Shortcuts…**.

Using the Timeline keyframe buttons

With any element selected, we can position the Playhead upon the Timeline and look to the left area of the Timeline panel to insert our keyframes. Any property which currently has a keyframe assigned to it will appear grouped beneath an element in the Timeline. These existing properties will include a small icon positioned to the right of the property name through which we can add new keyframes for that specific property. To add new keyframes to properties which do not appear beneath an element, we can simply right-click on the element name and choose **Add Keyframe** to insert them:

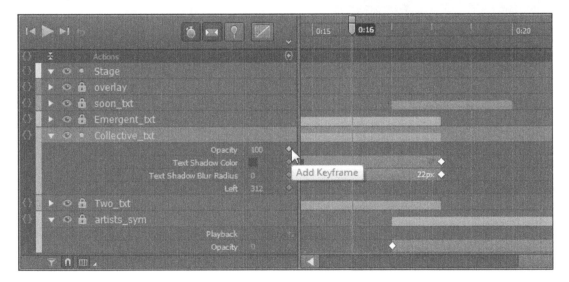

Using right-click for keyframe insertion

With any element selected, we can position the Playhead upon the Timeline and look to the Stage itself to insert our keyframes. Simply right-click on any element which exists on the Stage at that place in the Timeline, and choose **Add Keyframe** to insert any of the available properties for that element.

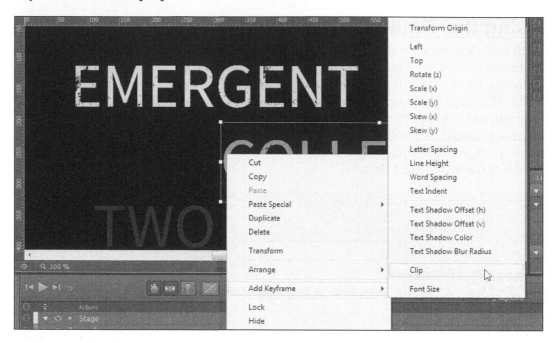

Animating with the Playhead

We will now do a simple animation of an element moving from one side of the Stage to the other, while rotating and changing color using the Playhead along with the Properties panel.

1. Create a new Edge Animate project and save it to your local disk.
2. Adjust the Stage as follows by using the **Properties** panel:
   - Stage **W**: 600 **px**
   - Stage **H**: 350 **px**
   - Background Color: #000000
   - **Overflow**: **hidden**

3. Using the Rectangle tool, draw out an element upon the Stage. We will modify its properties in the next step, so do not worry about dimensions or shape.

4. For each property listed, make the following adjustments within the **Properties** panel:

    ° Location **X**: 20 **px**
    ° Location **Y**: 230 **px**
    ° Size **W**: 100 **px**
    ° Size **H**: 100 **px**
    ° Background Color: #c0c0c0

5. Still using the **Properties** panel, click on the keyframe diamond next to the properties for Location, Background Color, and Rotation. This will set a keyframe for each property within the Timeline.

6. Be sure that Auto-Keyframe properties is in its selected state in the Timeline. Since we have already marked each of these properties with initial keyframes, any adjustments we make across time will be auto-keyframed.

7. Our project should now appear as shown in the following screenshot. We are ready to proceed with the remainder of this exercise.

8. Drag the Playhead over to the ruler marker labeled **0:04** and release.

9. Now, select the element with the Selection tool and in the **Properties** panel, modify the following properties:

    ◦ Location **X**: 480 **px**

    ◦ Background Color: #900000

    ◦ Rotation: 480 deg

10. Notice that we now have transition bars appear on the Timeline with another set of keyframes at the end of our animation sequence.

11. We can now either scrub through the Timeline by dragging the Playhead back and forth, or hit the **Play** button to view the full sequence.

    When played back, the element should appear to roll along the Stage from left to right, changing from gray to red as it does so. The resulting end state is displayed in the following screenshot:

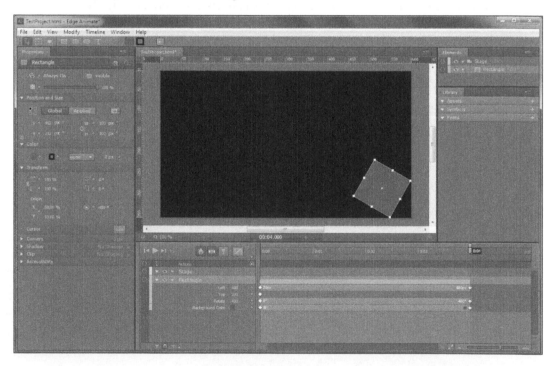

Note that any of the properties of an element can be keyframed, thus modified over time in the way we have done here.

Animating with the Pin

Now we will perform the preceding exercise, but this time we will employ the Pin to demonstrate an alternative way of creating motion in Edge Animate.

1. Create a new Edge Animate project and save it to your local disk.

2. Adjust the Stage as follows by using the **Properties** panel:
   - Stage **W**: 600 **px**
   - Stage **H**: 350 **px**
   - Background Color: #000000
   - **Overflow**: **hidden**

3. Using the Rectangle tool, draw out an element upon the Stage. We will modify its properties in the next step, so do not worry about dimensions or shape.

4. For each property listed, make the following adjustments within the **Properties** panel:
   - Location **X**: 20 **px**
   - Location **Y**: 230 **px**
   - Size **W**: 100 **px**
   - Size **H**: 100 **px**
   - Background Color: #c0c0c0

5. Drag the Playhead to **0:04** in the Timeline.

6. Now, go to the application menu and select **Timeline** | **Toggle Pin**. This will unsync the Pin from the Playhead. Again, the Pin is the small control directly beneath the Playhead when unsynced.

7. Grab the Pin and drag it to **0:00** in the Timeline. This will pin the element's current properties to the **0:00** point without the need to manually insert keyframes. Keep the Playhead itself at **0:04**.

8. Now, select the element with the Selection tool and in the **Properties** panel, modify the following properties:

    - Location **X**: 480 **px**
    - Background Color: #900000
    - Rotation: 480 deg

9. Notice that we now have transition bars appear on the Timeline without the need to set any keyframes whatsoever.

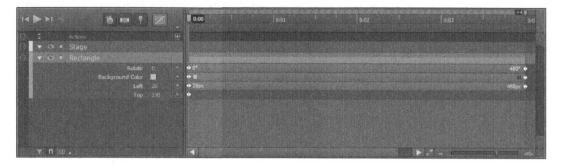

10. Go to the application menu and select **Timeline** | **Toggle Pin** to sync the Pin. We can also toggle the Pin through a keyboard shortcut as expressed earlier in this chapter.

11. We can now either scrub through the Timeline by dragging the Playhead back and forth, or hit the **Play** button to view the full sequence.

    When played back, the element should appear to roll along the Stage from left to right, changing from gray to red as it does so.

> Note that, while in this case the Pin was placed at an earlier time in relation to the Playhead within our Timeline—that need not be the case. We can also place the Pin at a later time than the Playhead and the same behavior will be exhibited: current properties are pinned to the Pin position while adjusted properties align to the position of the Playhead.

Editing transitions

Once a transition has been established, it can be adjusted through mouse interaction via the Timeline. In order to adjust the transition delay, duration, and end we simply click-and-drag the visual transition indicators within the Timeline itself.

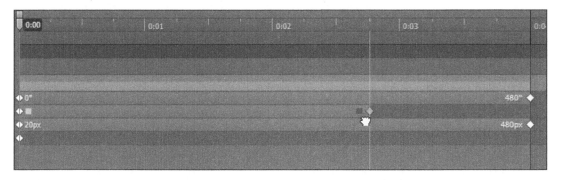

 Note that transitions can be adjusted on a per-object or per-property basis, allowing for a great amount of freedom when defining motion behavior.

Transition delay

This determines when the transition should begin, measured from the start of the overall Timeline. Modification of this value is accomplished by either moving the entire transition, or by dragging the right-most edge.

Transition duration

This represents the time taken up by the entire transition. Transitions can be extended or shortened easily by dragging the right-most edge.

Transition end

This is the time when the transition completes within the Timeline.

Modifying element properties based on transition

To select a transition to edit element properties within the **Properties** panel, use the mouse to select a Transition block within the Timeline. The cursor should change to a little grabby hand and clicking on the transition will cause it, along with any of its keyframes, to highlight.

We now know that the element is selected and can see that the **Properties** panel adjusts to reflect the properties of that element at the position of the Playhead. To adjust any properties across time, simply move the Playhead to see the **Properties** panel adjust to these changes.

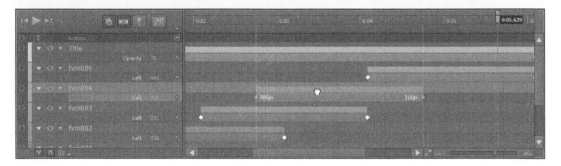

Note that when changing the easing behavior of a transition, we can select the entire element transition block or we may choose individual property transitions to apply a variety of transition types to the same element. It is quite flexible.

Transition easing controls

You may have noticed that the motions achieved through the examples presented so far have been plain, linear transitions from one value to another. To provide a greater sense of realism and a fuller, dynamic nature to individual transitions, we also have the ability to assign a variety of **easing** equations to our transitions.

There are many easing choices within Adobe Edge Animate. The default is **Linear**, which will simply express a transition from A to B in an entirely linear fashion. Often, an easing algorithm of a more dynamic nature is required to express a bit more realism in motion, or to achieve a specific effect. Edge Animate comes bundled with no less than 32 easing choices, to provide the user with a variety of options when determining transition easing.

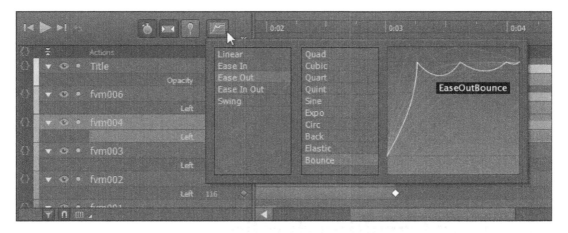

 The transition easing algorithms available in Edge Animate are similar to others found in many ActionScript libraries for animating Flash Professional content. Unlike in Flash Professional, Edge Animate does not yet have the ability to customize these presets.

Transition easing types

While Edge Animate does supply us with a large number of easing types, exactly what they do may not be obvious to many users at first glance. It is very simple to set up an Edge Animate project that allows us to adjust and visualize each of these easing types when applied to a simple transition. We've included such a project in the directory named EasingVisualization, for quick reference.

 Almost all easing types have three variants of themselves: *ease in*, *ease out*, and both *ease in and ease out* together.

Shifting transitions

Edge Animate makes it very easy to shift transitions back and forth across the Timeline. Simply use the mouse cursor to grab a transition (*click and hold*) and then move the mouse back and forth along the Timeline until the transition appears at the desired location. Release the mouse to complete the shift.

Changing transition duration

To adjust the duration of any transition, simply hover the mouse cursor over the beginning or end of any transition block until the cursor changes to indicate that adjustments are possible. Then, click-and-drag along the Timeline to adjust the length of a particular transition. We can also select multiple Transitions in this same way through use of the *Shift* key while we make additional selections along the Timeline.

 The cursor will adjust to look like two lines with arrows pointing to the left or right when hovering over a transition we can expand in this manner.

Selecting transition keyframes

To select individual keyframes, simply click on the desired keyframe and perform whatever modification is desired. Some possible options include hitting the *Delete* key on the keyboard to remove the selected keyframes, or modifying the transition through the right-click menu.

The cursor will adjust to look like a small pointing hand if we are able to select a keyframe. Of course, any locked element keyframes cannot be interacted with in any manner.

Selecting multiple transitions

Holding the *Shift* key down while keyframes are selected will enable the selection of multiple keyframes. Alternatively, a selection rectangle can be drawn across multiple keyframes, but this is imprecise, as full transitions will more than likely be selected as well.

Copy and paste keyframes

While keyframes are selected, we can easily copy and paste these keyframes from one spot in the Timeline to another by moving the Playhead to another position before we paste. This is a good mechanism for copying the exact properties we want and replicating them across the Timeline.

Generating transitions through keyframes

With multiple keyframes selected, we can choose to *right-click* on them in order to remove or create transitions between them. This is useful when we have used auto-transition mode but then decide to retain keyframes but remove the smooth transition between them, or perform the reverse intention.

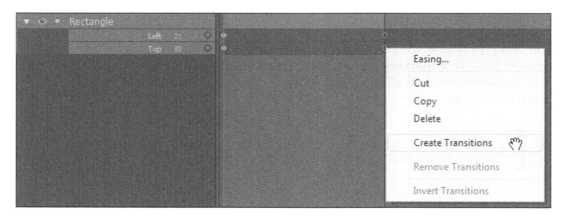

Expanding and contracting composition duration

By selecting all of the transitions within a composition, we can easily stretch or shrink the total duration in accordance with the adjusted composition length by dragging the transition head or tail in the appropriate direction.

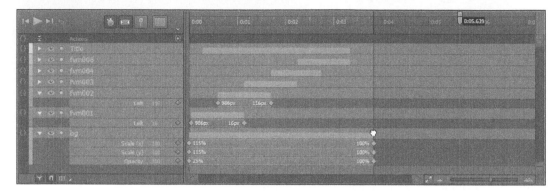

 When we adjust the length of a composition in this manner, all keyframes will shift accordingly. Be aware that timings across the entire composition will shift because of this.

Animating a website header

One of the basic use cases for Adobe Edge Animate is the creation of a simply animated website header. We will be authoring such a composition for a studio recording project of the name *An Early Morning Letter, Displaced*, who wish to have images of each of their releases animate in on the header itself. Thankfully, they have provided us with all of the assets necessary for the construction of this animated header.

 These assets are included as part of the files for this chapter and are in the folder named `banner_assets`.

Project setup, asset import, and general layout

The first step in this composition will be to set up our Edge Animate project, import all of the assets, and arrange them upon the Stage. We will begin by arranging the assets in their final form, as they should appear at the end of the animation once it has completed playback. The Pin makes it quite easy to animate "backwards".

1. Create a new Edge Animate project and save it onto the local disk.

2. Adjust the Stage as follows by using the **Properties** panel:
   - Stage **W**: 940 **px**
   - Stage **H**: 198 **px**
   - Background Color: #000000
   - **Overflow**: **hidden**

3. Go to the application menu and select **File** | **Import...** to bring up a file browser.

4. Select all of the .png files located within the provided assets folder and click on **Open**. The selected files will be placed upon the Stage and also added to the project **Library**.

5. The background image is the exact size of the Stage itself and should fill this entire area.

6. The album art can be arranged evenly across the bottom of the Stage as seen in the following screenshot. We can use the mouse or the **Properties** panel to arrange these images. Space them evenly apart from one another.

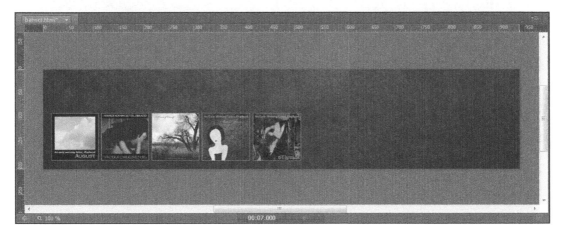

7. Finally, we need to add a title to this header animation. We'll use the Text tool to form the project's name along the top of the header. Choose **Text Tool (T)** now.

8. Add a new text element to the Stage and type the term `An Early Morning Letter, Displaced` into the field.

9. With this text element selected, enter the **Properties** panel and make the following adjustments:

   ° **ID**: `Title`

   ° Location **X**: `16` **px**

   ° Location **Y**: `11` **px**

   ° Font Name: **Arial Black, Gadget, sans-serif**

   ° Font Size: `40` **px**

   ° Font Color: `#bbbbbb`

10. We should now have a composition that appears as shown in the following screenshot:

Performing the animation of elements

We will now perform the animation of all elements on the Stage through use of the Playhead, Mark, and Properties panel.

Animating the background

We will create a transition lasting **00:07.000**, which will fade in the background element while slightly adjusting its scale.

1. Using the Selection tool, click on the bg element to bring up its properties.

2. In the Timeline, move the Pin to **00:07.000** and the Playhead to **00:00.000**.

3. Using the **Properties** panel, make the following adjustments:

   ° Scale (linked): 115 %

   ° Opacity: 25 %

4. In the Timeline, click on the transition that we have just created to select it.

5. In the Timeline, change the **Easing** selection to **Ease Out | Sine** to determine how the transition should occur upon playback. Leave the scale transitions as **Linear**.

Animating the cover art (do this for each cover art image)

For each image, we will create a transition lasting **00:02.000**, which will slide the image in from off-screen, resulting in a playful bounce before coming to a rest. We will stagger the transitions of each subsequent image to begin at the midpoint of the previous transition, creating a flurry of motion within the composition.

1. Using the Selection tool, click on the fvm001 element to bring up its properties.

2. In the Timeline, move the Pin to **00:02.090** and the Playhead to **00:00.000**.

3. Using the **Properties** panel, make the following adjustment:

   ° Location **X**: 986 **px**

4. In the Timeline, click on the opacity transition that we have just created to select it.

5. In the Timeline, change the **Easing** selection to **Ease Out | Bounce** to determine how the transition should occur upon playback.

6. Repeat the previous steps for each of the other album art images.

 Edge Animate also includes the option to paste various elements of a transition from one object to another. For repeatable transitions such as this one, we may want to have a look at the **Paste Special** commands under the application **Edit** menu.

Animating the title text

We will create a transition lasting **00:05.500**, which will fade in the title text element.

1. Using the Selection tool, click on the `Title` element to bring up its properties.
2. In the Timeline, move the Pin to **00:06.000** and the Playhead to **00:05.000**.
3. Using the **Properties** panel, make the following adjustment:
   - Opacity: 0 %
4. In the Timeline, click on the transition that we have just created to select it.
5. In the Timeline, change the **Easing** selection to **Ease In** | **Cubic** to determine how the transition should occur upon playback.

Finishing up!

Once all of the elements are added to the Stage, positioned correctly, and animated properly through transitions, the Edge Animate Timeline will look similar to what we see in the following screenshot:

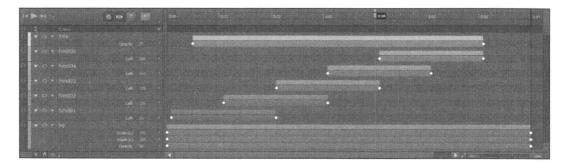

[Edge Animate makes it easy to see exactly what is going on in a composition through even fine-grained transition indicators, which correspond to individual element properties.]

The result of our animated banner appears in a web browser, as shown in the following screenshot. To publish an Edge Animate composition to the browser, we can choose **File** | **Preview in Browser** from the application menu.

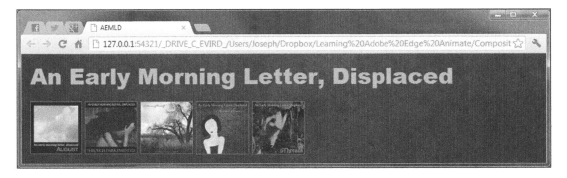

 Notice that there is no interactivity to any of the elements in this banner. In the next chapter, we'll wire up a number of ways to interact with individual elements within this composition.

Automated animation techniques

While it is always possible to perform animation upon individual elements, for reasons of precision or convenience, we may often wish to take advantage of special automations which Edge Animate makes available for our use. Consequently, workflow habits can be streamlined through the use of automation commands discussed next.

Pasting motion

For transitions that need to be replicated or even just copied and tweaked slightly, Edge Animate includes a number of commands for managing copied motion attributes from one element onto another.

Paste Transitions To Location

This command will replicate the exact motion from the copied element upon the selected element. The transition will terminate upon the element's present position.

Paste Transitions From Location

This command will replicate the exact motion from the copied element upon the selected element. The transition will begin at the element's present position.

Paste Inverted

This highly useful command allows us to paste a transition in reverse — very effective for creating back and forth motion.

Paste Actions

This commend will paste only any Actions present upon an element onto another element. See the next chapter for more information on Actions.

Paste All

This command, as implied by its name, will paste everything it possibly can between elements.

Automation example

In order to demonstrate what effect the Paste Transitions To Location, Paste Transitions From Location, and Paste Inverted commands would have upon a series of rectangular elements, we've prepared the following demonstration. The project files for this example can be found in the `PastingMotion` directory.

Initial state

In this first state, we have simply laid out four different-colored rectangle elements along the center of our Stage. We have named each element according to the paste behavior that will be applied to it, along with the uppermost block representing the original transition that the others will be pasted from.

For this original transition, we simply have the element move to the right of our Stage from its location in the center. The three other elements have no transition whatsoever at this point.

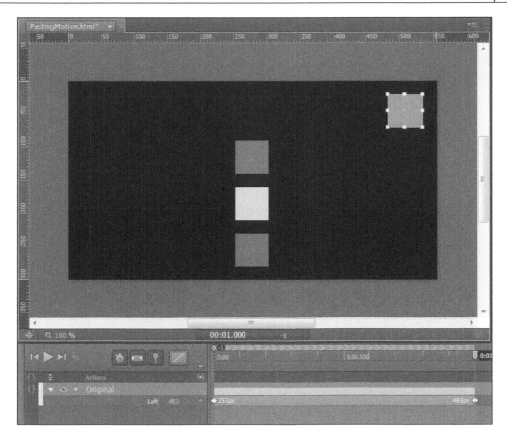

Transition begin state

This state represents the beginning of our composition. We have copied and pasted the transition information upon each element according to its name.

We can see that most of the elements appear in the center, like the original, except for the element which had a **Paste Transitions To Location** command applied to it:

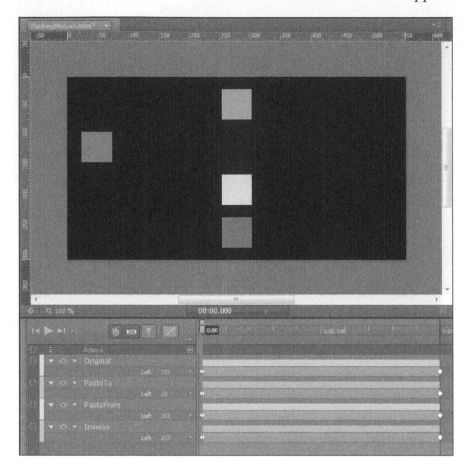

Transition end state

This state represents the composition end and when compared with the previous screenshot, we can understand precisely how each of the element transitions were affected by the type of *Paste* command applied.

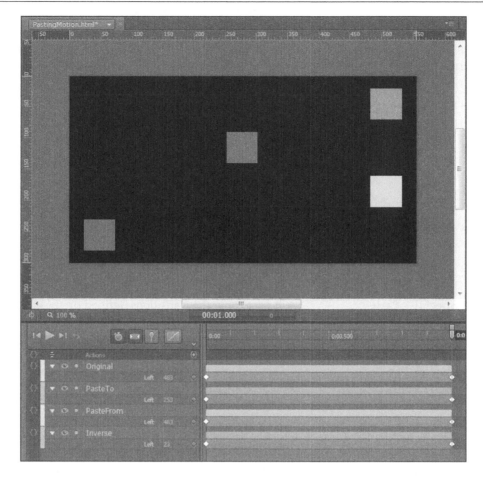

 We could probably benefit a great deal by going through a similar exercise ourselves, with our own assets and transitions in order to become more familiar with each behavior.

Adobe Edge Animate menu items

We'll now have a look at some of the Edge Animate menu items, which can be used along with transitions and the Timeline when dealing with motion.

Edit

The **Edit** menu allows for direct object manipulation through cut, copy, and paste commands, along with selection options and access to an undo/redo history.

Command	Description
Undo	Reverts the last action.
Redo	Re-performs an Undo action.
Cut	Removes the selection and places it into the clipboard.
Copy	Copies a selection and places it into the clipboard.
Paste	Pastes a selection from the clipboard.
Paste Special	This is actually a series of commands which allows the pasting of specific attributes. Like any Paste command, these attributes or an accompanying element must have been cut or copied previous to this.
Paste Special | Paste Transitions To Location	Will paste only the transitions defined on the element that has been copied or cut to a new element. The transition will terminate upon the element's present position.
Paste Special | Paste Transitions From Location	Will paste only the transitions defined on the element that has been copied or cut to a new element. The transition will begin at the element's present position.
Paste Special | Paste Inverted	Will paste an inverted (or reverse) sequence of what has been copied or cut into the Timeline, as explained earlier.
Paste Special | Paste Actions	We'll have a look at this option in the next chapter.
Paste Special | Paste All	Will paste the element which has been copied or cut as a new element along with all properties, Actions, and transitions into the Timeline.
Duplicate	Makes a copy of the selected element.
Select All	Selects everything visible on the Stage.
Transform	Toggles the Transform tool on.
Delete	Removes the selected element.
Keyboard Shortcuts...	Opens the **Keyboard Shortcuts** dialog.

Timeline

As Edge Animate is a motion and animation-focused tool, the **Timeline** commands listed in the following table are core to achieving the most we can through the application interface:

Command	Description
Play/Stop	Toggles playback of the Timeline.
Return	Returns the Playhead to the previous position.
Go to Start	Sends the Timeline Playhead to 0 milliseconds.
Go to End	Sends the Timeline Playhead to the very end of the established Timeline.
Go to Previous Keyframe	Jumps the Playhead to the previous keyframe.
Go to Next Keyframe	Jumps the Playhead to the next keyframe.
Auto-Keyframe Mode	Setting this will enable Edge Animate to generate keyframes for various properties automatically as they are adjusted along the Timeline.
Auto-Transition Mode	Informs Edge Animate to use immediate transitions between element property adjustments.
Add Keyframe	Adds a keyframe of a certain selected type. This command will bring up a menu allowing us to select the property to assign the keyframe to.
Insert Label	Adds a label marker at the current Playhead position. The label name can be edited.
Insert Trigger	Adds a new Trigger to the Actions layer along the Timeline at the current Playhead position.
Invert Transitions	Will basically reverse a transition completely.
Insert Time	Invokes a dialog which allows the insertion of time extending from the current Playhead position along the Timeline. This will extend the overall Timeline length as well.
Toggle Pin	Will toggle the Pin on and off—depending upon particular preferences when animating elements.
Flip Playhead and Pin	Toggles the position of the Playhead with that of the Pin. Only available when the Pin is active.

Command	Description
Snapping	Toggles snapping on and off.
Snap To	Specifies the snapping settings when snapping has been toggled on.
Snap To | Grid	Snaps to grid markers along the Timeline.
Snap To | Playhead	Snaps to the Playhead position.
Snap To | Keyframes, Labels, Triggers	Snaps to additional Timeline objects such as Keyframes, Labels, and Triggers.
Show Grid	Toggles display of the Timeline Grid.
Grid	Allows a choice in incremental gridline placement along the Timeline.
Zoom In	Scales the Stage in from its current scale.
Zoom Out	Scales the Stage out from its current scale.
Zoom to Fit	Scales the Stage to fit within constraints imposed by the size of the application window.
Expand/Collapse Selected	Expands selected elements within the Timeline to expose their individual keyframes.
Expand/Collapse All	Expands all elements within the Timeline to expose their individual keyframes.

Summary

In this chapter, we've examined how to create motion in Adobe Edge Animate by making use of the Timeline, Playhead, Pin, and Properties panel. Those who are familiar with Flash Professional or After Effects should recognize just how familiar many of these concepts are, and possibly how refined and evolved these concepts have become as implemented in the Edge Animate application interface. It is quite easy to both create and edit animation within an Edge Animate composition!

In the next chapter, we'll have a look at how to add interactivity to an Edge Animate project through the use of Actions and Triggers.

7
Interactivity with Actions, Triggers, and Labels

The Adobe Edge Animate Runtime API allows us to easily add basic interactivity to our compositions in the form of mouse interactions, touch interactions, and some core timeline and playback behaviors. This is all accomplished through different types of Edge Animate actions, depending upon the element they are being applied against. **Actions** in Adobe Edge Animate are specific instructions based upon the JavaScript scripting language used by all modern browsers. These instructions are an integral part of an Edge Animate composition that involves any sort of interactivity.

In this chapter, we will have a look at the following:

- Stage actions
- Element actions
- Timeline triggers
- Timeline labels
- Mouse cursors
- The **Code** panel
- Edge Animate events

We'll also have a look at adding interactivity to our sample web banner from the previous chapter, and will consider the Edge Animate Runtime APIs before moving on.

Working with Edge Animate actions

Actions are the primary way of creating interactivity within Adobe Edge Animate. They can be applied to either a single element, the entire Stage panel, or through certain points along the Timeline panel as triggers. The code utilized through the **Actions** panel is all JavaScript and relies on two JavaScript libraries: jQuery and Adobe Edge Animate Runtime. See the following example:

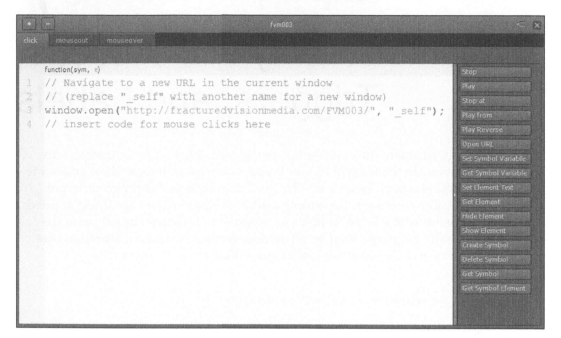

 Unlike with Adobe Flash Professional, code can be applied to any element—elements do not have to be created as symbols to receive actions upon them.

There are many types of actions which can be applied to a project depending upon the element receiving interaction, but they generally involve either playback instructions or element reference and manipulation.

The Actions panel

The **Actions** panel is the central place where actions and triggers are applied to elements within Edge Animate. The layout of this panel is unique, in that we have a number of controls which enable the manipulation of any actions applied to a specific element in a very robust way. The following diagram shows some actions:

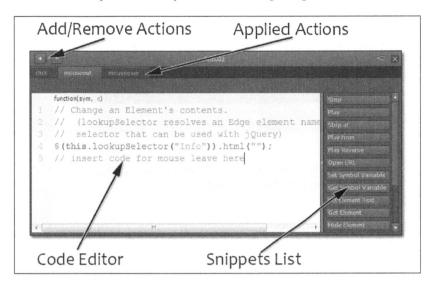

From this diagram, we can see the variety of controls we have available to us within this panel:

- **Snippets List:** This set of actions easily generates bits of code with a simple button click. They often require a small bit of code manipulations afterwards to become effective.

- **Add/Remove Actions:** These actions add new actions to an element, or removes existing Actions from the element.

- **Applied Actions**: These actions are represented as tabs along the top of the panel, and provide a quick way to see what actions are already applied to an element and a quick method of switching between them.

- **Code Editor**: This is the panel where manual manipulation of the preset commands takes place. We can also bypass the command list altogether if desired and simply write the code by hand.

Preferences in Actions panel

In the upper-right corner of the **Actions** panel is a small icon which allows us access to panel preferences. We can set a variety of preferences in this way, which will be preserved across Edge Animate projects.

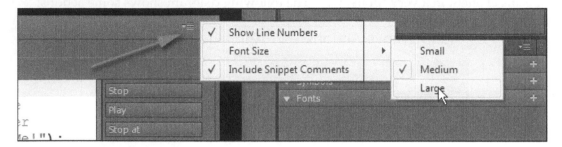

[Nearly all the panels in Edge Animate include a set of preferences that can be accessed in this way.]

Clicking upon the preferences icon will bring up the following preference selections:

Menu Item	Description
Show Line Numbers	This determines whether or not line numbers are visible in the **Actions** panel.
Font Size	This will adjust the font size of code displayed within the **Actions** panel. We have the choice of **Small**, **Medium**, or **Large**.
Include Snippet Comments	When snippets are inserted into the **Actions** panel code area, we have the option to include helpful comments which provide a bit of guidance on how to configure and customize the inserted snippet. This will toggle that feature on and off.

Applying actions to the Stage

Being that the Stage itself is, in fact, a symbol. It should come as no surprise that actions can be assigned directly to the Stage. To assign new action to the Stage click on the root `stage` node in the **Elements** panel, then from the **Properties** panel click on the **Actions** script icon command to configure a set of actions.

 Alternatively, the Stage actions can be set through the **Elements** panel in the same manner.

The Stage, due to its unique nature, can have some unique actions applied to it. These are listed as follows:

- **creationComplete**: With this action, code will execute upon Stage symbol creation.
- **beforeDeletion**: This action makes the code run immediately before the Stage is deleted.
- **compositionReady**: These instructions will fire immediately once the composition is loaded.
- **scroll**: This action lets us scroll the contents of the Stage.
- **keydown**: This action makes keyboard detection of keydown events possible.
- **keyup**: This action makes keyboard detection of keyup events possible.
- **orientationChange**: This detects an orientation change, more specific to mobile devices.
- **resize**: This action is fired when the Stage is resized.
- **onError**: This action runs when a JavaScript error occurs.

For instance, to listen for when the user hits the Space bar, Edge Animate will place this code upon a `keydown` action:

```
// The variable "e.which" tells you the key code of the key that was
pressed, e.g. 32 = space
if (e.which == 32) {
    // do something
}
```

Applying actions to individual elements

For many actions, such as mouse clicks, hover effects, and things of that nature, we will want to apply code directly to certain elements. The quickest way to do this is to go to the **Elements** panel and click upon the small brackets icon next to the desired element. This will open the **Actions** panel, within which we can specify an appropriate action as shown in the following screenshot:

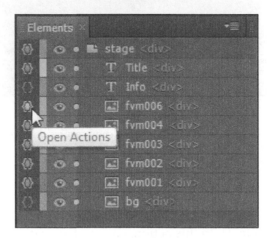

A common example of an individual element action would be a clicking event within which we direct the **Playhead** tool to **Play from** position 1000 along the **Timeline** panel:

```
// play the timeline from the given position (ms or label)
sym.play(1000);
// insert code for mouse clicks here
```

Changing the mouse cursor

To more clearly communicate that an element can be interacted with by the user, Edge Animate allows us to modify the appearance of the mouse cursor upon individual elements. This is especially useful when using interactivity through element actions, as it provides another level of user interaction.

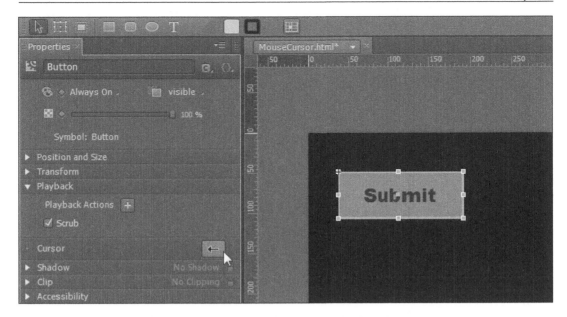

 While changing the cursor can assist with informing the user as to the purpose of an element, changing it to represent an incorrect action or some random purpose would be quite confusing. We must take care to only change the cursor when it is appropriate to do so.

Cursor types

Edge Animate allows for many cursor types within a composition. These can be used to assist in notifying the user of some action which can occur through the mouse, or that some process is occurring. In the following screenshot, we list all available cursor types along with their potential usage:

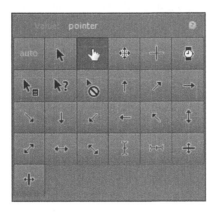

In that screenshot, we saw all of the cursors available to us within an Edge Animate project. The following chart shows what many of them are called and what they do.

Cursor	Description
auto	This allows the browser to determine which cursor to use.
default	This is the default arrow cursor.
pointer	This is useful for indicating that something can be clicked upon. It looks like a little hand.
move	This indicates movement along four directions. It is useful for click-and-drag.
crosshair	This is often used to choose elements on a page. It looks like a small crosshair.
wait	This indicates that something is happening and the user should be patient. It looks like a wristwatch.
context-menu	This is the default arrow with a little menu icon to the side.
help	This is the default arrow with a large "?" included.
no-drop	This is a smaller arrow with the circle-with-a-slash icon beneath it. It indicates that an operation cannot be performed.
n-resize	This is a resize arrow pointing north.
ne-resize	This is a resize arrow pointing northeast.
e-resize	This is a resize arrow pointing east.
se-resize	This is a resize arrow pointing southeast.
s-resize	This is a resize arrow pointing south.
sw-resize	This is a resize arrow pointing southwest.
w-resize	This is a resize arrow pointing west.
nw-resize	This is a resize arrow pointing northwest.
ns-resize	This is double-headed resize arrow pointing north and south.
nesw-resize	This is a double-headed resize arrow pointing northeast and southwest.
ew-resize	This is a double-headed resize arrow pointing east and west.
nwse-resize	This is a double-headed resize arrow pointing northwest and southeast.
text	This indicates selectable or editable text.
vertical-text	This indicates selectable or editable vertical text.
row-resize	This indicates the ability to reposition along the x axis.
col-resize	This indicates the ability to reposition along the y axis.

Triggers

Just as when dealing with element actions, the **Actions** panel is the place where triggers are applied to elements within Edge Animate. The layout of this panel is very similar to when dealing with element actions, though as triggers reside along the Timeline itself and are triggered by the **Playhead** tool rather than a chosen event, there are actually fewer options to deal with.

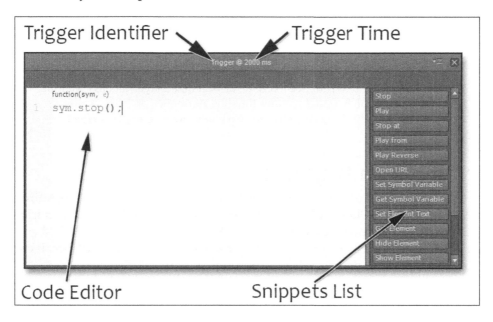

From this diagram, we can see the variety of controls we have available to us within this panel as follows:

- **Snippets List**: This set of actions easily generates bits of code with a simple button click. They often require a small bit of code manipulation afterwards to become effective.

- **Code Editor**: This is where manual manipulation of the preset commands takes place. We can also bypass the command list altogether if desires and simply write the code by hand.

- **Trigger Identifier**: This lets us know immediately that this is a Timeline-based trigger.

- **Trigger Time**: This is the time at which this trigger has been placed. Triggers can be shifted across the Timeline by click-and-drag.

The Timeline Actions layer

The Edge Animate Timeline includes a special layer set apart from all the others. This is called the **Actions** layer and is used explicitly for plotting special actions, called **triggers**, at various points along the Timeline:

 For many years, when working in Flash Professional, it has been the recommended practice to create a specialized layer labeled **Actions**, within which to include any timeline ActionScript. Edge Animate borrows this long-established workflow practice to great effect.

Working with triggers

Triggers can be created along the Timeline in a number of ways. The most direct method is to place the **Playhead** tool at a point where we want to include a trigger and then use the keyboard shortcut *Ctrl + T* (Windows) or *Command + T* (Mac). Alternatively, we can either click on the keyframe diamond in the **Actions** layer or go to the application menu and choose **Timeline | Insert Trigger**:

To edit an existing trigger, simply double-click upon it and the **Actions** panel will pop up, allowing us to make any adjustments. Triggers can also be dragged to any time along the Timeline panel using the mouse.

Working with labels

Labels in Edge Animate are a mechanism by which we are able to set textual markers along the Timeline panel. These markers are able to provide visual authoring cues or can be referenced through actions. For instance, if we were to set a label named **JumpPoint** at 0:02.000, we could then reference it as follows:

```
sym.play("JumpPoint");
```

in place of:

```
sym.play(2000);
```

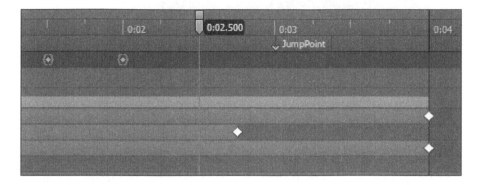

 Those used to working in Flash Professional will recognize this same concept. In that application, they are known as **frame labels** and can be used in exactly the same way.

Jumping to labels

As we have indicated, not only is it possible to jump to different specific timecodes along the Timeline panel, but we can also jump to established Timeline labels. The use of labels allows us freedom from absolute milliseconds in the case that we decide to shift content along the timeline — thus invalidating whatever the original timecode may have been.

For an example of how this works, have a look at the project within the directory named EdgeLabels.

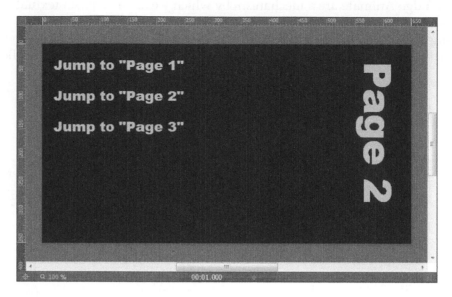

In this example, we set a Click event which then directs the **Playhead** tool position through a Stop at action. To apply such an action, perform the following steps:

1. Be sure and set the main Stage to disable **Autoplay** through the **Properties** panel. This will stop the **Playhead** tool at 0 milliseconds.

2. Create a label at a specific point in the Timeline (let's say at 0:00.500) by moving the **Playhead** tool to that position and then accessing the menu **Timeline | Insert Label** and naming the label Page 1.

3. Now create a text element upon the Stage which will receive our Click action. Have it read something like Jump to Page 1.

4. Add another text element to the Stage and simply have it read Page 1. Position this element in a unique place and set its **Element Display** property to be off at 0 milliseconds.

5. Move the **Playhead** to the previously created label and set the `Page 1` text element's **Element Display** property to `on` at the label. This way we'll know when we've jumped to that position.

6. Select the original `Jump to Page 1` element and enter the **Actions** panel by clicking upon its **Actions** icon in the **Elements** panel.

7. Add a Click event and choose to add a Stop at action. The following code will be placed within the code editor:

```
sym.stop(1000);
```

8. Change this to read as follows:

```
sym.stop("Page 1");
```

    This will allow the present action to use the **Label** name instead of a specific milliseconds entry.

9. Now test the composition in a web browser to demonstrate this implementation:

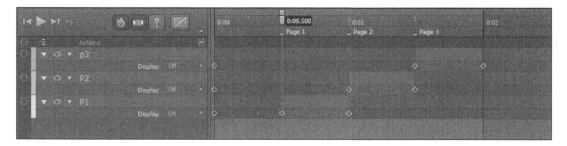

 Notice in this screenshot that we do not actually have any animation along our Timeline for this project. We are simply using a combination of actions and are toggling the visibility of elements on and off at specific points. We don't *have* to have transitions in a composition.

The Code panel

In many ways an expanded **Actions** panel — the **Code** panel provides a more complete view of all code within our project. It also provides an alternative way of adding event handlers to elements in a more code-focused way.

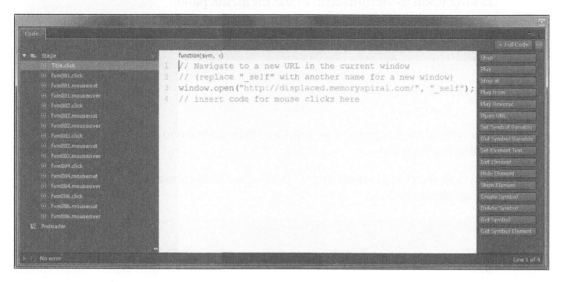

 The **Code** panel in Edge Animate is in some ways similar to the Flash Professional **Movie Inspector**, but much more useful in that the **Code** panel can be used as a direct management tool.

The **Code** panel is hidden by default, but can be accessed through the application menu **Window | Code**. It provides a project-level overview of the actions and triggers within a composition and also allows direct manipulation of the code through an interface similar to the **Actions** panel.

 Code panel keyboard shortcuts are *Ctrl + E* (Windows) and *Command + E* (Mac).

Unlike the **Actions** panel though, we have a column of all composition elements which have code attached to them along the left-hand side of the panel. From this column, we can easily add and remove actions with the project scope in full view.

 Right-click upon any action and select **Delete Action** to remove it entirely.

Full Code view

Aside from providing a different perspective on the assignment of all the actions within our composition, we also have the option of switching to a full code editor, which will display the entire {project}_edgeActions.js file in editable form. To access this, simply locate the **Full Code** button in the upper-right corner of the **Code** panel and click upon it to toggle between views:

 We must be particularly careful when editing in **Full Code** view, as the possibility to introduce JavaScript errors is much greater than through the normal view.

Code Error warnings

There is also a small notification in the lower-left corner of the **Code** panel through which we can view any errors that Edge Animate detects are present within the JavaScript. We can see the number of errors, a description of each, and are notified upon which line the error was detected:

Action and trigger breakdown

Edge Animate compositions are dependent upon the inclusion of both jQuery and Edge Animate Runtime JavaScript libraries in order to animate elements and provide interactivity.

For these examples, we will be looking at the raw code within the project {name}_edgeActions.js file after applying said actions.

This file is arranged as follows:

```
/***********************
 * Adobe Edge Animate Composition Actions
 *
 * Edit this file with caution, being careful to preserve
 * function signatures and comments starting with 'Edge' to maintain the
 * ability to interact with these actions from within Adobe Edge Animate
 *
 **********************/
(function($, Edge, compId){
var Composition = Edge.Composition, Symbol = Edge.Symbol; // aliases
for commonly used Edge classes

    //Edge symbol: 'stage'
    (function(symbolName) {

        Symbol.bindTriggerAction(compId, symbolName, "Default Timeline",
2000, function(sym, e) {
            sym.stop();

        });
        //Edge binding end
        Symbol.bindTriggerAction(compId, symbolName, "Default Timeline",
1505, function(sym, e) {
            // Navigate to a new URL in the current window
            // (replace "_self" with appropriate target attribute for a
new window)
            window.open("http://www.adobe.com", "_self");
            // insert code here

        });
        //Edge binding end
        Symbol.bindElementAction(compId, symbolName, "${_Rectangle}",
"mousedown", function(sym, e) {
            sym.playReverse();

        });
```

```
    //Edge binding end

})("stage");
//Edge symbol end:'stage'

//=========================================================

//Edge symbol: 'FaceSym'
(function(symbolName) {

})("FaceSym");
//Edge symbol end:'FaceSym'

})(jQuery, AdobeEdge, "EDGE-1161928078");
```

Composition actions

These general composition actions are tied to the Edge Animate Stage. Such events are fired when the composition is ready, when scrolling occurs, or when the keyboard is interacted with through keydown or keyup actions.

The following table shows the various events which can be applied in instances like this:

Action	Description
creationComplete	This fires upon creation of the entire composition.
beforeDeletion	This will be fired immediately prior to a composition's removal.
compositionReady	This is fired when the composition becomes available.
scroll	This is fired upon the scrolling of content within a scrollable element.
keydown	This is detected when a key is pressed down on the keyboard.
keyup	This is detected when a key that has previously been pressed down has been lifted.
OrientationChange	This fires on devices which support changes in orientation, such as tablets and mobile phones.
Resize	This detects when the composition has been resized.
onError	All composition errors are sent through this event.

For example, look at the following code:

```
Symbol.bindElementAction(compId, symbolName, "document",
"compositionReady", function(sym, e) {
sym.play();
// insert code for compositionReady event here
});
//Edge binding end
```

Read up on the DOM at: http://www.w3.org/DOM/.

Mouse actions

These are normal mouse events which are registered upon individual Edge Animate elements. Use these when targeting when a user presses or releases the mouse button, among other things.

The following table shows the various events which can be applied in instances like this:

Action	Description
click	This represents a simple mouse click.
dblclick	This represents a mouse double-click.
mouseover	This is activated when the cursor enters the bounds of an element.
mousedown	This event is fired when the mouse button is held down.
mousemove	This detects and responds to the cursor moving across an element.
mouseup	This event is fired when the mouse button is released.
mouseout	This is activated when the cursor exits the bounds of an element.

For example, consider the following code:

```
Symbol.bindElementAction(compId, symbolName, "${_Rectangle}",
"mousedown", function(sym, e) {
// stop the timeline at the given position (ms or label)
sym.stop(1000);
// insert code for mousedown here
});
//Edge binding end
```

 Generally these actions can be applied to the Stage as well.

Touch actions

Touch actions are to be used when targeting touch-enabled devices such as smartphones and tablets; we can listen for when a touch begins, touch movements, and touch end events to perform certain functions within an Edge Animate composition.

The following table shows the various events which can be applied in instances like this:

Action	Description
touchstart	This indicates that a touch event has been detected.
touchmove	This will fire after a detected touch event as the touchpoint is moved across an element.
touchend	This indicates that a previously detected touch event has ended.

For example, consider the following code:

```
Symbol.bindElementAction(compId, symbolName, "${_Rectangle}",
"touchstart", function(sym, e) {
// Navigate to a new URL in the current window
// (replace "_self" with another name for a new window)
window.open("http://www.adobe.com", "_self");
// insert code for touchstart here
});
//Edge binding end
```

 Similar to mouse events, these actions can also be applied to the Stage or individual elements.

jQuery actions

These are jQuery-specific events that we can listen for and respond to within an Edge Animate composition, as listed in the following table:

Action	Description
mouseenter (jQuery)	This is the code to be run when the mouse enters an element.
mouseleave (jQuery)	This is the code to be run when the mouse leaves an element.
focus (jQuery)	This is the code to be run when an element gains focus.

For example, consider the following code:

```
Symbol.bindElementAction(compId, symbolName, "${_Rectangle}",
"mouseenter", function(sym, e) {
        sym.$("Status_txt").html("Mouse Enter detected!");
});
```

 Similar to mouse and touch events, these actions can also be applied to the Stage or individual elements.

Action and trigger events

Events are added to actions that can be set upon the Stage, individual elements and symbols, or along the Timeline as triggers. Any action can contain many different events.

The following table shows various events which can be applied in instances like this:

Action	Description
Stop	This stops the timeline.
	sym.stop();
Play	This plays the timeline.
	sym.play();
Stop at	This stops the timeline at the given position (milliseconds or label).
	sym.stop(1000);
	sym.stop("Label");
Play from	This plays the timeline from the given position (milliseconds or label).
	sym.play(1000);
	sym.play("Label");
Play Reverse	This plays the timeline in reverse from the current position.
	sym.playReverse();
Open URL	This navigates to a new URL.
	window.open("http://www.adobe.com", "_self");
Set Symbol Variable	This sets the value of a symbol parameter.
	sym.setParameter("myParameterName", "parameterValue");

Action	Description
Get Symbol Variable	This gets the value of a symbol parameter.
	var myParameter = sym.getParameter("myParameterName");
Set Element Text	This changes an element's textual contents.
	sym.$("ElementID").html("NewText");
Get Element	This resolves an Edge Animate element name to a DOM element that can be used with jQuery.
	var element = sym.$("ElementID");
Hide Element	This hides an element.
	sym.$("ElementID").hide();
Show Element	This shows an element.
	sym.$("ElementID").show();
Create Symbol	This creates an instance element of a symbol as a child of the given parent element.
	var mySymbolObject = sym.createChildSymbol("Symbol", "ParentElement");
Delete Symbol	This deletes an element that is an instance of a symbol.
	sym.getSymbol("Symbol").deleteSymbol();
Get Symbol	This looks up the Edge Animate Symbol JavaScript Object from an element that is an instance of a symbol.
	var mySymbolObject = sym.getSymbol("Symbol");
Get Symbol Element	This gets the element node for an Edge Animate Symbol JavaScript Object.
	var symbolElement = sym.getSymbolElement();

Many of these actions, such as Stop at, have close counterparts in the world of Flash Professional and ActionScript.

Adding interactivity to a website header

Now that we've had a solid overview of how to apply interactivity through actions within an Edge Animate composition, let's revisit our example project from the previous chapter. If you recall, we have created an animated website header for a studio recording project of the name **An Early Morning Letter, Displaced**.

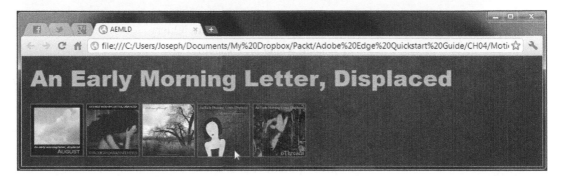

They liked what we've done with the composition so far but now request that we make it a bit more interactive. Specifically they want a hover effect where rolling over each piece of album art brings up some basic information about that release. Additionally, they would like to have their website open when a user clicks upon the title text and direct links to each album page when the album art is clicked on.

Creating the text element

First we must open the project and create a new text element on the Stage to contain the hover text they wish to display:

1. Open the website header project from the previous chapter.
    If desired, a completed version of that project can be located
    within the `MotionBanner` folder.

2. Save this project to a new location so that if we make a disastrous mistake,
    the original project is not lost. Note that it is always important to version
    or back up our files in an organized fashion.

3. Using the **Text** tool, drag a new text element out onto the Stage.

4. Upon releasing the mouse button, the **Selection** tool will activate
    automatically with the new text element selected. We will want to leave
    the text element empty for now, so simply insert a space using the Space bar.

Creating a text element with no text at all attributed to it will result in no text element being created. This is why we must insert, at least, a space.

5. Within the **Properties** panel, make the following adjustments:

   ID: Info

   Location X: 530 px

   Location Y: 83 px

   Size W: 392 px

   Size H: 96 px

   Font Name: Arial Black, Gadget, sans-serif

   Font Size: 18 px

   Font Color: #808080

The text element is now set up properly.

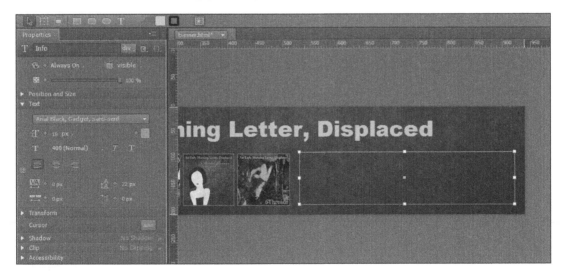

 As the text element actually contains no text at this point, when unselected, we may have a difficult time locating it for any further manipulation. This is not a problem; simply click upon it in the **Elements** panel to select it once again.

Adding interactivity to the title

We will need to add a click action to the title element, allowing a user to click off into the artist's website. To do so, we perform the following steps:

1. Within the **Elements** panel, click on the script icon next to the **Title** element. This will bring up the **Actions** panel.

2. We are immediately presented with a number of actions to choose from. Select the click action.

3. From the right-hand side column, select **Open URL**. Some code along with comments are inserted into the editor.

4. Change the code that appears to read as follows:

   ```
   window.open("http://displaced.memoryspiral.com/", "_self");
   ```

5. In the **Properties** panel, change the Cursor property to pointer, indicating the element can be clicked on.

This portion of the example is now complete, as shown in the following screenshot:

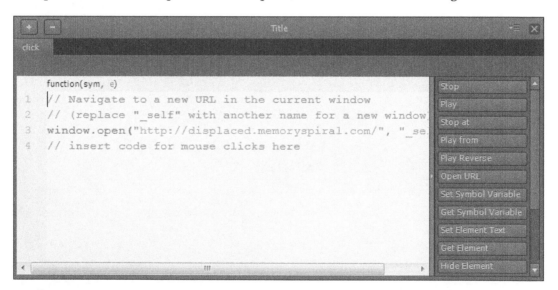

Adding interactivity to the album art

There are three separate actions that we need to assign to each of the album images in this composition: click, mouseover, and mouseout. We will repeat the following steps for each element, changing the necessary parameters as needed:

1. Within the **Elements** panel, click on the script icon next to one of the album art image elements. For this example, we'll choose the `fvm004` element. This will bring up the **Actions** panel.

2. We are immediately presented with a number of actions to choose from. Select the click action.

3. From the right-hand side column, select **Open URL**. Some code along with comments are inserted into the editor.

4. Change the code that appears to read as follows:

    ```
    window.open("http://fracturedvisionmedia.com/FVM004/", "_self");
    ```

5. We need to select two more actions to choose from. First, we click on the little plus icon at the top of the **Actions** panel and select the `mouseover` action.

6. From the right-hand side column, select **Set Element Text**. Some code along with comments are inserted into the editor.

7. Change the code that appears to read as follows:

    ```
    sym.$("Info").html("Shudderflowers (2009)");
    ```

    This will change our dynamic text element to display information regarding this album.

> Notice that we are changing text within the `Info` text element that was previously created. **Element IDs** are important not only for our own recognition, but are also used to target specific elements in cases like this.

8. For the final action, we will click on the little plus icon at the top of the **Actions** panel and select the `mouseout` action.

9. From the right-hand side column, select **Set Element Text** just as before. Code will be inserted into the editor.

10. Change the code that appears to read as follows:

    ```
    sym.$("Info").html("");
    ```

    This will clear out any of the text inserted through our mouseover command.

11. In the **Properties** panel, change the `Cursor` property to `pointer`, indicating the element can be clicked on.

We have now enabled three separate actions upon this element; a **click** action to open more details in the web browser, a **mouseover** action, to display some general text to the user upon hover, and **mouseout** action to remove that text when the cursor is no longer present over the element.

We have demonstrated how to accomplish this for one of the five album image elements. To complete the exercise, we will need to repeat this for each element. A completed example of this project can be found in the InteractiveBanner folder.

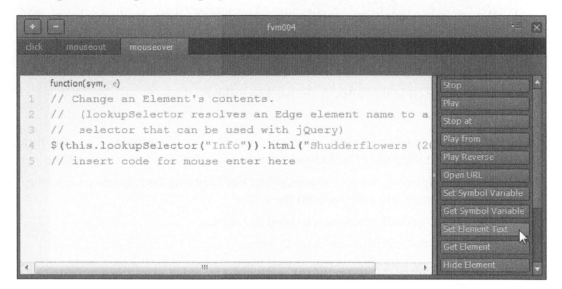

 Note that if desired, entire sets of actions can be copied from one element to be pasted within another. To accomplish this, use the **Selection** tool and select the element containing the desired actions. Copy the element through the application menu **Edit | Copy**. Now select the element to receive the actions and return to the application menu **Edit | Paste Special | Paste Actions**. Now we can simply open the **Actions** panel and tweak the pasted actions as desired.

Completing the final website header composition

We are now ready to produce the final files for our client. To publish our Edge Animate composition to the browser, we can choose **File | Preview in Browser** from the application menu. This will write all necessary files and open the completed composition in a web browser.

Now that we have added interactivity to this banner, we can hover over each image to get more information about it. The cursor will change from the default arrow to a pointer, indicating that the user can click upon the element. Clicking upon the image will open details within the browser. Clicking upon the title will also open a website.

 This is just an example of the types of interactivity that can be achieved through Adobe Edge Animate. We can have a look at the Edge Animate Runtime API and documentation for more examples.

Using touch actions for mobile devices

The previous example uses mouse-specific events for a variety of purposes. Edge Animate compositions can also employ events for touch. Let's create a simple project that employs touch events and provides some user feedback for mobile devices.

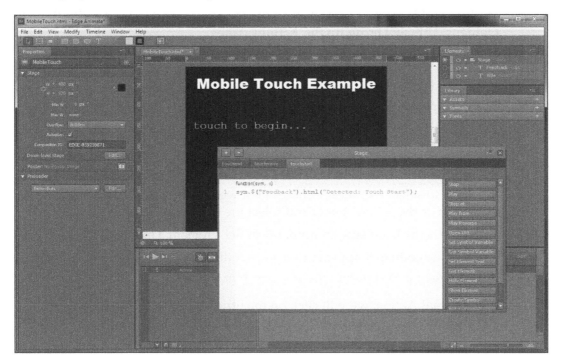

To reproduce the `MobileTouch` example, take the following steps:

1. Create a new project and modify the Stage properties as follows:

   Background Color: #000000

   Stage W: 480 px

   Stage H: 920 px

2. If desired, use the **Text** tool to draw out a text element upon the Stage for use as a simple title. The example project uses the name `Mobile Touch Example`.

3. Using the **Text** tool create another element with the following properties:

   ID: Feedback

   Location X: 20 px

   Location Y: 126 px

   Size W: 440 px

   Size H: 250 px

   Font Name: Courier, Courier New, monospace

   Text Color: #00ff03

4. Within the **Elements** panel, click on the script icon next to the **Feedback** text element. This will bring up the **Actions** panel.

   We are immediately presented with a number of actions to choose from.

5. Select the `touchstart` action.

6. From the right-hand side column, select **Set Element Text**. Some code along with comments are inserted into the editor.

7. Change the code that appears to read as follows:

   ```
   sym.$("Feedback").html("Detected: Touch Start");
   ```

8. We need to select two more actions. First we click on the little plus icon at the top of the actions panel and select the `touchmove` action.

9. From the right-hand side column, select **Set Element Text** as before.

10. Change the code that appears to read as follows:

    ```
    sym.$("Feedback").html("Detected: Touch Move");
    ```

11. For the final Action, we will click on the little plus icon at the top of the **Actions** panel and select the `touchend` action.

12. From the right-hand side column, select **Set Element Text** just as we have been doing. Code will be inserted to the editor.

13. Change the code that appears to read as follows:

```
sym.$("Feedback").html("Detected: Touch End");
```

We now have a small composition that will react to all three touch events supported by the Edge Animate Runtime, by writing a message to the user within a predefined text element. When uploaded to the Web and viewed within a tablet running Android 4.0, the project appears as shown in the following screenshot:

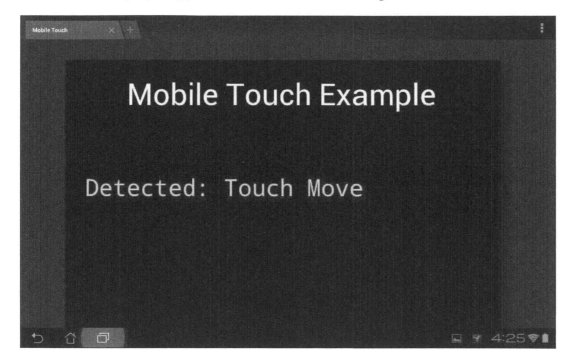

 It is important to note that just because something is built using HTML, it will not necessary be tuned for mobile or be more performant than other technologies. Much of this depends upon the particular project, and the intent and skill of those working on it.

Adobe Edge Animate menu items

We'll now have a look at some of the Edge Animate menu items which can be used when copying and pasting elements with actions applied to them.

Edit

The **Edit** menu allows for direct object manipulation through cut, copy, and paste commands, along with selection options and access to an undo/redo history:

Command	Description
Paste Special	This is actually a series of commands that allow the pasting of specific attributes. Like any **Paste** command, these attributes or an accompanying element must have been cut or copied previous to this.
**Paste Special	Paste Actions**	Will paste only the actions defined on the element that has been copied or cut to a new element.
**Paste Special	Paste All**	Will paste the element which has been copied or cut as a new element along with all properties, actions, and transitions into the Timeline.

Summary

In this chapter, we've examined how to use the **Actions** panel to add interactivity to an Edge Animate composition through element actions and Timeline triggers. Adobe Edge Animate uses JavaScript as its scripting language through the Edge Animate Runtime APIs due to its adherence to web standards. Those familiar with ActionScript versions 1 or 2 from Flash Professional should feel quite at home, as will anyone coming from another JavaScript-based coding environment.

In the next chapter of this book, we'll have a look some more advanced element handling within Edge Animate such as the use of symbols, nesting elements, and the grouping mechanism.

8
Making Use of Symbols, Nested Elements, and Grouping

Symbols in Adobe Edge Animate are self-contained objects that have their own unique attributes and functionality, separate from other base elements within a composition such as rectangles and text. Symbols themselves are stored in the Library of an Edge Animate project and can be instantiated upon the Stage. These instances can then be modified separately, as needed by the author. This chapter will explore symbols with respect to the following aspects:

- Comparison between symbols and other elements
- How to create and manage symbols
- The usage of symbols in Edge Animate
- The export and import of symbols
- An exploration of unique properties of symbols

We'll also have a look at some similar functionality in regard to the nesting of elements within one another, and explore the grouping mechanism available to us within Edge Animate.

What are Symbols in Edge Animate?

Symbols in Adobe Edge Animate are encapsulated objects that may consist of one or more base elements, contain their own Timeline, and provide a mechanism by which they can be packaged and shared across compositions.

Those readers with a background in Flash Professional, Fireworks, or Illustrator should immediately understand the concept and benefits of symbols. There are many similarities to take advantage of!

Differences between Symbols and other elements

Symbols in Adobe Edge Animate are quite different from other elements that may be created through the application tools or via external asset import. It is important to recognize the various differences here, as they do matter when considering usage of a Symbol instance in an Edge Animate project.

Symbols are self-contained

One of the great benefits of symbols is that they exist outside of Stage. Because of this fact, they are edited within a special, isolated edit mode and behave in complete isolation from the main Timeline. When a Symbol entity has entered into isolated edit mode, the Stage obtains a texture effect represented by a diagonal line pattern. You will see the following when you open the **BasicSymbol.html**:

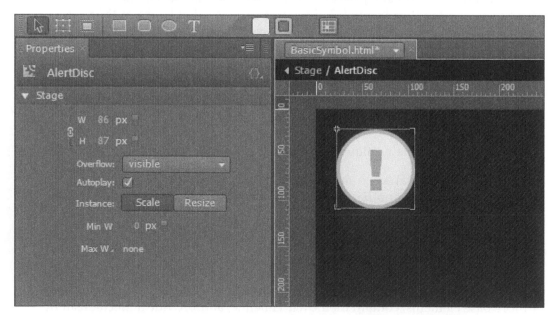

In this screenshot, we see that the Symbol instance has been placed in isolated edit mode. To exit edit mode, simply click upon the text that reads **Stage** along the top of the window.

Symbols exist within the Library panel

Unlike basic drawn elements that exist solely upon the Stage in Edge Animate, Symbols reside within the Library of the project and instances of Symbols can be created upon the Stage by dragging them out from within the **Library** panel:

This is a very similar model to that employed by Flash Professional. Even the icon for Symbol in Edge Animate is very similar to that of a MovieClip symbol in Flash Professional.

Symbols are instantiated upon the Stage

As mentioned earlier, Symbols in Edge Animate reside in the project library and are used by creating an isntance of the Symbol, placing the instance upon Stage, and manipulating that instance in some way.

In the next screenshot, we see how a number of Symbol instances can be created upon the Stage and have individual instance properties such as opacity, rotation, and scale manipulated at random without affecting other instances.

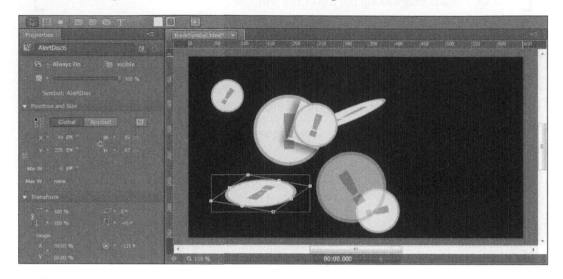

 The manipulation of Symbols instances upon that the Stage does not actually modify the **Symbol** instance itself unless we are in **Symbol Edit** mode. If we do change the properties of a Symbol instance itself, these changes will cascade across all instances of the Symbol.

Symbols have their own Timeline

Unlike other elements which are tied directly to the **Timeline** of the main project, symbols employ their own isolated Timeline, which can be manipulated in isolation from the primary Timeline. This allows us to create motion within symbols that moves independently from whatever is going on in the main Timeline. This also opens up the possibility of nested animations.

 Though the Timeline within a Symbol instance is independent of the Stage Timeline, the Timeline of that Symbol can be controlled from the main project Timeline scope through both **Actions** and **Playback Actions**.

Symbols can employ Playback Actions

Playback Actions are only available upon symbols and are accessed through either the **Properties** panel or **Timeline**. They allow us to control the Timeline within a Symbol instance through actions such as **Stop**, **Play**, or **Play Reverse** — and the ability to specify the specific time code to perform that action from.

[This functionality can allow specific embedded animated segments within a Symbol instance to be accessed at proper times from the Stage Timeline. A good example of this would be controlling a walk animation sequence—issuing commands to have the character walk to the right, stop and hold, run to the left, and so forth.]

Comparison of Symbols in Edge Animate with Symbols in Flash Professional

Symbols in Edge Animate obviously borrow a lot of qualities from MovieClip symbols in Adobe Flash Professional. Let's break down both the similarities and differences between these two implementations.

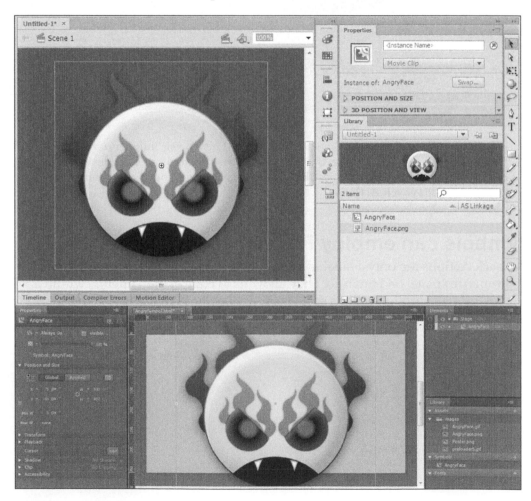

Similarities

Many of the basic properties and functionality are shared by these two platforms. Here are some of the more easily identifiable similarities:

- In both cases, symbols are self-contained, isolated objects
- Symbols must be instantiated upon the Stage
- Symbols can be instantiated through the use of code
- **Playback** can be controlled from code upon both the main Timeline and from within the symbol itself
- Visibility can be toggled from the main Timeline

Differences

There are some definite differences to be aware of between these two implementations as well. These differences are outlined as follows:

- Internal animation in Flash Professional MovieClip symbols cannot be scrubbed along the Timeline—though the **Graphic** symbols do behave this way.

- Symbols in Edge Animate cannot have advanced compositional features such as blend modes or filter effects applied to them.

- Symbols in Edge Animate do not have 3D rotation and translation options.

- Symbols in Edge Animate can employ clipping to hide portions of the symbol. Symbols in Flash Professional can employ masking to the same effect.

- In Flash Professional, it is possible to create empty Symbols. Within Edge Animate, Symbols are always created through the conversion of other elements.

 While we cannot create empty Symbols in Edge Animate, it is possible to convert a symbol into an empty Symbol by deleting all elements within it after its creation.

Creating and managing Symbols

Symbols can be created and managed through the Adobe Edge Animate application in a number of ways. Each time we want to create a new Symbol, we must first create one or more elements, which will make up its parts. We can do this through use of the drawing tools, text tool, or through the import of image assets created in other applications.

The command to convert one of more selected elements to a Symbol is located in the Edge Animate application menu. Choose **Modify | Convert to Symbol** to achieve this.

We can also use the keyboard shortcut for this command: *Ctrl + Y* (Windows) or *Command + Y* (Mac).

As with many Adobe creative applications, the same command can be accessed in a variety of ways. Aside from the ways detailed previously, it is also possible to right-click upon many elements for a contextual list of options:

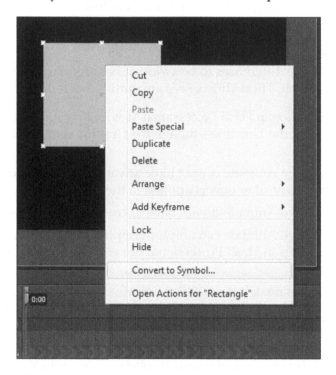

As seen in the previous screenshot, aside from using the Edge Animate application menu or keyboard shortcuts; we can also employ right-clicking on the menu in the conversion of elements to symbols.

Converting assets into Symbols

Symbols in Adobe Edge Animate reside in Library and are self-contained objects with their own timelines and behaviors. Instances of symbols can be dragged out of the Library and placed upon the main Stage, or even within other symbols, where their properties can be adjusted like any other element.

 The **Autoplay timeline** option in this dialog determines whether the symbol will play on its own or will require a manual command from the Edge Animate Runtime API to begin playback.

To create a Symbol instance in Edge Animate, perform the following steps:

1. Create a new project and save it to the local disk.
2. Use the **Rectangle** tool to draw out an element upon the Stage.
3. If you wish, adjust the properties of your element before proceeding.
4. Be sure that your element is selected using the **Selection** tool.
5. In the Edge Animate menu, choose **Modify | Convert to Symbol...**.
6. A small **Create Symbol** dialog will appear, which provides the option to give the Symbol a custom name. Type a meaningful name and click on **OK**.

As indicated by this screenshot, there are certain restrictions upon which characters can be used within a symbol name.

The Symbol instance will now exist within the project library and the original element will be converted into a Symbol on the Stage. To edit a Symbol, simply double-click upon the small cogwheel icon to the left-hand side of the Symbol name in the **Library** panel. Alternatively, double-click upon an instance of Symbol upon the Stage. This will bring us into the Symbol itself for isolated editing.

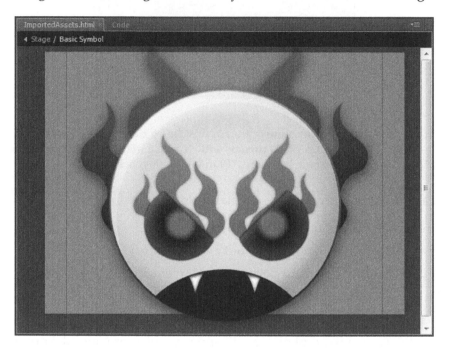

Return to the main **Stage** panel by clicking upon the term **Stage** from the black header within edit mode.

 Create many instances of the same Symbol by dragging them from the **Library** panel to the Stage panel. Adjusting properties of a Symbol will not change the original Symbol whatsoever.

Managing Symbols through the Library panel

Aside from editing Symbols in-place through their instances placed upon the Stage, we can also edit the Symbol itself through the Library, directly. To do so, simply right-click on the Symbol and choose whichever option is desired:

[We can also rename a Symbol in the **Library** panel by double-clicking on its name.]

Edit

This command will bring the Symbol into an edit mode that is slightly different from the one described previously. Within direct edit mode, the Symbol is not in any way tied to the Stage and appears by itself within edit mode, enabling a much more focused edit experience.

Delete

This command will delete a Symbol entirely from the project. If there are instances of this Symbol in use within the project, Edge Animate will provide a warning dialog telling us so.

Rename

This command allows us to rename a Symbol by typing a new name or modifying the current one. Changing the name of a Symbol will not affect any instances of this Symbol in a negative way—it is perfectly safe to do so even with many instances already upon the Stage.

Duplicate

This will clone the selected Symbol and create an entirely new Symbol within the Edge Animate project that can be edited without affecting the original Symbol whatsoever. When a Symbol is duplicated—each is its own unique object so editing either one will not affect the other in any way.

 Note that the new Symbol will be named the same as the original, but with the text _{x} appended to that original name. (x representing a number; for example if you have Symbol_1 and duplicate it, the duplicate will be Symbol_2.) It would be a good idea to rename such a **Symbol** immediately for clarity.

Export...

This command will open the **Export Symbols to File** dialog, which allows us to save Symbols from the Library into portable .ansym files.

Sharing Symbols across Edge Animate compositions

It is often desirable to share certain Symbol assets across Edge Animate projects for use in many compositions. Edge Animate makes it fairly simple to do this through the .ansym file format. This format contains everything associated with a particular Symbol and can be stored on a local hard drive, uploaded to a network resource, sent over email, or otherwise shared between groups and devices.

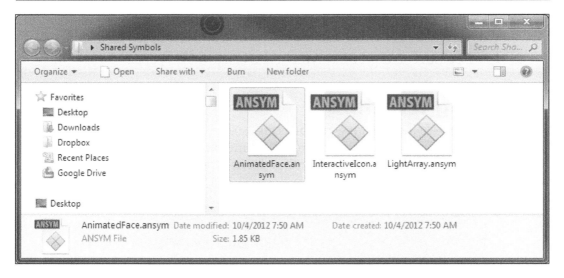

Exporting a Symbol

To export a Symbol from Edge Animate and create a portable .ansym file, perform the following actions:

1. Open the Edge Animate project that contains the Symbol to be shared.

2. In the library of the project, right-click on the Symbol to be exported. A small context menu will appear.

3. Choose **Export…** from this context menu to select the destination the file will be saved to. We can also provide a specific name to the file if desired.

4. Click on **Save** to export the Symbol and create a .ansym file.

Importing a Symbol

Now that we have exported our Symbol as an .ansym file, we are able to import that into a new or existing Edge Animate project for immediate use. To import an .ansym file and create the associated Symbol within the new project library, perform the following actions:

1. Create a new, blank Edge Animate project.

2. In the **Library** panel, click on the small plus sign icon to the right-hand side of the **Symbols** section.

3. Choose **Import Symbols…** from the context menu that appears. This will open the **Import Symbols** from the **File** dialog.

4. Browse to the .ansym file we wish to import and click on **Open**.

5. The selected Symbol will now exist within the project library and can be used and edited just like any other Symbol.

Properties unique to Symbol instances

Symbol instances and **Symbols** themselves both have a set of properties unique to them. When an instance is created upon the Stage, it inherits all of the internal Symbol properties from its parent, and a number of items are also exposed through the **Properties** panel once an instance is selected. The unique properties of Symbol instances are shown in the next diagram:

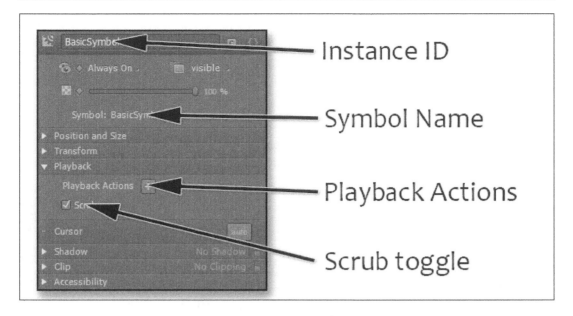

Instance ID

This is a unique identifier given to an individual Symbol instance in order to distinguish it from other instances and elements within a given project. The instance ID also allows us to target a specific instance through **Actions** or **Triggers**.

> Note the small cogwheel icon to the left-hand side of the instance ID. This is only visible when interacting with a Symbol instance and is a quick indicator that we are dealing with a Symbol instance.

Symbol name

The **Symbol** name is not editable—though it performs the important function of alerting or informing us which specific Symbol this element is an instance of.

Scrub toggle

This checkbox determines whether or not the Symbol Timeline animation will scrub along with the Stage Timeline. This setting has no effect upon published compositions but exists only for convenience when authoring.

Note that the **AutoPlay** property internal to the Symbol must also be enabled for this feature to function.

Playback Actions

These are not the same as **Actions,** which are defined within the **Actions** panel, but are more like primitive behaviors for Symbol instances. They allow us to influence the Timeline of the Symbol itself through commands placed upon the Stage Timeline.

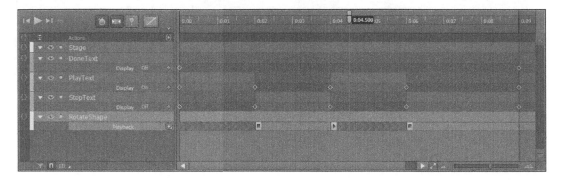

Using Playback Actions to control Symbol playback

This example will demonstrate how to set up and use **Playback Actions** to influence the playback of a Symbol instance across the main Timeline:

1. Create a new Edge Animate project and save it to the file system.

2. Now, use the **Rectangle** tool to draw out a rectangle element upon the Stage.

3. With the new element selected, choose **Modify | Convert to Symbol...** from the application menu. Provide a name for that Symbol and click on **OK**.

4. Double-click on the Symbol instance upon the Stage to enter edit mode and perform at least five seconds of animation across the internal Timeline.

5. Exit edit mode by clicking on Stage in the navigation bar atop the Symbol Stage. We'll now be at composition Timeline.

6. Select the Symbol instance once again and focus on the Timeline.

7. Move the **Playhead** to two seconds in and click on the little plus button with the term **Playback** to the left-hand side of it. All Symbol instances will have this option within the Timeline.

8. We can select from a number of options from within this menu. In the case of this example, we will choose **Stop**:

9. This inserts a **Playback Action** of type **Stop** upon the Timeline, bound to our Symbol instance. This command instructs Timeline the Symbol instance to stop once the main Timeline gets to this point upon playback. In this way, we can control Symbol instances easily from the main Timeline.

10. Test the composition to see that the animation within our Symbol instance will stop at the 2-second point.

Available Playback Commands

When we apply a **Playback Command** along the main Timeline, we have a number of choices for which type we want to apply. The different command types are as follows:

Command	Description
Play	This will play the Symbol instance from its current internal Timeline position.
Play from...	This will play the Symbol instance in reverse from specified internal Timeline position or **Label**.
Play Reverse	This will play the **Symbol** instance in reverse from its current internal Timeline position.
Play Reverse From...	This will play the Symbol instance in reverse from the specified internal Timeline position or **Label**.
Stop	This will stop the Symbol instance at its current internal Timeline position.
Stop At...	This will stop the Symbol instance at its specified internal Timeline position or **Label**.

Here we see how to specify timecode through the **Play from...** command:

Note that we can alternatively specify a defined **Label** to **Play From...** in place of the exact time code.

Internal Symbol properties

Internal Symbol properties are accessed by placing a Symbol instance or Symbol into edit mode and selecting internal Symbol Stage. A number of properties will then be revealed through the **Properties** panel, which we can then manipulate.

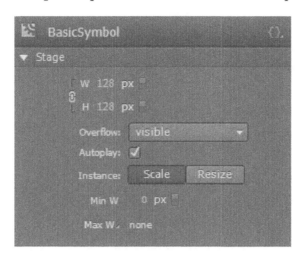

Property	Description
Symbol Name	This is the name given to the Symbol (not the **Instance ID** of Symbol) upon creation. This value can be changed from within the project library by right-clicking upon Symbol and choosing the rename option. This is also set upon Symbol creation.
Actions	Clicking upon the **Actions** icon within the **Symbol Properties** panel allows us to edit Symbol-level events. These events are detailed within the following section.
Symbol Stage dimensions	These properties function in the exact same way as for the main composition Stage properties. Use this to adjust the width and height of our Symbol.
Overflow	Just as is the case with any visible element, overflow determines how nested elements appear.
Autoplay	This determines whether or not the Symbol Timeline should play by default—or await a command from Edge Animate. This is also set upon Symbol creation.
Instance	This can be set to **Scale** or **Resize**. This affects the behavior of Symbol instances.
Min W , Max W	These options set limits upon how much the instance size can be adjusted.

Symbol-level events

The **Symbol-level events** are events that can be fired off upon the creation of or previous to the deletion of a Symbol instance. The following table explains the two panes of **beforeDeletion** and **creationComplete** events:

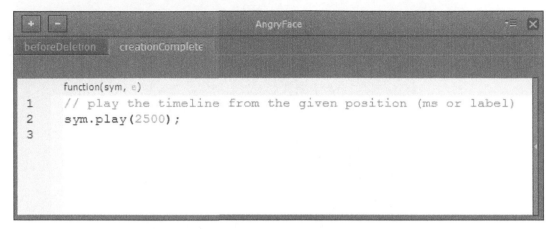

Event Name	Description
creationComplete	The included code will be run when the **Symbol** is created.
beforeDeletion	The included code will be run just before a **Symbol** is deleted.

Nesting elements

Nesting one or more elements within another creates a sort of grouped relationship where one element is the container for others. Doing this can have many advantages; for instance, elements that have been nested are essentially grouped to their container element, allowing all elements to be moved and adjusted along with and in relation to the container.

Nested elements can also be hidden when out of bounds from their container element. This almost works like masking in some regards, as certain nested elements or portions of a nested element can be revealed through the container element. All that needs to be done is for the container element's **overflow** property to be set to `hidden`.

Note that nesting elements is quite different from converting elements into a symbol. Nested elements do not get their own timeline or any of the special properties of symbols and retain all their original attributes.

How nesting works

To actually nest one or more elements with Edge Animate is deceptively simple. All that needs to be done is to access the **Elements** panel and then drag-and-drop elements into one another.

In the next screenshot, we see all of the elements within an Edge Animate composition as basically child elements of the Stage. None of these elements is nested within another and there is no visual indicator to show that there is any relationship between these elements at all.

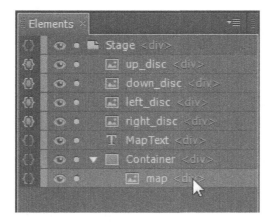

To nest one element within another, simply click-and-drag one element in this panel and drop it onto another element. In the next screenshot, we can see as an example that the **map** element has been nested within the **Container** element in this manner.

We can easily see that there is now a nesting relationship between these elements because of the twirl next to the container element and as the nested element is now indented underneath:

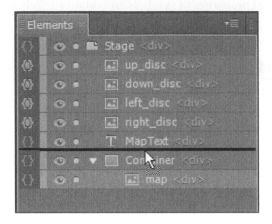

[To un-nest a nested element, simply drag and drop back out of the container element.]

Nesting assets

Library assets can easily be nested within rectangular elements through use of the **Elements** panel. Nesting basically encapsulates one element within another and allows us to perform grouping of elements in this way, as many elements can be grouped within a single parent element.

[It's important to note that for nesting to occur, the parent element must be either **Rectangle**, **Rounded Rectangle,** or **Ellipse** <div/>.

An image, a Symbol instance, or a text element cannot be the parent element in this case. These can all be child elements, but not the target of a parent.]

Modifications made to the properties of a parent element will essentially affect all of the nested children as well—though properties of each child can also be adjusted independently of both the parent element and one another.

We can tell that an element is nested within another by looking at the **Elements** panel. Nested elements are indented below their parent, and the parent itself has a small twirl next to it, allowing us to collapse and expand display of the child elements whenever we wish.

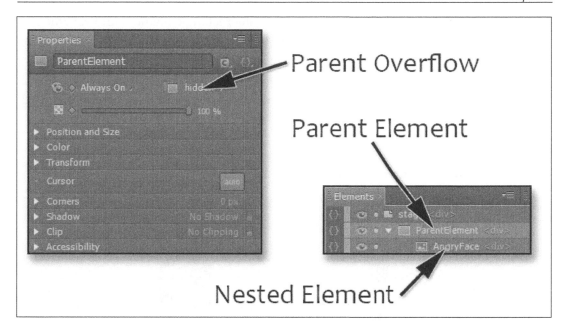

Parent Overflow

Parent Element

Nested Element

 We can even think of the Stage panel as a big nested element as it contains all other elements within it.

Let's have a look at nesting an imported image within a basic rectangle element:

1. We'll first create a new Edge Animate project and modify the properties of the Stage to our liking.

2. Using the **Rectangle** tool, draw out a rectangle element onto the Stage.

3. With this rectangle element selected, visit the **Properties** panel and make the following adjustments:

   Background Color: #404040

   Border Color: #2eff00

   Border Style: solid

   Border Thickness: 12 px

   Overflow: hidden

4. We will now import an image asset into our project by either using the **File | Import...** feature or by dragging-and-dropping into the project. We should now have two elements on the Stage.

5. In the **Elements** panel, double-click on the rectangle element and rename it to `ParentElement`. We do not need to do this but it is helpful for clarity.

6. While still in the **Elements** panel, click upon the image asset element node and drag it directly over the `ParentElement`.

7. Release the mouse and we will see the image element node become indented and a small twirl will appear aside `ParentElement`, indicating that nesting has occurred.

8. To verify this fact, we can see that the image is partially hidden due to the **Overflow:** `hidden` setting we created in step 3.

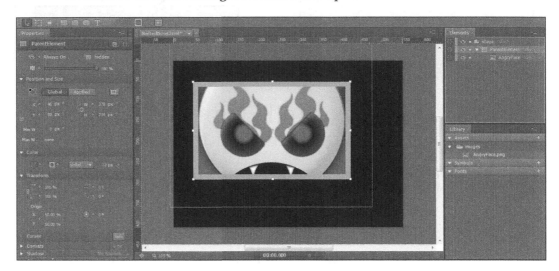

 At this point, it would be useful to play around with the properties of each element to see how they behave together now that they are nested.

Nesting text

To further illustrate the usage of nested elements within Edge Animate, we are going to go through a few small examples of nesting. In the first example, we see how text can be nested within an element, allowing for scrollbars to appear in order to scroll through and read all of the text, which has been hidden from the bounds of the container element through an overflow setting.

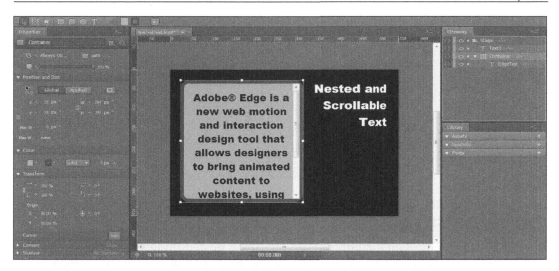

The files for this project are located in the `NestedText` directory.

To replicate this project:

1. Create a new Edge Animate project.
2. Using the **Rectangle** tool, draw out a rectangle element upon the Stage panel.
3. In the **Properties** panel, set the `Overflow` property to `auto`.
4. Now, using the **Text** tool, create a text element on the Stage and fill it with a lot of text. The goal here is to make sure the text element is larger than the rectangle element we just created.
5. To nest the text element within the rectangle element, in the **Elements** panel, click on the text element and drag it onto the rectangle element.
6. Once the cursor is over the rectangle element, release the mouse button to perform the nesting function.
7. The text element is now nested within the rectangle element, as indicated by the downward arrow to the left-hand side of the rectangle element.

As we have set the `Overflow` property of this element to `auto`, we can now scroll through the text using the scrollbars that automatically appear.

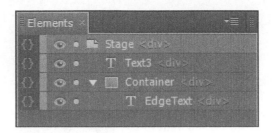

Controlling nested content

Taking this concept even further, we can employ a nested image so that we not only reveal only a portion of that image at any given time, but we can control which areas are revealed through a set of custom controls and a little JavaScript.

This example will feature a large map image nested within a rectangle element, similar to the previous example. Instead of having the browser render scrollbars automatically, we will fashion a set of controls and wire them up through actions for a truly customized experience.

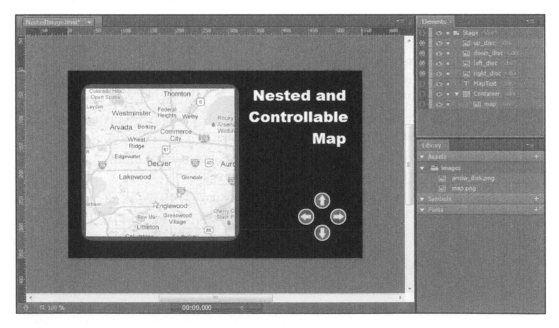

The files for this project are located in the NestedImage directory.

To replicate this project:

1. Create a new Edge Animate project.

2. Using the **Rectangle** tool, draw out a rectangle elements upon the **Stage** panel.

3. In the **Properties** panel, set the Overflow property to hidden.

4. Now, we'll need to import a large image file into our composition. Choose **File | Import** from the menu, or simply drag-and-drop a prepared image into the application window.

5. Once the image has been imported, make sure there is an instance on the **Stage**. Remember that the goal here is to make sure the image element is larger than the rectangle element we just created.

6. To nest the image element within the rectangle element, in the **Elements** panel, click on the image element and drag it onto the rectangle element.

7. Once the cursor is over the rectangle element, release the mouse button to perform the nesting function.

8. The image element is now nested within the rectangle element, as indicated by the downward arrow to the left-hand side of the rectangle element.

9. Be sure to provide a sensible ID to the nested image element. We will need this later on.

As we have set the Overflow property of this element to hidden, even though the image is much too large for its containing element, content that extends beyond these borders remains hidden with no way to scroll or reveal the hidden portions.

To allow the user to scroll around and view other portions of the image, we'll have to create a set of custom controls within our interface.

To create the controls:

1. Either design a small directional arrow image in something like Photoshop, draw one out using Edge Animate tools, or import the example provided in this project. However you choose to create it, be sure it is available in your project.

2. Replicate the arrow element three times so that there are four instances of this element upon the Stage panel. You may choose to replicate through copy and paste or by simply *Alt* + dragging instances from the original.

3. Using the **Transform** tool, rotate each of the three arrow elements so that they point: up, down, left, and right. Arrange these upon the Stage in whichever way makes the most sense to you.

4. Give each of these arrow elements a sensible ID. This will make things much easier when it comes time to make adjustments to the composition later on, and is good for clarity.

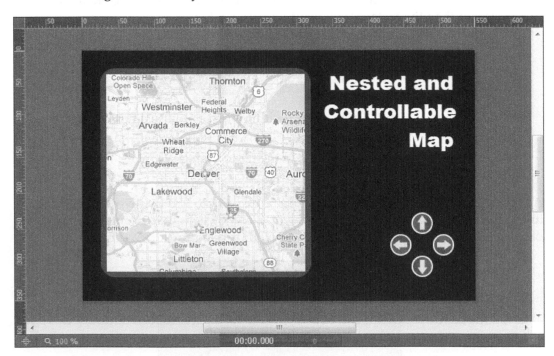

Now to make this all work, we need to wire together the directional arrow elements with some actions which influence the nested content.

To prepare the element actions:

1. Choose the upward arrow element first and click upon the curly-brace icon to the left-hand side of this element within the **Elements** panel. This will open up the **Actions** editor.

2. Add an action instance of type Click and insert the following code (where map is the ID of our nested image element):

    ```
    var element = sym.$("map")
    element.animate({top: +=20})
    ```

3. Open the **Actions** editor for the right-side arrow element.

4. Add an action instance of type Click and insert the following code (where map is the ID of our nested image element):

    ```
    var element = sym.$("map");
    element.animate({left: "-=20"});
    ```

5. Open the **Actions** editor for the downward arrow element.

6. Add an action instance of type Click and insert the following code (where map is the ID of our nested image element):

    ```
    var element = sym.$("map");
    element.animate({top: "-=20"});
    ```

7. Open the **Actions** editor for the left arrow element.

8. Add an action instance of type Click and insert the following code (where "map" is the ID of our nested image element):

    ```
    var element = sym.$("map");
    element.animate({left: "+=20"});
    ```

9. Close the **Actions** editor, then save and test your composition.

So what is happening here? We are tapping into the jQuery "animate" method in order to shift the image element around within its container. This allows us the ability to provide the user with a set of customized controls and not have to rely on simple scrollbars generated by the browser.

Grouping and ungrouping within Edge Animate

While nesting is a great mechanism for more complex, intentional relationships, sometimes we just need to temporarily group a set of items to position or transform them all in some way, without having to manage each element individually. The ability to group and ungroup a set of elements is a useful mechanism in such situations.

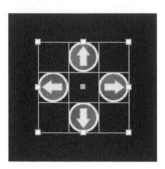

To actually group a set of elements, we must first select the elements we intend to form the group with. We can manage our selection through the Stage panel, the **Elements** panel, or really any avenue of interaction that allows selection of multiple elements within a composition. Once the elements are selected, there are a few ways of constituting a new group:

- The first method of grouping elements is performed by right-clicking on one of the selected elements and choosing **Group Elements in DIV** from the context menu that appears.

- Another method of grouping is to access the application menu and choose **Modify | Group Elements in DIV**.

- A third method is through the simple keyboard shortcut: *Ctrl* + *G* (Windows) or *Command* + *G* (Mac).

To ungroup an established group of elements, we can take these very same steps but choose the **Ungroup Elements** option. Keyboard shortcuts to ungroup are: *Ctrl* + *Shift* + *G* (Windows) or *Command* + *Shift* + *G* (Mac).

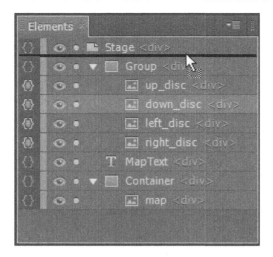

 We are also able to ungroup elements through the **Elements** panel in the same way that we remove elements from a nested parent element—simply drag-and-drop.

Adobe Edge Animate menu items

We'll now have a look at some of the Edge Animate menu items that can be used when dealing with the creation and editing of Symbols.

Modify

The **Modify** menu includes two commands particular to Symbols involving element conversion and the editing of Symbols and groups.

Command	Description
Group Elements in DIV	This wraps all selected elements within an empty DIV element.
Ungroup Elements	This removes any grouped elements for a container DIV and removes the container.
Convert to Symbol...	This will convert the selected elements to Symbol and place this new Symbol in the **Library**. An instance of the newly created Symbol is created on the Stage in the exact spot within which the element(s) previously existed.
Edit Symbol	If Symbol has been selected, Edge Animate switches the view to an isolation mode within that Symbol in order to edit its contents.

Summary

Both Symbols and nested elements are ways in which we can expand the base capabilities and creative borders of elements within Adobe Edge Animate. With Symbols, we have access to what could almost be considered to be sub-compositions within our overall project. With the power available to us within Edge Animate Symbols, the creation of rich, engaging compositions is not so far away. When Symbols are overkill, but we require something beyond basic elements, we can employ the nesting of elements in the form of grouping or to perform other associations.

In the next chapter, we'll have a look at some mechanisms that can be used for "masking" or clipping content, as well as the use of sprite sheets and other advanced animation features within Edge Animate.

9
Advanced Animation Techniques

In this chapter, we look at a number of advanced tools and techniques which are available to us in Adobe Edge Animate. While much can be done through calculated motion across the timeline, there are many more possibilities which can be realized through further exploration. These advanced techniques provide a greater amount of control and expressive potential within our compositions through the following features:

- Clipping
- The **Clipping** tool
- Animating with sprite sheets
- Animating with PNG sequences

We'll employ the content examined within the pages that follow in order to take animated compositions to the next level and expand the use of Edge Animate with complementary tooling, such as that found in Flash Professional CS6 and other Adobe Creative Suite applications.

Clipping

Clipping is a mechanism by which we can define a clipping rectangle upon the selected element to hide portions of that element from view. This is similar to the concept of **masking** found in some other applications—but is more limited as we are constrained to a rectangular clipping mask. By default, an element **clipping rectangle** is set to show all of any particular element, with no portion being hidden whatsoever.

This is similar to setting the **Overflow** property of an element to `hidden` when nesting elements within it to hide portions of the parent elements' children—though clipping provides no overflow settings.

Clip properties

Depending upon the type of the element selected when clipping, we can modify a number of properties related to the **Clipping** tool (C). If an image element is selected, we can modify the **Clip** positions, `top`, `bottom`, `left`, and `right` properties, as well as the image source **Background** position. For any other element, we have access to only the four **Clip** position properties as shown in the following properties:

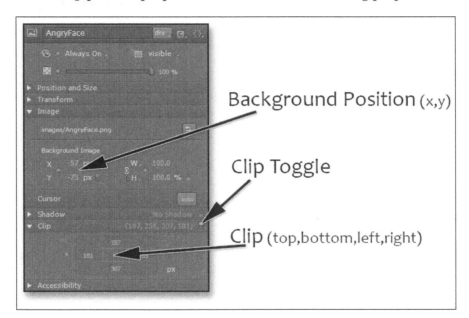

We may initially think it strange that the image element **Background** position can be controlled in line with **Clip** properties. However, if coming to Edge Animate with Adobe InDesign experience, this pairing will seem immediately familiar.

The Clipping tool

Edge Animate includes a dedicated tool for visually clipping elements upon the Stage. The **Clipping** tool (C) is accessed from the toolbar and is placed to the right-hand side of the **Transform** tool, as shown in the following screenshot:

 The **Clipping** tool appears as a small, filled box enclosed within a larger box that is indicated by a dashed border.

Selecting the **Clipping** tool allows us to adjust the **Clip** properties of any visual element. Simply choose the **Clipping** tool and select any element on stage to adjust the top, bottom, left, and right **Clip** properties. Refer to the following screenshot:

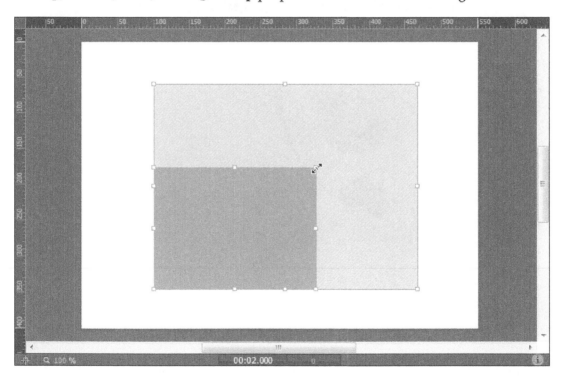

An element selected with the **Clipping** tool will appear as shown in this screenshot. The clipping rectangle is displayed with green borders. Anything being hidden behind the clipping rectangle will appear as a shadow with a diagonal line pattern.

We can also make adjustments to the **Background** position of our image elements with this tool.

Image elements and the Clipping tool

When an image element is selected with the **Clipping** tool (*C*), we will see a small icon overlay in the very center of the image. This is the **Background** position adjustment overlay and appears almost like a little donut. It is known as the **content grabber**. If we click upon this small control and drag it around the Stage, it will shift the **Background** position of the image source past the bounds of our clipping rectangle. This works similar to adjusting the clipping rectangle directly, but in this case the rectangle itself is not altered—just the contents within.

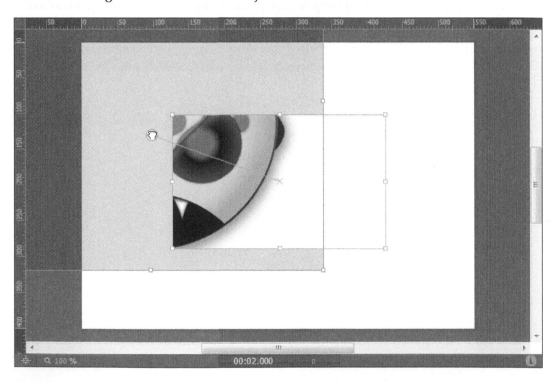

The previous screenshot demonstrates displacement of an image source through visual manipulation of the small **Background** position adjustment content grabber overlay, originally located in the center of an image element.

Revealing image and text elements through clipping

Clipping is an excellent way of revealing elements within our composition through animation. In the following example, we'll reveal a number of text and image elements by animating the **Clip** properties of each element upon the Stage.

 This completed project example is located in the directory named Clipping Text.

To perform this example, we will begin by creating a number of elements upon the **Stage**:

1. First establish the Stage properties for this project. Use any values you like. In this example, we've created our Stage with **Width** having a value of 650 pixels, a value of 350 pixels for **Height**, and with **Background Color** of the value of #000000.

2. We have also included a textured image as a background wash for this example. This element is not going to be animated so it is inconsequential in terms of the example itself—though it is nice to have a more interesting background within our Edge composition.

3. Now import an image (via **File** | **Import...**) onto the Stage panel directly or through the **Library**. In this example, we're using the Adobe Edge Animate logo and have centered it upon the Stage. This will provide experience in clipping with image elements.

   We have three distinct text elements to establish for this project. One should read **Adobe Edge**, another should read **Rich Motion and Interactivity**, and the third should be **using web standards**.

4. For the first text element, position it above the logo and adjust the properties as follows:

   Font Name: Tahoma, Geneva, sans-serif

   Font Size: 66 px

   Text Color: #15ea83

   Bold: on

   Italic: off

5. For the second text element, position it below the logo and adjust the properties as follows:

   Font Name: Arial Black, Gadget, sans-serif

   Font Size: 37 px

   Text Color: #caecdb

   Bold: off

   Italic: off

6. For the third text element, position it below the second text element and adjust the properties as follows:

   Font Name: Arial Black, Gadget, sans-serif

   Font Size: 30 px

   Text Color: #629d8d

   Bold: off

   Italic: on

Now that we have completed the layout for this example, we can begin animating each of these elements across the Timeline:

7. Let's begin with the image element, as this is the most complex. Choose the **Clipping** tool (*C*) and select the image element. You will notice that there is a small donut-shaped content grabber overlay that appears on the image. This is a control that allows us to adjust the **Background** position of the source file for this image element with the **Clipping** tool. It may make sense to explore this tool before moving on, by clicking on it and dragging it around the screen.

8. When we are ready to move on, we will enable **Pin** (*P*) upon the Timeline and position it at **00:01.500** — move the **Playhead** to **00:00.500**. Click-and-drag each side of the clipping rectangle until the image is totally obscured.

9. Before moving on, let's make a few more adjustments. Set **Scale X** and **Scale Y** to **125**% and the **Opacity** to **18**% — this will provide some interesting effects along with the clipping reveal of this image element.

10. Now select the first text element with the **Clipping** tool (*C*). Notice that there is no donut overlay this time. That's because this element has no image associated with it.

11. We are going to use the same exact span of time already established for our transition, so we simply grab the blue transition indicator between the **Playhead** and **Pin** and drag it backwards along the Timeline to the very beginning of our sequence. **Playhead** will read **00:00**.

12. Upon Stage, adjust the clipping rectangle so that the **Clip** (right-hand side) property reads **0**. This will enable a wipe reveal from the left-hand side.

13. We will again click-and-drag the blue transition indicator between the **Playhead** and **Pin** and this time drag it forward along the Timeline until **Playhead** reads **00:01**.

14. Using the **Clipping** tool, select the second text element directly beneath the image and adjust the clipping rectangle so that the **Clip** (left-hand side) property reads **0**. This will enable a wipe reveal from the right-hand side.

15. For a final time, we again click-and-drag the blue transition indicator between the **Playhead** and **Pin** and drag it forward along the Timeline until the **Playhead** this time reads **00:01.500**.

16. Using the **Clipping** tool, select the third and final text element and adjust the clipping rectangle so that the **Clip** (top) property reads the exact same number as the **Clip** (bottom) property. This will enable a wipe reveal from the bottom.

17. Disable the **Pin** (*P*) and test the animation by either dragging the **Playhead** along the Timeline, clicking on the **Play** button, or performing a browser preview via **File | Preview in Browser**. We can see all of our elements being revealed through staggered segments.

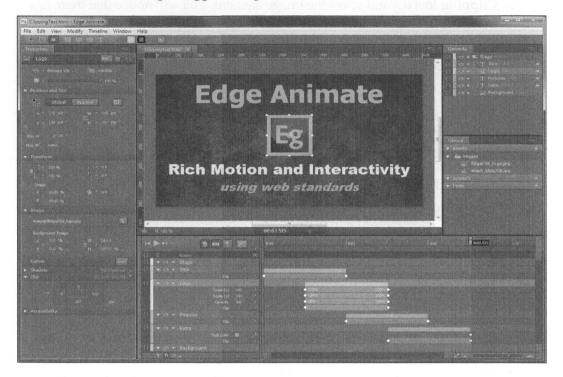

 In this example, we have authored an Edge Animate composition that includes the animated clipping of both text and image elements.

The completed example will appear as shown in the previous screenshot. Notice how we've staggered the transitions so that they overlap one another somewhat. This keeps the animation moving and there is no *dead time* within the sequence. To further adjust this composition, we can experiment by assigning a variety of easing properties to each transition. Within a short, directed animation such as this, keeping momentum is key.

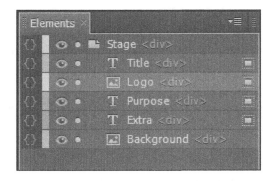

 Notice how in the **Elements** panel, any clipped elements have a clipping icon displayed to the very right-hand side. This makes it easy to determine which elements are clipped and which are not with a quick glance.

Animating with sprite sheets

Sprite sheets are image files composed of all the representative frames of an animation sequence, packed into a single file—usually with accompanying data that describes how the animation should be interpreted. Sprite sheets are used heavily in gaming and have even had resurgence over the past few years with the increased popularity of Flash runtimes and HTML5 gaming engines.

In the previous image, we see how the various single frames of an animated walk sequence are rendered within a single sprite sheet.

Generating sprite sheets from Flash Professional CS6

There are many applications which can be used to generate sprite sheets for use in Edge Animate. Flash Professional CS6 is an excellent choice due to the variety of rich animation tooling and maturity of the application. Using Flash Professional, we can create an animation sequence and export it as a sprite sheet with total control over the image aspect as well as the data format to be exported.

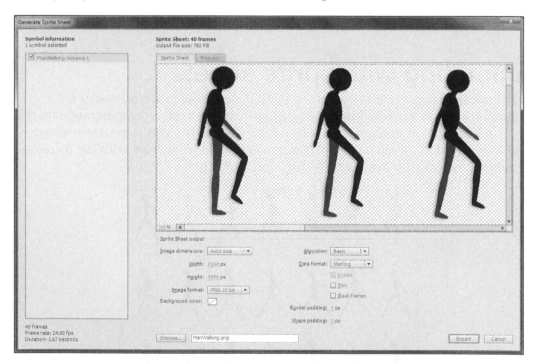

The previous screenshot represents the **Generate Sprite Sheet** dialog available in Flash Professional CS6.

To generate a sprite sheet in Flash Professional CS6 for use within an Edge Animate composition, perform the following steps:

1. Create an animation and enclose that animation within a MovieClip symbol. In this example, we are creating a simple walk sequence using the Inverse Kinematics tools available in Flash Professional.

2. From Stage or Library, right-click upon the MovieClip to convert to a sprite sheet and choose the option Generate Sprite Sheet.

 Note that when generating a sprite sheet from the **Stage**, any filters and effects we have applied will carry over as well!

3. The **Generate Sprite Sheet** dialog will appear. There is really no reason to tweak any of these settings for use within Edge Animate, so we can simply click on **Export** to proceed.

 Note that we can specify a filename and location through the **Browse** button, if desired.

We now have a sprite sheet image and accompanying data file. We will only be using the Sprite Sheet image and so can discard the data file, if desired. Note for later that we are using a 24 frames per second (fps) animation. This will be important when it is brought back into Edge Animate.

 If Flash Professional CS6 is not immediately accessible, there are many other sprite sheet generators available for download via the web—many of them for free.

Using a sprite sheet within Edge Animate

Although Edge Animate does not directly support the use of sprite sheets through any sort of automation, it is possible to use sprite sheets within a composition by employing a sprite sheet image file along with the **Clipping** tool and **Auto-Transition Mode** disabled.

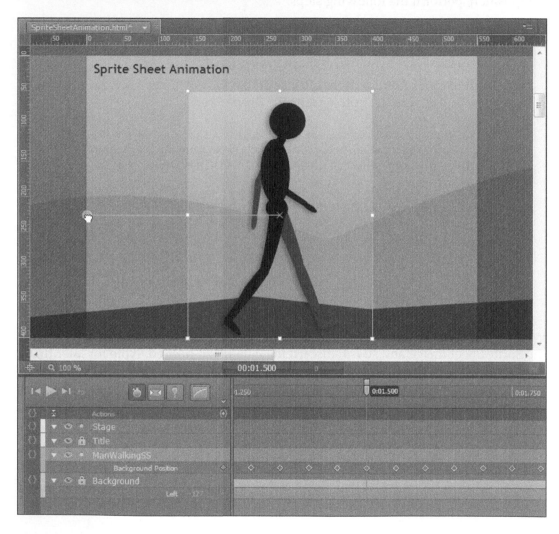

To use a generated sprite sheet within an Edge Animate composition, perform the following steps:

1. Create a new Edge Animate project and set up the Stage according to the specifications of the project. Generally, be sure it is large enough in resolution to accommodate the sprite sheet we will be using.

2. Place the sprite sheet image file upon Stage by using either the **File | Import...** command from the application menu, or via drag-and-drop from the desktop.

3. Now position the image so that the first frame of the animation is at the coordinates that make the most sense to the project. The image element itself does not necessarily need to move in order to provide animation—in fact, this method of animation involves moving the source position only.

4. Select the **Clipping** tool from the toolbar and click upon the image element to select it.

5. We now must adjust the clipping rectangle to hide all other frames represented within the sprite sheet so that only the initial frame of the animation is visible. As sprite sheets tend to be rather large, we may need to make our initial **Clipping** adjustments through the **Properties** panel and then fine-tune them on Stage with the **Clipping** tool.

6. The next set of actions are similar to frame-by-frame animation, so we will disable the **Auto-Transition Mode** (X).

7. To assist with placement, we can change the Timeline grid overlay in order to easily snap to a certain sequence of time. In this case, we will choose the **Show Grid** option and set the snapping to **24 fps**. This matches the settings from Flash Professional.

8. Here is the tedious part! Depending on the complexity of the sprite sheet animation sequence, we may have to repeat this step many, many times. For each and every sprite sheet in the sequence, we must adjust the **Playhead** so that it is a few milliseconds forward on the Timeline from the last keyframe and then use the content grabber available from within the **Clipping** tool to adjust the **Position** of our image element source.

9. With each frame in the sequence, nudge the **Playhead** forward a bit (to the next grid marker) and adjust the image source position with the content grabber. It makes good sense to test our animation every couple of frames in to be sure the sprite sheet sequence is animating properly. We can make small adjustments with the content grabber wherever it may be needed as we test.

While this is by no means a quick way of animating content within Edge Animate, if a project requires or could benefit from this sort of animated content, it is definitely worth the effort as the result is extremely difficult to achieve otherwise.

[This is also a great example of how to repurpose content across platforms. For instance, create sprite sheets for use in a Flash game targeting iOS with Stage3D and Starling through Adobe AIR, while employing the very same sprite sheet within a website about the game with content produced in Adobe Edge Animate.]

Animating with PNG sequences

Another method of employing representative frames-based content from other applications is through the use of image sequences. The most versatile type of image to use when working in this way is the PNG format because of the range of transparency it allows.

PNG sequences themselves can be generated by a number of CS6 applications, including Fireworks, Premiere Pro, After Effects, and Flash Professional. For this example, we'll use Flash Professional to create an animated sequence and export it as a series of images.

Generating PNG sequences from Flash Professional CS6

One of the major advantages of using Flash Professional when generating an animated sequence of this nature, is that Flash Professional has an abundance of tools within it for drawing and modifying objects within its timeline—tools and workflows that simply do not exist within Edge Animate. We can leverage these tools to create complex animations to bring over into our Edge Animate projects and used as symbols.

The first step in this workflow is to author a short animated sequence in Flash Professional. To make things simple, it is advised that we create a new **MovieClip** symbol and then create animation within that because it can then be easily exported as a PNG sequence from the Flash Professional project library.

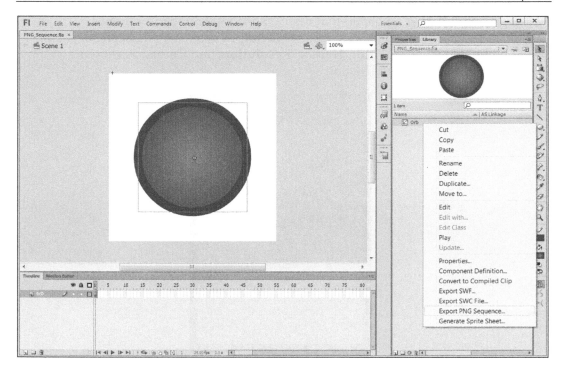

 Keep in mind that when an image sequence is exported, one image is generated for every single frame of animation. To reduce the number of exported images, we can reduce the project frames per second in the **Properties** panel, and make sure the animation is not too lengthy.

Now that we have our animation, we need to export it as a PNG sequence. This will create a series of individual files for us to use within our Edge Animate composition.

Flash Professional makes this task very simple:

1. Open the **Library** panel and right-click on the **MovieClip** symbol containing our animated sequence.

2. Choose **Export PNG Sequence...** from the menu that appears.

3. We will now need to browse to a location on the hard drive within which to save our image sequence. We can also provide a custom name for this sequence. Choose a location we can easily access later on.

4. A small dialog will open that displays the total number of frames to be exported, along with a series of output properties that can be adjusted such as **Width**, **Height**, **Resolution**, and **Colors**, as shown in the following screenshot:

5. Click on **Export** to complete the generation of our image sequence. The files will now be created within the previously specified location.

Normally, the default settings within the Export PNG Sequence dialog will work just fine for use in Adobe Edge Animate.

Note again that we are using a 24fps animation when authoring in Flash Professional. This data will simplify our animation tasks within Edge Animate.

Using PNG sequences in Edge Animate

Similar to the use of sprite sheets in Edge Animate, there is no import tool to assist in the use of image sequences. The image assets must be imported into Edge Animate and all positioning and property adjustments must be completed manually. For this reason, it is best to use short sequences to avoid having to perform a lot of manual adjustments within the project.

There are two initial steps to getting this all working within an Edge Animate composition. The first is to create a new Edge Animate project, which we will be importing the image sequence into. The second is to locate the generated image sequence images on our local machine, as shown in the following screenshot:

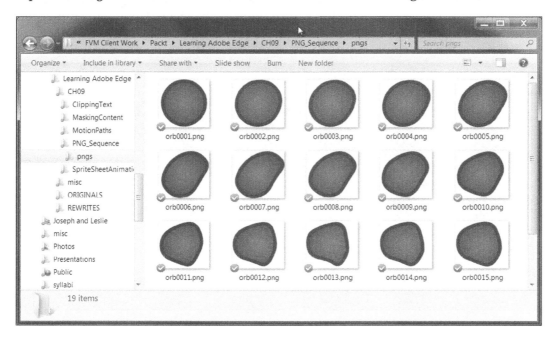

 The image sequence as generated by Flash Professional will appear as shown in this screenshot. Notice that each image retains the filename provided during the export process with a number appended to it. Each number corresponds to a single frame within the Flash timeline.

To get the image sequence into Edge Animate, perform the following steps:

1. Create a new symbol within the Edge Animate project by drawing out a temporary object using the **Rectangle** tool and then choosing **Modify | Convert to Symbol...** from the application menu.

2. Edit the symbol by either double-clicking on its instance on the Stage panel, or by editing through the **Library** window by right-clicking upon **Symbol** and choosing **Edit** from the menu that appears.

3. Remove the temporary asset used in creation of the symbol by selecting it and hitting *Delete*.

4. Now select all of the images which are part of the PNG sequence we want to use within our project.

5. Drag the selected images from the operating system file explorer onto the Stage of the symbol. Before dropping the images within Edge Animate, be sure the cursor aligns with the **(0, 0)** point of the Stage panel in the upper-left corner of the symbol:

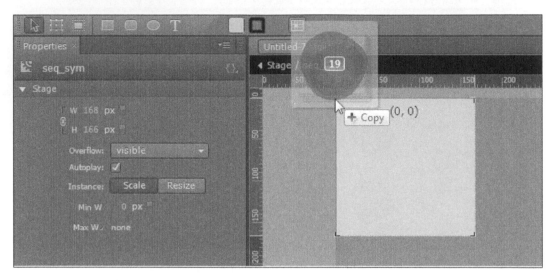

You will notice that our Timeline, **Library Assets**, and **Elements** panels are now filled with the sequenced images. We can now go about performing animation with these images upon the Symbol timeline.

We'll be disabling **Auto-Transition Mode** to toggle the **Display** property of each image on and off at a set time sequence across the timeline. This is very similar to frame-by-frame animation in that we are simply changing the entire image at set spans of time. For this example, we are changing these properties at every **00.042** mark in the timeline, or every 24 frames per second.

We can also change the Timeline grid overlay in order to easily snap to a certain sequence of time. In this case, we will choose the **Show Grid** option and set the snapping to **24 fps**. This matches the settings from Flash Professional.

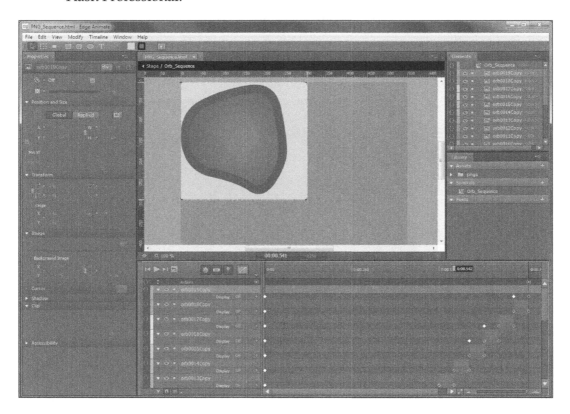

Perform the following steps in order to animate our image sequence:

6. Toggle **Auto-Transition Mode** to off through use of the button in Timeline or by pressing *X* on the keyboard.

7. Toggle the **Display** attribute to off, for all images in the sequence.

8. Using **Playhead**, or the time display controls beneath the Stage panel, set the current time to **00:00.042**.

9. Toggle the **Display** attribute to on for the first image in the sequence.

10. Move the **Playhead** forward to **00:00.083** and toggle the **Display** attribute of our first image in the sequence to off.

11. Toggle the **Display** attribute of our second image in the sequence to on.

12. Now, we must step through every next grid marker for each image in the sequence and perform steps 5 and 6 for each one. It is a time consuming process and calculations on how much time is proper to be used between transitions should be calculated ahead of time.

Once all the adjustments in the Timeline have been set up properly, by toggling each image in the sequence either on and off at a set interval, we will have a resulting animated sequence that should correspond closely to that which was created in Flash Professional.

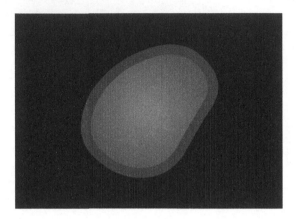

 Running our composition in a web browser will produce a fully animated symbol instance. Note that we can use multiple instances of the same symbol instance within a composition to create some rather striking effects.

Summary

In this chapter we have seen ways in which we can build upon simple timeline transitions, using a variety of other tools within Edge Animate to perform more complex animation through clipping, the use of spite sheets, and image sequences.

In the next chapter, we'll examine a number of features in regard to preparing Edge Animate compositions for distribution.

10
Publishing Edge Animate Compositions

This chapter describes a number of features in regard to preparing Edge Animate compositions for distribution. There are a number of ways in which Adobe Edge Animate facilitates a good experience for end-users by making the distributed code as light as possible, providing them with a preloader or notification while content is initialized, and being aware of browsers that may not be quite up to fulfilling the demands of the Edge Animate Runtime.

We'll explore the following topics over the course of this chapter:

- Publish Settings
- Capturing a poster image
- The Down-level Stage
- Using project preloaders
- Publishing a composition

Publishing an Edge Animate composition

While it is entirely possible to simply deploy the Edge Animate files that make up a composition without going through any sort of publish activity, this is not ideal. Why not? Because all of the code that makes up our composition can be tightened up and made to be much, much lighter than what we work with directly in Edge Animate.

There are also a number of other concerns with deployment such as support for unsupported browsers, tapping into a CDN to lighten the load even further, and the use of preloaders when displaying a composition. The steps toward publishing a composition takes into account all of these concerns.

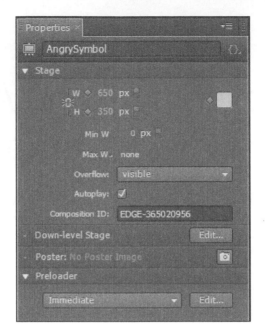

Publish Settings

The **Publish Settings** dialog provides a way for us to make some important decisions around how an Edge Animate composition will be packaged upon publication. Choices around whether to target the web directly or rather publish for ingest via some other Adobe application, and the decision to use a **content delivery network** (**CDN**) for distributed JavaScript libraries or not. All of this is handled from within this dialog.

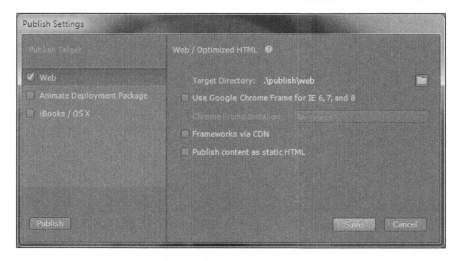

Targeting the Web / Optimized HTML

As Edge Animate projects are based in HTML, CSS, and JavaScript, when most think of Adobe Edge Animate, they immediately think of some website as the distribution point. In most cases, this is probably quite accurate as this is the primary target of Edge Animate (and the most widely talked about).

To target the Web when publishing an Edge Animate project:

1. From the application menu, choose **File | Publish Settings**.

2. We see a list of **Publish Target** entries along the left-hand side. Choose **Web**. The **Publish Target** will now read **Web / Optimized HTML**.

3. The **Target Directory** can be adjusted if desired. By default, Edge Animate will publish to a **.\publish\web** directory within the root of a project.

4. We may also decide to use the distributed frameworks via CDN through use of a checkbox, use **Google Chrome Frame for IE 6, 7, and 8**, or **Publish content as static HTML** (more on these options later).

5. When satisfied, click on **Save** to preserve these choices and publish later, or click on **Publish** for immediate publication according to the choices indicated.

Using the Frameworks via CDN option

Choosing the **Frameworks via CDN** option will write out a link to the content distribution network (CDN) address of jQuery. This bypasses the need to bundle and distribute the jQuery library along with our Edge Animate composition and can reduce the overall file size by quite a bit. As this URL is shared between any applications that use jQuery over CDN, and these files are cached locally, chances are good that the user actually already has the necessary jQuery files stored locally before the browser even needs to make a request for our Edge Animate composition.

The Edge Animate Runtime libraries are also distributed via CDN and we can choose to include them when publishing. While the Edge Animate Runtime is not as widespread as jQuery, this still takes a lot of weight from our final output—placing it into what can be a one-time download. Not only does this benefit our published Edge Animate composition upon subsequent visits, it also makes it so that other Edge Animate compositions spread out over the Web will benefit from the already-downloaded and cached libraries.

Using the Google Chrome Frame for IE 6, 7, and 8 option

Google Chrome Frame is a plugin that allows a user of the Microsoft Internet Explorer (IE) browser to experience web content within that browser—but rendered as though it were being viewed upon Google's Chrome browser. This is especially useful for older versions of IE, which do not support many of the recent advances in web technology.

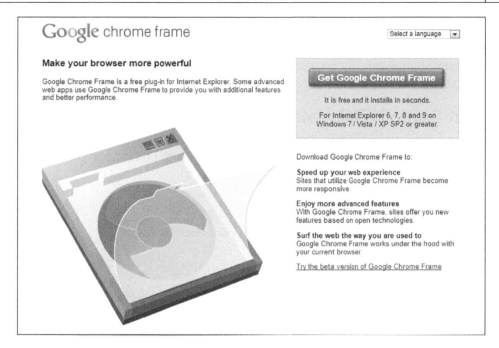

 Download the Chrome Frame plugin from Google at `http://www.google.com/chromeframe`.

Selecting to use Chrome Frame only applies to Internet Explorer 6, 7, and 8 on the Windows platform. When a user of Internet Explorer attempts to view this Edge Animate project, they will be presented with the option to install Chrome Frame within their current browser.

Publishing with this option selected will inject a small bit of code into the project HTML, just above the preloader JavaScript within the `<head>` of our document:

```
<meta http-equiv="X-UA-Compatible" content="chrome=IE8">
<script type="text/javascript" src="http://ajax.googleapis.com/ajax/
libs/chrome-frame/1/CFInstall.min.js"></script>
```

Using the Publish content as static HTML option

The **Publish content as static HTML** option will render the various HTML elements that are normally created by JavaScript and injected into the composition at runtime. This can be used to improve searchability and indexing on certain platforms.

Without Static HTML selected

Here follows the generated HTML without the Edge Animate static HTML option selected. Notice how there is simply one DIV representing the entire composition:

```
<!DOCTYPE html>
<html>
<head>
    <meta http-equiv='Content-Type' content='text/html;
charset=utf-8'>
    <title>ClippingText</title>
<!--Adobe Edge Runtime-->
<meta http-equiv="X-UA-Compatible" content="chrome=IE8">
    <script type="text/javascript" charset="utf-8" src="ClippingText_
edgePreload.js"></script>
    <style>
        .edgeLoad-EDGE-415806110 { visibility:hidden; }
    </style>
<!--Adobe Edge Runtime End-->

</head>
<body style="margin:0;padding:0;">
    <div id="Stage" class="EDGE-415806110">
    </div>
</body>
</html>
```

With static HTML selected

Here follows the generated HTML with the Edge Animate static HTML option selected. In this case, we not only have the composition Stage rendered as HTML—but also a variety of other elements which are part of our composition:

```
<!DOCTYPE html>
<html>
<head>
    <meta http-equiv='Content-Type' content='text/html;
charset=utf-8'>
    <title>ClippingText</title>
<!--Adobe Edge Runtime-->
```

```
<meta http-equiv="X-UA-Compatible" content="chrome=IE8">
    <script type="text/javascript" charset="utf-8" src="ClippingText_
edgePreload.js"></script>
    <style>
        .edgeLoad-EDGE-415806110 { visibility:hidden; }
    </style>
<!--Adobe Edge Runtime End-->

</head>
<body style="margin:0;padding:0;">
    <div id="Stage" class="EDGE-415806110">


        <div id="Stage_Background" class="edgeLoad-EDGE-415806110"></
div>
        <div id="Stage_Extra" class="edgeLoad-EDGE-415806110">using
web standards</div>
        <div id="Stage_Purpose" class="edgeLoad-EDGE-415806110">Rich
Motion and Interactivity</div>
        <div id="Stage_Logo" class="edgeLoad-EDGE-415806110"></div>
        <div id="Stage_Title" class="edgeLoad-EDGE-415806110">Adobe
Edge</div>
    </div>
</body>
</html>
```

Note that though these elements are injected into the HTML — they are not styled until the runtime initializes. That is still taken care of by the Edge Animate Runtime library.

Targeting InDesign/DPS/Muse

Adobe InDesign is a software application that allows us to design and pre-flight page layouts for print or digital distribution with the built-in creative toolset. It includes robust control over visuals and typography and can generate output in a number of formats.

More information on InDesign can be found on the Adobe website at: http://www.adobe.com/products/indesign.html.

The **Adobe Digital Publishing Suite** (**DPS**) is a solution for content producers that want to create, distribute, monetize, and optimize content produced in InDesign for tablet devices.

[More information on DPS can be found on the Adobe website at:
`http://www.adobe.com/products/digital-publishing-suite-family.html`.]

Adobe Muse is a software application built upon Abobe AIR (Flash Platform) that allows us to design and publish websites through use of an interface and tooling familiar to print designers. Muse features tight integration with other Adobe services such as TypeKit for an integrated font library, and Business Catalyst for simple web publication.

[More information on Muse can be found on the Adobe website at:
`http://www.adobe.com/products/muse.html`.]

When specifying **Animate Deployment Package** as a **Publish Target** entry as shown in the following screenshot, Edge Animate will publish an `.oam` file that can be used within InDesign CS6 for use as part of a larger project. The simplest way to accomplish this is to drag the `.oam` file into InDesign CS6, which will allow us to embed the full Edge Animate composition via the **Place** command as is normally done with external assets.

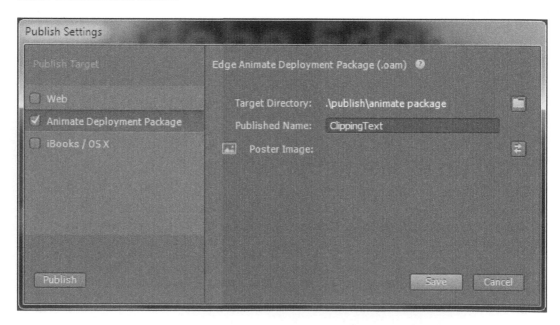

We are able to specify a **Target Directory** of our choosing. By default, the output will be located in the root of our project under /publish/ animate package/ClippingText.oam. (**Published Name** will be different for your composition, which is **ClippingText** here.)

Placing a composition within InDesign

To insert the Edge Animate composition within InDesign CS6, we open an InDesign document and choose **File | Place… | Edge Package** from the application menu. Locate the .oam file we wish to include. Then click upon the document to place the composition as we would a photo or any other imported file type.

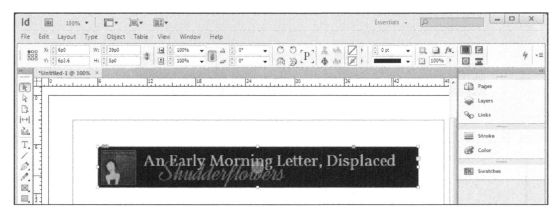

Once in InDesign, we can use the included DPS workflow tools to publish to the Adobe Digital Publishing Suite.

Placing a composition within Muse

To insert the Edge Animate composition within Adobe Muse, we open a Muse document and choose **File | Place… | Edge Animation** from the application menu. Locate the .oam file we wish to include.

Then click upon the document to place the composition as we would an image or any other imported file type that is compatible with Muse.

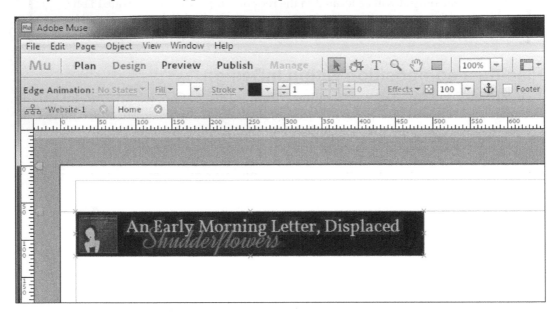

Using Adobe Muse, we can publish a website to upload later, via **File Transfer Protocol** (**FTP**) — or, alternatively, publish to the Web using the integrated Adobe Business Catalyst platform: http://www.adobe.com/products/business-catalyst.edu.html.

Targeting iBooks / OS X

Apple iBooks Author (only available on OS X) is a free application on the Mac App Store that allows users to create multi-touch textbooks which target the iPad (note that iBooks Author targets only iPad — no other tablet devices).

More information on iBooks Author can be found on the Apple website at http://www.apple.com/ibooks-author/.

When specifying **iBooks / OS X** as a **Publish Target** entry, Edge Animate will publish a .wdgt file — which is basically an uncompressed directory of files for consumption through iBooks Author. These iBooks widgets are very easy to use. We can simply drag-and-drop the .wdgt file into iBooks Author or import as an HTML widget within our iBooks project.

 As is the case with **Animate Deployment Package**, we are able to specify a **Target Directory** entry of our choosing. By default, the output will be located in the root of our project under /publish/iBooks/ClipingText.wdgt. (**Published Name** will be different for your composition, which is **ClippingText** here.)

Capturing a poster image

A **poster image** is a flattened image file that is used in place of the Stage panel, for use within browsers that do not support the Edge Animate Runtime as a placeholder or fallback image. This is accomplished by adding a captured poster image to the **Down-level Stage**. The format used for a poster image is PNG.

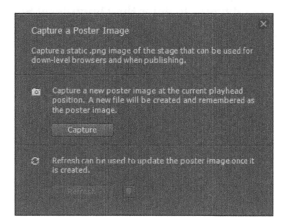

This is very similar to the practice of serving a static image in place of a SWF when it is detected that the user does not have Flash Player installed on their machine. It can provide a minimum level of support or a warning—depending upon the content.

Saving a poster image

Before we can use a captured poster image in our project, we must first perform the image capture itself. To do so, we must complete the following steps:

1. Find a place in the Timeline that visually represents the current project well.

2. Move **Playhead** to that exact position. This will be the scenario captured as an image.

3. Access the **Properties** panel for the Stage by deselecting all other elements.

4. Within the **Properties** panel is the **Poster** property, which has next to it a small icon that looks like a camera. Click upon this button to summon the **Capture a Poster Image** overlay.

5. The overlay will now change to let us know that a **Poster Image** instance has been captured successfully (the image can be found within Library under **Assets**) and present us with some immediate choices.

6. Choose **Publish Settings...** to access the **Publish Settings** dialog.

7. Choose **Edit Down-level...** to enter **the Down-level Stage** and perhaps place the newly acquired poster image within it.

In case this dialog is dismissed early through a misplaced click, **Publish Settings** can also be invoked from the **File** menu and **Edit Down-level Stage** can be invoked from the **Properties** panel with the document selected.

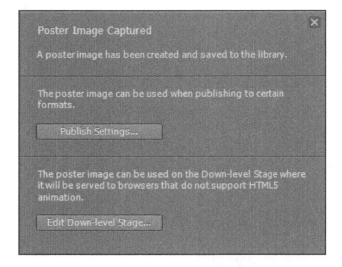

 Note that to actually see the **Down-level Stage** panel in action, we will need to use a browser which is not compatible with Adobe Edge Animate compositions.

Down-level Stage

The **Down-level Stage** panel exists for older or less-compliant browsers that are incapable of rendering normal Edge Animate content. This is a mechanism by which we can present some content (a static image basically) to the user. This allows the user to know that something exists in the space which would be occupied by our full Edge Animate composition. If desired, a text message can also be placed within the **Down-level Stage** panel, alerting the user as to their poor choice of browser.

Editing the Down-level Stage panel

In order to access and edit the **Down-level Stage** panel, we must look to the **Properties** panel with nothing but the **Stage** panel selected to access the Stage properties. Click upon the button labeled **Edit...** to enter the **Down-level Stage** panel for manipulation:

Once within the **Down-level Stage**, we can use a few of the Edge Animate tools to add content, insert a previously captured **Poster Image** from the main Stage panel, or use an imported image to communicate to the viewer. As seen in the next screenshot we can add text to the **Down-level Stage** panel using the **Text** tool—but that is about all aside from using imported or captured image media:

[

By default, the **Down-level Stage** panel is composed of simply a white fill.
]

Using a poster image

Edge Animate make things very easy when it comes to substituting items for use in these fallback scenarios. Any captured **Poster Image** can be used within the **Down-level Stage** panel by simply choosing **Insert** from the **Properties** panel (assuming that we've already captured a **Poster Image** entry).

If we already have a **Poster Image** instance in the **Down-level Stage** panel, the **Insert** button command does not detect this; so if the end user clicks on it again, the command will insert the last generated **Poster Image**. At worst, it's easy to have replicas of a **Poster Image** one on top of another, which is something that should be avoided.

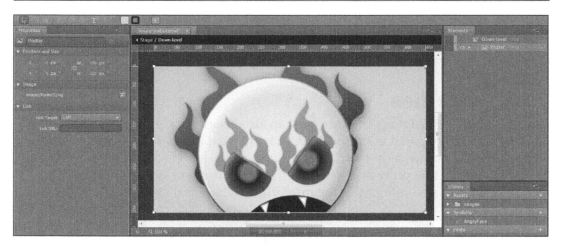

 In this screenshot, a **Poster Image** instance is inserted from a snapshot of our animation. This can serve as alternate content when a user's browser simply cannot display Edge Animate compositions.

Image properties

Once a **Poster Image** instance has been added to the **Down-level Stage** panel, we can perform edits to its location, width, and height. We can also change its **ID**, swap it out with another image through the **Select Image** icon to the right-hand side of the **Source** property, or even set some **Link URL** to activate upon interaction by the user:

The **Link URL** could possibly take the user to a different page on a website, or send them off to download a more modern web browser.

Text properties

Aside from a **Poster Image** instance, we can also insert text elements upon the **Down-level Stage** panel using the **Text** tool. The **Text** tool here works very similar to that when used upon the main Edge Animate Stage and text elements are created using the exact same process. The main differences here are simply limitations in what can be adjusted in terms of the properties of these text elements.

 The text element properties within **Down-level Stage** are much more limited that what we are used to in a full Edge Animate project. This is due to addressing only the most basic of support options.

Creating custom Down-level Stage

We do not have to be constrained to using a basic **Poster Image** instance with some text elements with our **Down-level Stage**. A more complex (or more customized) visual can be created in something like Adobe Photoshop and then imported into Edge Animate for use explicitly with the **Down-level Stage** panel.

For this example, we will create an image in Photoshop the exact size of our Edge Animate project stage. In the case of the example project, in the folder named `CustomDLS`, this is a 650 x 350 resolution.

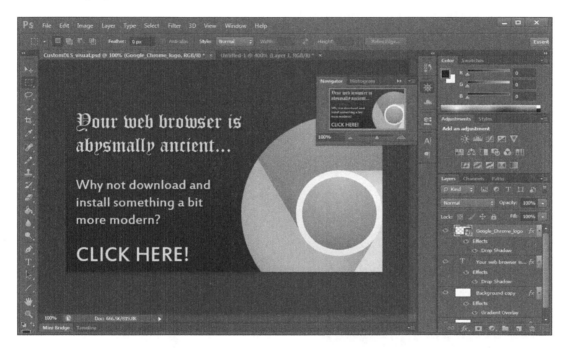

To maintain the widest amount of compatibility possible, we will export this image as a JPG file. The **Poster Image** instance produced by Edge Animate is saved as a PNG file, which is not compatible with very old browsers.

To create a fully customized **Poster Image** for the **Down-level Stage** panel, perform the following steps:

1. First, we create our visual in Photoshop (or whatever is preferred) and choose **File | Save for Web...**.

2. When the **Save for Web** dialog appears, choose **JPG** and export the image file.

3. Within our Edge Animate project, edit the **Down-level Stage** by accessing the **Properties** panel with the main Stage selected and click upon the **Edit...** button next to **Down-level Stage**.

4. Now, drag-and-drop the JPG image file that we have just exported from Photoshop onto the **Down-level Stage** panel. Notice it is added to the library of our project as well. Reposition if necessary.

5. Finally, as our image indicates the user should click to download Google Chrome, let's add a link to our imported image. With the image element selected, type `https://www.google.com/chrome/` into the **Link URL** property in the **Properties** panel.

We now have a custom **Down-Level Stage** panel using any visuals and effects we want. As this is a flattened image, we do not rely upon the limitations of Edge Animate tooling and can make our visual include compositing effects, blend modes, drop shadows, and whatever else is needed to convey our message to the user.

Using project preloaders

Preloading is a mechanism that has been used for years in other media to download enough material to ensure a good user experience, previous to the user being able to view or interact with the main content. This function is often accompanied by a visual preloader notice or animation, which alerts the user as to what is happening and reassures them that they only need to wait for a small amount of time before experiencing the downloaded content. This helps tremendously with large pieces of content as the user will otherwise simply think that the content is broken, which no one wants to happen.

 Long-time users of Adobe Flash Professional have no doubt built many preloaders over the years. In Flash Professional, preloaders must be built from scratch. In Edge Animate, we have this capability built into the Edge Animate Runtime—simplifying the entire process.

Preloaders in Edge Animate compositions are a way in which we can provide this sort of visual feedback to the user when waiting for some amount of the composition content to load up. There are two behaviors we can apply to our **Preloader** in Edge Animate, **Immediate** or **Polite**, with the following features:

Preference	Description
Polite Preloading	When it is selected, Edge Animate will not load anything beyond the preloader until the document load event occurs. At this point, it will load.
Immediate Preloading	When it is selected, Edge Animate will load as quickly as possible as though everything was directly embedded as part of the web page.

Using a built-in preloader

Adobe Edge Animate ships with a number of quite lovely preloader assets that can be freely used within our projects. These assets are basically small animated GIF files that are designed to indicate that something is loading and the user should wait. In essence, these are more akin to animated "throbber" assets than true preloaders—but they do get the job done.

To use a built-in preloader for our composition:

1. Select the main Stage by deselecting all other elements, or by selecting the Stage from the **Elements** panel.

2. From the **Properties** panel, find the **Preloader** area. Choosing **Edit...** will allow us to edit the **Preloader** panel within a special **Preloader Stage**:

3. From within the **Preloader** Stage, choose **Insert Preloader Clip-Art...** from the **Properties** panel. This will reveal an overlay dialog containing a variety of prebuilt preloader assets to choose from:

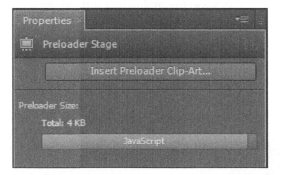

 We can also keep tabs on the weight of our preloader from the **Properties** panel. In the previous example, our **Preloader** contains only JavaScript and so weighs in at a light 3 kB. Adding preloader assets will definitely increase this total preloader file size.

4. We may now choose whichever preloader asset we wish to use within our composition by clicking upon it and choosing the **Insert...** button. It will automatically be added to the center of our **Preloader** Stage.

5. Once we save and publish our composition, if a preloader is needed, it will be shown to the user while the rest of the composition code and assets are downloaded for playback:

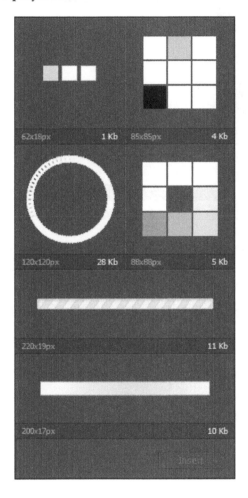

 Edge Animate comes bundled with a number of different pre-built preloader assets that can easily be inserted into an Edge Animate composition. When choosing a particular asset from this menu, we can view dimensions and file size along with a static preview.

Once a preloader image has been selected and inserted, it will appear at the center of the **Preloader** Stage as seen in the next screenshot:

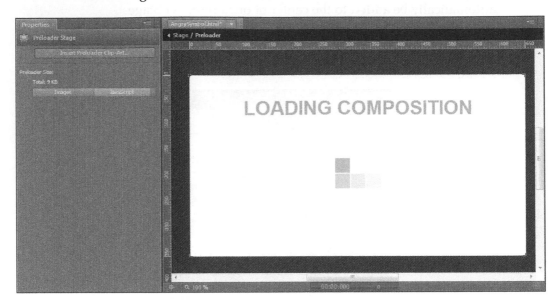

Upon inserting preloader assets, we will be able to preview full **Preloader** upon Stage, add text elements to describe what is happening for the user, and view the amended **Preloader** file size within the **Properties** panel.

Notice how these additional assets add weight to the preloader. We must always keep this in mind.

Creating a custom preloader

As **Preloader** assets are basically simple animated GIF files, we are actually able to create our own animated assets for use in the construction of an Edge Animate **Preloader**. Any application capable of authoring animation and outputting an animated GIF will work. In this example, we'll use Adobe Flash Professional CS6 to create a small animation, and export as a GIF file for inclusion in our **Preloader**.

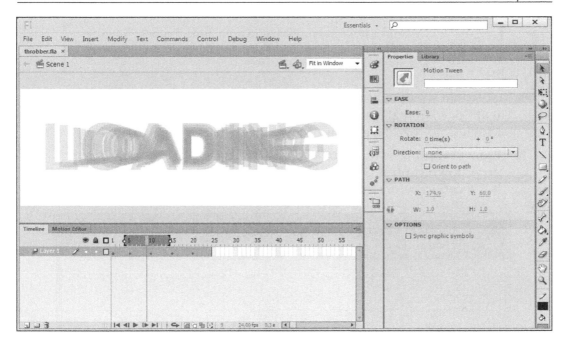

 Be sure not to make the preloader assets too heavy in terms of file size, else it defeats the whole point of having a preloader as the preloader assets themselves will take an inordinate time to load!

To create a custom preloader asset in Flash Professional for use in our Edge Animate composition:

1. Open Flash Professional and create a new document through **File | New…** (ActionScript 2.0 or ActionScript 3.0 will both be fine as we are simply outputting a GIF file). In this example, we will save the document as `throbber.fla`.

2. Change the dimensions of the Stage within the **Properties** panel to a smaller resolution—remember that we need tiny files for our preloader assets! In this example, we change the Stage to a width of 350 px and a height of 120 px.

3. Now select the **Text** tool from the toolbar and create a text field upon the Stage. Simply type the message we wish to convey to our users `LOADING`.

4. We will then access the **Motion Presets** panel (**Window | Motion Presets**) with our text field selected and choose the preset called `pulse`. This automatically applies the animation to our text field. That's all there is to it!

> Of course, if we are proficient in animating content within Flash Professional, we can choose to author the animation in any way we please.

5. Now that we have a quick animation, we need to export it in a format that Edge Animate can easily understand. Choose **File | Export | Export Movie...** to reveal the **Export Movie** dialog window.

6. We will want to select **Animated GIF (*.gif)** from the **Save as Type** drop-down control. We may also rename the file to be exported from this location before clicking on the **Save** button.

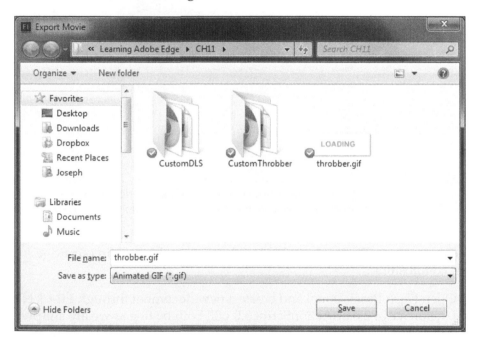

The **Export GIF** dialog will now appear, allowing us to adjust the following options:

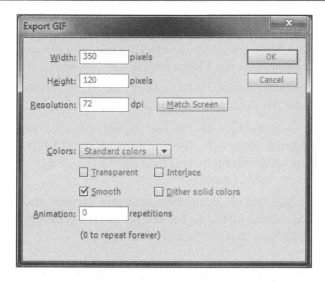

The following table describes the various properties available to us using this method:

Property	Description
Width	This represents the width of our exported image.
Height	This is the height of our exported image.
Resolution	The **Dots or Pixels per Inch (DPI)** of our exported image. A value of 72 is normal for desktop and laptop displays. Mobile displays will vary.
Colors	Choose a color palette made from 4 to 256 colors. Remember that the fewer colors in use, the smaller the file size will be.
Transparent	It determines whether to write transparent pixels or not in the final output.
Interlace	This determines whether we interlace horizontal rows or not.
Smooth	This determines whether to apply a smoothing algorithm to our output or not.
Dither solid colors	This determines whether to use dithering when approximating colors.
Animation	This determines the number of times to loop the animation. (0 for endless loop.)

7. Clicking on the **OK** button will complete the export process.

8. We now have an animated GIF file that can be imported into Edge Animate and used as a preloader asset. Nice!

To actually use our custom preloader within an Edge Animate composition:

1. Select the main Stage panel by deselecting all other elements, or by selecting the Stage element from the **Elements** panel.

2. From the **Properties** panel, find the **Preloader** area. Choosing **Edit…** will allow us to edit the **Preloader** within a special **Preloader** Stage.

3. Now, simply drag the GIF file we just exported from Flash Professional onto the **Preloader** Stage. The file will be added to **Library** | **Assets** of the project and an image element will be added to the Stage panel displaying our animated preloader asset.

4. We can also place text elements or even more images upon the **Preloader** Stage—just be careful not to not make the preloader too large, else it will take too long to load and become useless.

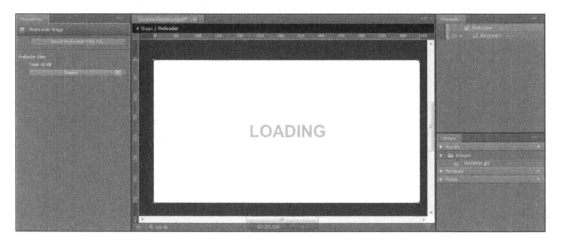

 In this example, we've used Flash Professional to author and generate an animated GIF file. Any application that allows us to author and export animated GIF files can be used in this same way. The process within Edge Animate does not change.

Publishing a composition

To actually publish our composition, including all of the **Publish Settings** defined, our **Down-level Stage** panel, and **Preloader**—we must choose **File** | **Publish** from the application menu. This will go through and minify the entire project JavaScript code by minifying any relevant files. This will make our compositions cleaner and lighter when considering distribution.

The two main JavaScript files in an Edge Animate project are the `Edge.js` and `Edge Actions.js` files. Each Edge Animate project will prepend the project name to the files as they are unique to each project, whereas the Edge Animate Runtime and jQuery files are not and can be shared either locally or through use of a CDN.

In the next section, we can see the differences in file size when comparing these two files in an unpublished project to those same files in a published project.

Before publishing

The following table shows the file size in bytes of both the `Edge.js` and `EdgeActions.js` files before publication. The name of the project file given by the user, is represented in the curly brackets.

File	Size
{xxx}_Edge.js	6,301 bytes
{xxx}_ EdgeActions.js	1,292 bytes

After publishing

This next table shows the file size in bytes of those same files (from the same project) but after publication. The name of the project file given by the user, is represented in the curly brackets.

File	Size
{xxx}_Edge.js	2,689 bytes
{xxx}_ EdgeActions.js	539 bytes

Summary

In this chapter, we have seen all the options available to us when publishing content through Edge Animate to the Web, to InDesign, or to iBooks Author. We've also explored an array of options used to make the user experience a bit more pleasant. These include use of the **Down-level Stage**, capture of **Poster Images**, and the use of **Preloaders** within our projects.

The final chapter of the book will delve into some of the more isolated and less-apparent aspects of Edge Animate not already covered in the chapters which have preceded it.

11
Further Explorations with Adobe Edge Animate

This chapter covers an assortment of topics related to Adobe Edge Animate which are either beyond the scope of previous chapters, or simply do not categorically fit within them. These can be considered as some of the more obscure or even advanced topics, and include the following :

- The Adobe Edge Animate Runtime API
- Modifying existing web content in Edge Animate
- Integrating Edge Animate content into existing websites
- Embedding more than one Edge Animate composition
- Measuring page load through Chrome Developer tools
- Advanced CSS treatments in Edge Animate
- Video support with Adobe Edge Animate
- Compositional audio integration
- Using Adobe Edge Inspect with Edge Animate

The Adobe Edge Animate Runtime API

Adobe Edge Animate comes equipped with its own JavaScript API for manipulating compositional content. Not only does this API allow for any necessary time-based and user-based interactions within a composition, it also manages the compositional preloader and a number of composition management APIs. When integrating an Edge Animate composition into a larger application, it would be beneficial to study the Edge Animate Runtime API documentation.

The inclusion of the runtime itself occurs through a basic JavaScript include within the HTML document:

```
<!--Adobe Edge Animate Runtime-->
<script type="text/javascript" charset="utf-8" src="{project-name}_
Edge AnimatePreload.js"></script>
<!--Adobe Edge Animate Runtime End-->
```

The Adobe Edge Animate Runtime API documentation is available on the web at `http://www.adobe.com/devnet-docs/edgeanimate/api/current/index.html`

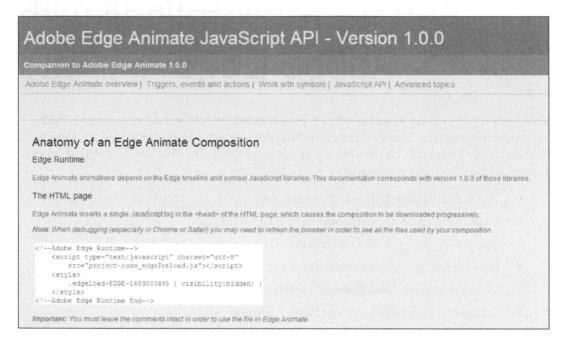

Adobe Edge Animate JavaScript API - Version 1.0.0

Companion to Adobe Edge Animate 1.0.0

Adobe Edge Animate overview | Triggers, events and actions | Work with symbols | JavaScript API | Advanced topics

Anatomy of an Edge Animate Composition

Edge Runtime

Edge Animate animations depend on the Edge timeline and symbol JavaScript libraries. This documentation corresponds with version 1.0.0 of those libraries.

The HTML page

Edge Animate inserts a single JavaScript tag in the <head> of the HTML page, which causes the composition to be downloaded progressively.

Note: When debugging (especially in Chrome or Safari) you may need to refresh the browser in order to see all the files used by your composition.

```
<!--Adobe Edge Runtime-->
    <script type="text/javascript" charset="utf-8"
        src="project-name_edgePreload.js"></script>
    <style>
        .edgeLoad-EDGE-1689000495 { visibility:hidden; }
    </style>
<!--Adobe Edge Runtime End-->
```

Important: You must leave the comments intact in order to use the file in Edge Animate.

 Adobe is also developing an online reference, which covers a lot of Edge Animate examples and resources that can be accessed from the following URL:

`http://html.adobe.com/edge/animate/.`

Modifying existing web content in Edge Animate

Throughout this book, we have been examining all of the tools and techniques made available to us in Edge Animate for the purpose of creating compositions from scratch. It is, however, very important to recognize the fact that what all Edge Animate is really doing is manipulating HTML… we can also open existing web pages in Edge Animate in order to perform animation upon various pre-existing elements.

Animating existing web content

In this example, we will open an existing web page in Edge Animate and apply a simple opacity transition upon an existing image element. A sample HTML document is located in the downloadable resources for this chapter: `ExistingWeb/originals/index.html`.

The following steps illustrate this concept:

1. Within Edge Animate, choose to open a document by accessing **File | Open...** from the application menu.

2. In the file browser that appears, we now navigate to and choose the HTML file we wish to work with.

3. Select some element which exists upon the Stage panel. In the referenced example, we choose the existing image element.

4. Employ **Pin** to create a Transition instance, which animates the value of image opacity property from 0 to 100 over two seconds.

5. Perform a quick preview to verify that everything is animating properly:

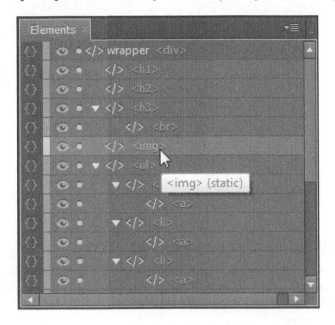

Note that when editing pre-existing HTML content within Edge Animate, all elements will be in an unmanaged, *static* state, and will appear as such within the **Elements** panel.

Now that we have adapted our content using Edge Animate, there is really no further action needed. Opening the HTML file which is produced will display the web page as normal—but with any added Edge Animate motion and interaction.

This does not mean that there have been no changes in our documents however. If we look within the directory that the HTML file was being edited in, we will now see all of the extra files and directories that we would expect to see in any Edge Animate project. This is because in order to employ the Edge Animate runtime, all of the proper libraries must be included with targets and dependencies written in, just as with a dedicated Edge Animate composition.

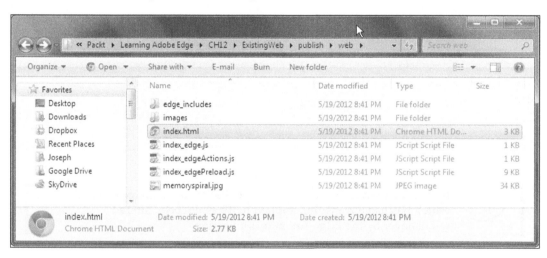

 When publishing the modified HTML document, just as with any Edge Animate composition, do not forget to include all the files which are needed for Edge Animate to function!

Opening the HTML document within a text editor or web-focused IDE such as Adobe Dreamweaver will reveal that only a few lines of code have been inserted within the head of our document in order to include the Edge Animate Runtime:

```
<!--Adobe Edge Animate Runtime-->
    <script type="text/javascript" charset="utf-8" src="index_
EdgePreload.js"></script>
    <style>
```

```
        .EdgeLoad-EDGE ANIMATE-335531406 { visibility:hidden; }
    </style>
<!--Adobe Edge Animate Runtime End-->
```

```
60  }
61  </style>
62  <!--Adobe Edge Runtime-->
63      <script type="text/javascript" charset="utf-8" src="index_edgePreload.js"></script>
64      <style>
65          .edgeLoad-EDGE-335531406 { display:none; }
66      </style>
67  <!--Adobe Edge Runtime End-->
68
69  </head>
70
71  <body>
72
73
74  <div id="wrapper">
75  <h1>The Memoryspiral</h1>
76
77  <h2>This is the website gateway of Joseph Labrecque</h2>
78
79  <h3>Senior Interactive Software Engineer - Artist - Author - <br />Adobe Education Leader -
    Adobe Community Professional</h3>
80
    <img src="memoryspiral.jpg" alt="Joseph Labrecque" title="Joseph Labrecque" />
82
83  <ul>
84      <li><a href="http://inflagrantedelicto.memoryspiral.com/">In Flagrante Delicto!</a></li>
85      <li><a href="http://twitter.com/JosephLabrecque">Twitter Profile</a></li>
86      <li><a href="http://www.linkedin.com/in/josephlabrecque">LinkedIn Profile</a></li>
```

 In this screenshot for example, we see that even the image element which has had a transition applied to it has not been altered whatsoever by the Edge Animate application.

Integrating Edge Animate content into existing websites

While some Edge Animate compositions make sense on their own, we will generally want to integrate content produced with Edge Animate into an existing website. In fact, as Edge Animate, by default, produces a simple, unstyled, blank HTML document for the composition to reside, we will most assuredly want to at least make things a little nicer to look at, even if it is a standalone piece we are dealing with. This is also necessary for content such as web banners.

The example project for this example can be found within the directory called `WebBanner` in the book assets.

We'll need to include everything in the Adobe Edge Animate Runtime code block. This includes moving this entire code block into the `<head>` area of another HTML document, moving all of the actual files into the existing website directory structure, and then updating any references that may have changed.

```
<!--Adobe Edge Runtime-->
    <script type="text/javascript" charset="utf-8" src="Untitled-8_
edgePreload.js"></script>
    <style>
        .edgeLoad-EDGE-1427881954 { visibility:hidden; }
    </style>
<!--Adobe Edge Runtime End-->
```

We'll also need to copy and paste the Stage panel itself into our existing document. This is the easy bit; simply copy and paste the following `<div>` element into the document `<body>` area and then position as desired through CSS:

```
<div id="Stage" class="EDGE-1427881954 edgeLoad-EDGE-1427881954">
</div>
```

Embedding a composition

To embed an Edge Animate composition within an existing website, there are basically two steps:

1. Copy the included JavaScript/CSS from the HTML generated by Edge Animate, into the `<head>` area of the existing document.

2. Copy the elements from the same generated HTML document into the `<body>` area of the existing document.

Additionally, we can also target the Edge Animate composition through CSS (via ID and class) to perform advanced positioning and size manipulation.

Embedding content

This method involves removing pieces of code from the HTML document generated by Edge Animate and including it within the target document. In this example, we are using the publish option without any modification.

JS/CSS

The following code snippet is located within the document head:

```
<!--Adobe Edge Runtime-->
    <script type="text/javascript" charset="utf-8" src="WebBanner_
EdgePreload.js"></script>
    <style>
        . edgeLoad-EDGE-686136729  { visibility:hidden; }
    </style>
<!--Adobe Edge Runtime End-->
```

HTML

The following code snippet is located within the document body:

```
<div id="Stage" class="EDGE-686136729"></div>
```

Embedding with static content

This secondary method also involves removing pieces of code from the HTML document generated by Edge Animate and including it within the target document. In this example, we are using the static publish option from within the **Publish Settings** dialog.

JS/CSS

The following code is located within the document head:

```
<!--Adobe Edge Runtime-->
    <script type="text/javascript" charset="utf-8" src="WebBanner_
edgePreload.js"></script>
    <style>
        .edgeLoad-EDGE-686136729 { visibility:hidden; }
    </style>

 <!--Adobe Edge Runtime End-->
```

HTML

The following code is located within the document body:

```
<div id="Stage" class="EDGE-686136729">
    <div id="Stage_Album" class="edgeLoad-EDGE-
686136729">Shudderflowers</div>
    <div id="Stage_Artist" class="edgeLoad-EDGE-686136729">An Early
Morning Letter, Displaced</div>
    <div id="Stage_Shudderflowers" class="edgeLoad-EDGE-686136729">
        <div id="Stage_Shudderflowers_Cover"></div>
    </div>
</div>
```

 This method is more robust, as much of our content is generated for us as static HTML rather than being injected into the DOM at runtime.

Packaging with <iframe>

One of the most useful (and simple) methods of distributing Edge Animate content is to simply supply some `<iframe>` code, which points to the HTML file generated by Edge Animate. Using this method, there is no need to copy and paste code out of the generated files—we simply include it as-is within whatever HTML documents require it. This method is perfect for banner ads, as you can see with the following `<iframe>` code:

```
<iframe src="WebBanner.html" width="468" height="60" scrolling="no"
frameborder="0"> </iframe>
```

Embedding more than one Edge Animate composition within a web page

The task of embedding multiple compositions within a web page is actually fairly simple so long as we follow a few important steps. Each composition has a composition ID and this is what can be used to target one specific composition over another. Additionally, it is also important to be sure to include all of the JavaScript and image files from each composition and to retain the proper paths to reference these files.

If each composition is using the same version of the Edge Animate Runtime libraries, they can all share the same set of includes.

In the following examples, we can see one way of employing multiple compositions by simply inserting our includes and container elements at opportune places.

JS/CSS

The following code snippet is located within the document head:

```
<!--Adobe Edge Runtime-->
    <script type="text/javascript" charset="utf-8"
src="Composition001_edgePreload.js"></script>
    <script type="text/javascript" charset="utf-8"
src="Composition002_edgePreload.js"></script>
    <style>
        .edgeLoad-EDGE-686136729 { visibility:hidden; }
        .edgeLoad-EDGE-686136730 { visibility:hidden; }
    </style>
<!--Adobe Edge Runtime End-->
```

HTML instance 01

This line of code is located anywhere within the document body:

```
<div id="Stage001" class="EDGE-686136729"></div>
```

HTML instance 02

The following code is located anywhere within the document body:

```
<div id="Stage002" class="EDGE-686136730"></div>
```

To position each of our compositions, simply target them through CSS and apply positioning rules to them, as follows:

```
#Stage002 {
    position:relative;
    top:100px;
}
```

Measuring page load through Chrome Developer tools

Not only is Google Chrome one of the most stable and cutting Edge Animate browsers available — but it also comes equipped with a slew of developer tools which we can leverage to monitor the lifecycle and progress surrounding our Edge Animate compositions when running in the browser.

The Chrome Developer tools can be accessed from within Chrome by clicking on the **Customize** icon to the right-hand side of the address bar and choosing **Tools | Developer tools**. In the following screenshot, Google Chrome (version 19) on Windows 7 is shown.

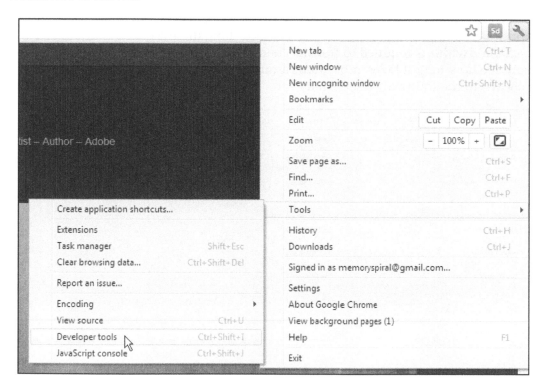

Once the tools are opened, we have the choice of either docking them within the browser window or through the use of a floating window which can be positioned independently of the browser.

We can select a number of tools from within this panel such as **Elements**, **Resources**, **Network**, **Scripts**, **Timeline**, **Profiles**, **Audits**, and **Console**. All of these can be used when monitoring our Edge Animate composition—but we will pay special attention to **Network** and **Audits**.

 It is advisable not only to use these tools when monitoring the content rendered directly from Edge Animate—but also once a composition has been published and integrated into some other system, for a true picture of performance and load.

Network

The **Network** tab allows us to monitor what components your web page or application is requesting from web servers, how long these requests take, and how much bandwidth is required to transfer them. Using the included timeline, we can easily see how long it takes individual resources within our composition to load up, as shown in the following screenshot:

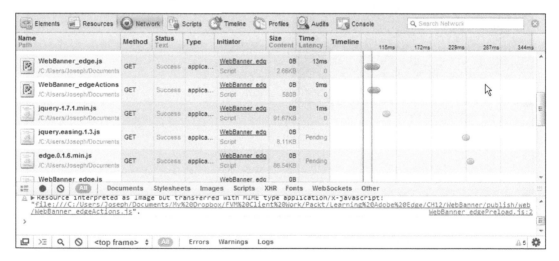

Audits

The **Audits** tool allows us to run an examination of our content in order to receive **Network Utilization** and **Web Page Performance** recommendations. While some of these options are beyond our control being tied directly to the runtime libraries, there are other recommendations which we can put into practice depending upon the composition being audited.

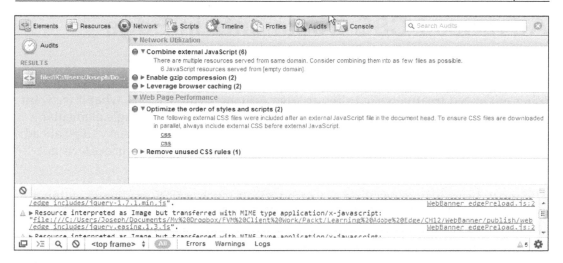

Other development tools

Aside from the tools previously outlined, we can also make use of any of the others included in Google Chrome when troubleshooting our application. Of special note are the **Profiles** and **Console** tools when troubleshooting JavaScript within an Animate composition.

 If you are using the Apple Safari browser, you will notice the development tools in that browser are very similar to the ones available in Chrome. This is because these tools are a core part of WebKit, which both of these browsers utilize.

While we are paying special attention to Google Chrome in this book, it is important to note that just about all modern web browsers do come equipped with some sort of developer tools. Recent versions of Mozilla Firefox and Microsoft Internet Explorer each come with a set of developer tools, and there are always third party options to consider as well.

Advanced CSS treatments in Edge Animate

While it is fabulous that we are able to make use of web fonts, text shadows, and other advanced treatments within our Edge Animate compositions, what if we want to include effects such as gradient backgrounds upon certain rectangle elements? Fortunately, as this is all just HTML, CSS, and JavaScript, it's fairly easy to go ahead and edit our published Edge Animate composition files in order to use effects not supported in the Edge Animate application itself.

The most direct way of enabling advanced effects (such as CSS gradients) within a composition is by leveraging the CSS classes and other designators used by Edge Animate during authoring. One of the most direct ways of doing this is through leveraging CSS specificity rules. We also have the ability to tag certain elements within Edge Animate with class names. This is much more precise and is what we will do for this demonstration.

There are a few other ways of increasing CSS specificity upon elements within Edge Animate. For instance, we could apply a unique ID to an element and also set the element type to `<p>` rather than the generic `<div>` element that Edge Animate normally creates for text elements. The ID can be used to specify CSS rules and the paragraph designation can assist with specificity.

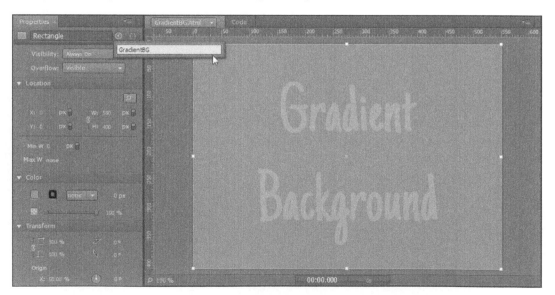

This project is located in the directory called `GradientBG` in the book's project files.

To apply some CSS to our composition, we must now either test or publish to render the proper files. Viewing the composition in a web browser such as Google Chrome, we can inspect the composition to be sure of the specific identifier to be used in targeting certain elements.

In the following code, we are targeting an element with the `GradientBG` class. This is a pretty specific designation and will allow us to isolate this particular element through the `background` CSS rules in order to render a complex gradient using nothing but CSS:

```
<!DOCTYPE html>
<html>
<head>
    <meta http-equiv="Content-Type" content="text/html;
charset=utf-8">
    <title>Gradient</title>
<!--Adobe Edge Runtime-->
    <script type="text/javascript" charset="utf-8" src="GradientBG_
edgePreload.js"></script>
    <style>
        .edgeLoad-648104304 { visibility:hidden; }
        .GradientBG {
            background: #f28c26;
            background: -moz-linear-gradient(-45deg,  #f28c26 0%,
#191919 47%, #631e1e 100%, #0e0e0e 100%, #d83511 100%);
            background: -webkit-gradient(linear, left top,
right bottom, color-stop(0%,#f28c26), color-stop(47%,#191919),
color-stop(100%,#631e1e), color-stop(100%,#0e0e0e), color-
stop(100%,#d83511));
            background: -webkit-linear-gradient(-45deg,  #f28c26
0%,#191919 47%,#631e1e 100%,#0e0e0e 100%,#d83511 100%);
            background: -o-linear-gradient(-45deg,  #f28c26 0%,#191919
47%,#631e1e 100%,#0e0e0e 100%,#d83511 100%);
            background: -ms-linear-gradient(-45deg,  #f28c26
0%,#191919 47%,#631e1e 100%,#0e0e0e 100%,#d83511 100%);
            background: linear-gradient(135deg,  #f28c26 0%,#191919
47%,#631e1e 100%,#0e0e0e 100%,#d83511 100%);
            filter: progid:DXImageTransform.Microsoft.gradient(
startColorstr='#f28c26', endColorstr='#d83511',GradientType=1 );
        }
```

```
</style>
<!--Adobe Edge Runtime End-->

</head>
<body style="margin:0;padding:0;">
    <div id="Stage" class="EDGE-516055382 edgeLoad-EDGE-516055382">
    </div>
</body>
</html>
```

 Note that we are also using a `filter` attribute along with our various `background` gradient specifiers in order to target older versions of Internet Explorer.

Once we save this modification and run the composition within a web browser which supports CSS gradients, we will see the gradient rendered perfectly along with our base rectangle element.

 While this example specifically allows for gradients upon rectangle elements—it can be used for just about any property modification through CSS. It simply must be applied outside of Edge Animate.

Video support in Adobe Edge Animate

While Edge Animate does not yet support the inclusion of video elements within a composition, that doesn't mean it cannot be done. The most effective way of including video within an Edge Animate composition is to use the **Set Element Text** action, in order to replace the contents of a rectangle element with a `<video>` or `<iframe>` tag pointing directly to the video source or to some intermediary document.

When using video on the web today, we have two main choices: the HTML5 <video> tag or a SWF file to be used with Adobe Flash Player.

The HTML5 <video> tag

The most prevalent mechanism to distribute video on the web is through the use of Adobe Flash Player. The second most popular way is via the HTML5 <video> tag. This method is becoming increasingly utilized by web authors—especially for those who wish to target hardware running iOS and other devices which do not support Flash Player in the web browser.

The <video> tag itself is really quite simple, yet depending upon the browser and a number of codec concerns, implementation can be less than ideal. Here we see the <video> tag in one of its most simple implementations:

```
<video width="560" height="315" controls="controls">
  <source src="testmovie.mp4" type="video/mp4" />
  <source src="testmovie.mp4" type="video/mp4" />
  <source src="testmovie.ogg" type="video/ogg" />
</video>
```

There are generally three video formats which are supported by the various browsers at this time. Let's take a general look at each of these.

MP4

MP4 is a widely supported, industry standard format for delivering video across desktop and devices. The major drawback with MP4 is that it does have certain patent requirements. Many devices include hardware-based H.264 decoders, making MP4 most desirable for use on smartphone and tablet devices.

WebM

The WebM format was formerly known as VP8. Google acquired the specification from On2 and have open-sourced it as a specification named WebM. It is not widely supported but has a lot of industry backing as there are (supposedly) no patents and it enables a similar compression and quality as MP4.

OGG

The OGG format is an entirely open source format with no patents attached to it. It is only used in limited ways by certain, specific browsers. The format does not have a lot of industry support outside of the browser community and is generally of much poorer quality than either of the other formats.

Adobe Flash Player

As an Edge Animate composition is actually just HTML5, we can use the full range of HTML tags, including `<object>` and `<embed>`. If we do not care for iOS compatibility, it is perfectly acceptable to employ a SWF file for enhanced video playback within our Edge Animate composition. As mentioned previously, Flash Player is still the most utilized method of enabling video playback on the web—not only for advanced capabilities such as streaming through **real time messaging protocol** (**RTMP**) and the **digital rights management** (**DRM**) protections it allows, but also simply because it can be a great experience when used properly.

Embedding a YouTube video within an Edge Animate composition

In this example, we will embed a video from YouTube (`http://youtube.com/`) into an Edge Animate composition.

 Note that this sort of external asset inclusion can actually be accomplished with all sorts of external media—not just video!

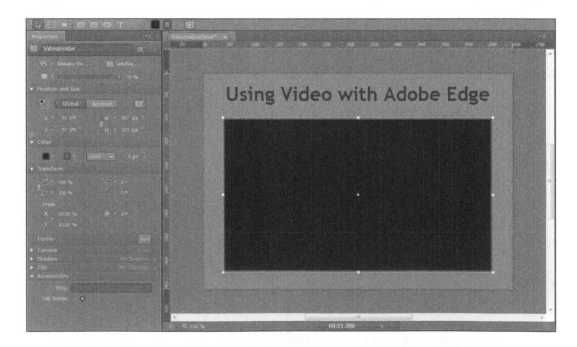

The first step in getting a video inside of Edge Animate is to create a container element. In this example, we will draw out a simple rectangle element using the **Rectangle** tool. As shown previously, we provide an ID of VideoHolder to this element and size it to the dimensions of the video we wish to use.

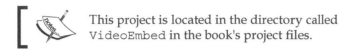

This project is located in the directory called VideoEmbed in the book's project files.

To actually load in a video, we will be employing a Trigger instance along the Timeline panel, as shown in the following screenshot:

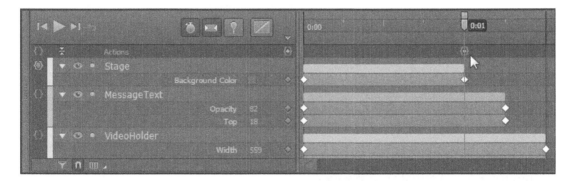

Here, we are animating our video placeholder in from off-screen and so will want to set the value for Trigger sometimes after the element animation completes. In this case, we set a new Trigger at 0:01.

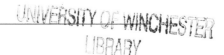

Now we need to select a video to embed within our composition. In YouTube, we must choose **Share** for sharing the chosen video and choose to reveal the embed code by clicking on **Embed**.

This will provide us with the `<iframe>` tag, which must be copied for insertion within the Edge Animate composition:

```
<iframe width="560" height="315" src="http://www.youtube.com/
embed/2MyNO_ecQag" frameborder="0" allowfullscreen></iframe>
```

 Note that this is a good way to get the exact dimensions to be used for our video container element, in case we do not know how large to make the initial rectangle element within Edge Animate.

Back in Edge Animate, open the **Actions** panel for the Trigger instance we have created upon the Timeline panel and insert the code for **Set Element Text** from the code snippets. The following snippet will be inserted but will require modification:

```
sym.$("Text").html("NewText");
```

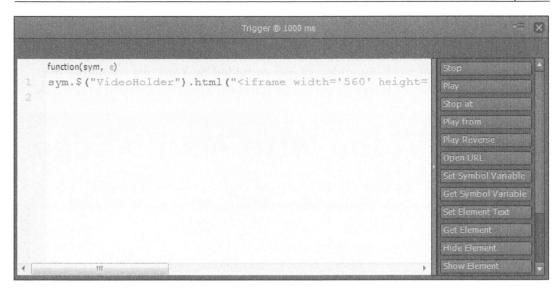

 We could, instead of having tied this event to a Trigger instance, had performed the **Set Element Text** action on **compositionReady**. It would work but could cause some jarring lag in any animation, while the video loads up into our composition.

Now we change the target element to `VideoHolder` and replace the text to be inserted with the `<iframe>` code from YouTube, as shown in the following code snippet. A very important step here is to replace all of the double quotes within the `<iframe>` code with single quotes, to avoid interference with the Edge Animate JavaScript code, which utilizes double quotes.

```
sym.$("VideoHolder").html("<iframe width='560' height='315'
src='http://www.youtube.com/embed/2MyNO_ecQag' frameborder='0'
allowfullscreen></iframe>");
```

 Note again that we absolutely must replace the double quotes with single quotes on any attributes of the `<iframe>` tag in order to avoid conflict with the Edge Animate APIs.

We will not be able to preview this within Edge Animate itself, but when publishing our composition or previewing in a browser, the animation will play and the video will load into our container element as expected. We will be able to employ any of the controls provided in the video player provided by YouTube—whether the HTML5 `<video>` player is served up or the standard Flash Player based playback.

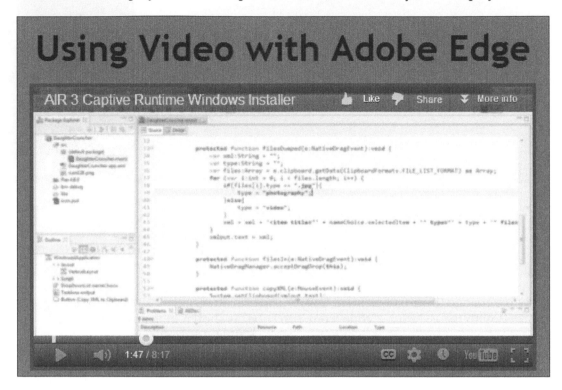

The great thing about this technique is that it can be used to include all sorts of external content provided by a variety of web services. Generally, if we can embed content in HTML, we can embed the same content within an Edge Animate composition!

Compositional audio integration

Whereas in the early days of the Internet, many settled for MIDI files playing back through SoundBlaster 16 as acceptable audio playback on the Web… today there is a higher expectation, especially now that people are used to rich playback through the various full Flash Player based solutions of the past decade, still quite prevalent today. In the following screenshot, we see the default audio tag skin as rendered by Google Chrome. The look and even default control elements differ across browser implementations.

In order to provide a browser-based solution for audio playback which does not rely upon the Adobe Flash Player or other additional solutions, the standards bodies have drafted an <audio> tag as part of the HTML5 specification.

The HTML5 audio tag

The HTML5 <audio> tag can be used to provide progressive playback of certain audio files along with optional, browser-styled controls. As an HTML tag, it can be implemented just as any other tag is through syntactical markup. This is very similar to how the <img> or <video> tags work, as follows:

```
<audio src="audio.mp3" />
```

Alternatively, the tag can be arranged as shown in the following code:

```
<audio>
    <source src="audio.mp3" type="audio/mp3" />
    <source src="audio.ogg" type="audio/ogg" />
</audio>
```

The following details the current audio tag attributes which are available to us:

Attribute	Description
autoplay	This determines whether the audio should playback on its own or wait for some external command.
controls	This specifies that the browser should render playback controls for the user to interact with the audio.
loop	This determines whether the audio file should repeat upon playback completion.
preload	This lets the browser know how the author wants it to handle loading the file. The browser can override this attribute or ignore it.
src	This is the path to a specific audio file.

Note that, instead of providing a `src` attribute upon the audio tag directly, we can nest a number of `<source>` tags within `<audio>` parent elements in order to provide alternative files for various browsers.

Working with audio

As Edge Animate does not support audio playback directly within a composition, we cannot bind playback events to Actions or Triggers. However, it is a fairly simple matter to get some basic background audio playback along with any generated composition.

The following screenshot represents the composition we wish to add audio to. It is a landing page for an experimental music that introduces visitors to the latest recording, and upon interaction, will navigate to another website where the user can preview and acquire the full album.

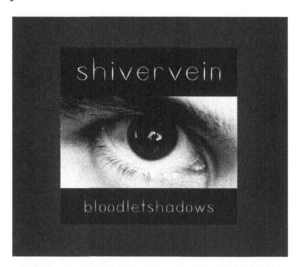

Refer to the `AudioIntegration` source folder to reference this entire project, or visit `http://shivervein.memoryspiral.com/` to view the result.

As Edge Animate does not support audio within the composition directly, we will need to provide the audio playback adjacent to our composition by adding an audio tag to the body of our published web page.

We must first author the composition in Edge Animate and then publish for the Web. Then we open the published HTML file within a text editor and add the audio tags manually. In the case of our example composition, the source will appear as follows:

```html
<!DOCTYPE html>
<html style="height:100%;">
<head>
    <meta http-equiv="Content-Type" content="text/html;
charset=utf-8">
    <title>shivervein</title>
    <link rel="shortcut icon" href="favicon.ico" />
<!--Adobe Edge Runtime-->
<meta http-equiv="X-UA-Compatible" content="chrome=IE8">
<script type="text/javascript" src="http://ajax.googleapis.com/ajax/
libs/chrome-frame/1/CFInstall.min.js"></script>
    <script type="text/javascript" charset="utf-8" src="shivervein_
edgePreload.js"></script>
    <style>
        .edgeLoad-EDGE-506590799 { visibility:hidden; }
    </style>
<!--Adobe Edge Runtime End-->

</head>
<body style="margin:0;padding:0;height:100%;">

    <div id="Stage" class="EDGE-506590799 edgeLoad-EDGE-506590799">
    </div>
    <audio autoplay="true" loop="">
        <source src="12_shiverechos.mp3" type="audio/mp3">
        <source src="12_shiverechos.ogg" type="audio/ogg">
    </audio>
</body>
</html>
```

This code will provide background ambience to our Edge Animate composition by automatically playing back the specified audio track. We've excluded any controls, making the audio element both invisible and out of the control of the user. We've also provided both .mp3 and .ogg files in order to target a variety of web browsers.

 Note that any text provided within an `<audio>` tag will be presented as a fallback message, for those browsers which do not support this tag.

Using Adobe Edge Inspect with Edge Animate

Edge Inspect is a new product from Adobe which seeks to lessen some of the pain involved in mobile web development by streamlining the process of device preview and testing. One of the great things about Inspect is that it is being built with considerations toward content produced in Edge Animate and is part of the Adobe Edge Tools and Services family of products.

At the time of this writing, Adobe Edge Inspect is available as a free download from Adobe Creative Cloud. We will need to visit `http://creative.adobe.com/` to download and install the application to continue.

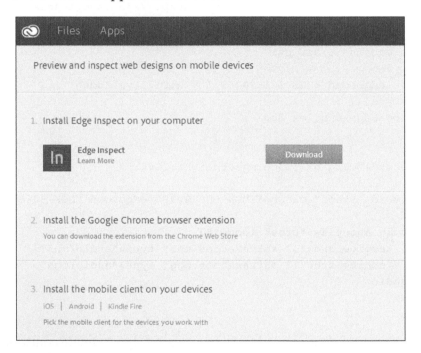

Note that in order to make full use of Inspect, the extension for Google Chrome and the mobile client for Android or iOS must also be downloaded and installed upon the test device. These clients can be accessed via each platform's designated app store and the Inspect download page has full instructions for Inspect configuration.

Edge Inspect works in sync with the Google Chrome browser. Once Inspect is installed upon a host computer, we must then be sure that the Chrome extension for Adobe Inspect is also installed.

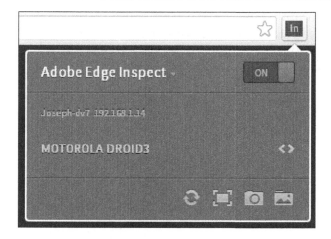

 The Google Chrome extension can be downloaded from
`http://www.adobe.com/go/inspect_chrome_app`.

Once installed, the Google Chrome extension can be managed through the Chrome Extensions manager, available through the options menu in **Tools** | **Extensions** or by typing `chrome://chrome/extensions` into the Chrome address bar.

 If running Windows, we may also need to take the additional step of installing the Bonjour service. Luckily, Adobe has packaged the Bonjour installer in the Inspect installation directory and we will only be notified to install this if we do not already have it.

Once we have all three fragments of Edge Inspect running in the host OS, the mobile OS, and within the Chrome browser, we can then continue with connections and setup:

1. Be sure the Adobe Edge Inspect host utility is running. A small indicator will appear in the system taskbar where Inspect can be managed.

2. Run the Inspect app upon a device connected over the same network as the host machine. The Inspect app will scan for connections and present the host machines it finds.

3. Either click upon the desired host listed, or we can manually add a connection via IP address through the app. A connection will be established and a passcode is then shown upon the mobile device.

4. Within Google Chrome, a small icon will be present to the right-hand side of the address bar. Click upon this icon and enter the given passcode into the input field.

5. Now open a project in Edge Animate and perform a browser preview in Chrome. The composition will run in Chrome and we will also be able to view the composition running with the aid of the Inspect app upon our mobile device.

In the following screenshot, we can see an Animate composition running within the Inspect view on an Android device. Notice that the Inspect app displays the name of the host machine in the top toolbar.

 While Edge Inspect provides a great workflow for testing and previewing Edge Animate content on mobile devices, it is also advisable to be sure to test the published composition upon normal device browsers as well.

Summary

In this chapter, we've looked over a variety of additional options we have when working in Adobe Edge Animate. These options include alternative inclusion strategies, tricks to get more out of Edge Animate, and the use of other tools such as Edge Inspect.

Edge Animate is a great new tool for interactive and motion design. It is planned to have quarterly releases for Edge Animate, which expand upon and add to previous functionality. Version 1.0 is quite impressive and as time goes by, it will become even more powerful.

Index

Symbols

<audio> tag 3
<canvas> tag 3
.edge file 156
<iframe> tag 323
<video> tag 3

A

About Adobe Edge Animate...command 53
Accessibility property
  about 107
  Tab Index 107
  Title 107
action
  composition actions 209
  Create Symbol 213
  Delete Symbol 213
  Get Element 213
  Get Symbol 213
  Get Symbol Element 213
  Get Symbol Variable 213
  Hide Element 213
  jQuery actions 211
  mouse actions 210
  Open URL 212
  play 212
  play from 212
  play reverse 212
  raw code 208
  Set Element Text 213
  Set Symbol Variable 212
  Show Element 213
  stop 212
  stop at 212

  touch actions 211
Actions, Edge Animate 22
Actions panel
  about 195
  Add/Remove Actions 195
  Applied Actions 195
  Code Editor 195
  menu item 196
  preferences 196
  Snippets List 195
actions property 103
actions, stage
  beforeDeletion 197
  compositionReady 197
  creationComplete 197
  keydown 197
  keyup 197
  onError 197
  orientationChange 197
  resize 197
  scroll 197
Actual Size command 110
Add Web Font dialog 128
Adobe AIR 14
Adobe Digital Publishing Suite. *See* **DPS**
Adobe Edge Animate. *See* **also Edge Animate**
Adobe Edge Animate
  about 1
  Adobe Flash Professional 19, 20
  advance tools 255
  clipping 255
  drawing elements 57
  drawing tools 56
  Edge Runtime 6
  Ellipse tool (O) 57

Flash Player restrictions 1, 2
Guides 72, 73
history 14, 15
HTML technology maturity 3
installing 23-26
Layout preferences 70
menu items 110
mobile, deploying 5
need for 1
PNG sequences 268
project, creating 28-30
project, Save As option 31
project, Save option 30
Rectangle tool (M) 56
roles, shifting 3, 4
Rounded Rectangle tool (R) 57
Rulers 55, 72
Selection tool (V) 58
sprite sheets 263
starting with 7
target users 7
using 5
using, for web animation 6
welcome screen 27
Adobe Edge Animate menu items
about 75, 110
Edit menu 75
Modify menu 76, 77
View menu 76
View menu, commands 76, 110
Adobe Edge Animate Runtime 15, 18
**Adobe Edge Animate Runtime API 193,
303, 304**
Adobe Flash Professional
Adobe Edge Animate 19, 20
Adobe Illustrator
about 149
bitmap image asset, exporting 149
SVG image asset, exporting 150
Adobe InDesign 281
Adobe Integrated Runtime. See AIR
Adobe Muse 282
Adobe Photoshop
image asset, exporting 151
**Adobe Product Improvement Program...
command 53**

Adobe TypeKit
URL 125
AIR 18
AJAX 16
Animation property 299
Apple iBooks Author 284
Application interface overview
Application window 34
panel layout, customizing 35, 36
workspaces, managing 36, 37
assets
exporting, from Adobe Photoshop 151
exporting, from Creative Suite applications
148
exporting, from Fireworks 152, 153
exporting, from Flash Professional 158
exporting, from Illustrator 149, 150
assets, exporting from Fireworks
about 152, 153
Edge Animate extension, using 153-155
extension, using 155-157
Asynchronous JavaScript and XML. See
AJAX
audio integration
about 324
audio, working with 326, 327
HTML5 audio tag 325, 326
auto cursor 200
automated animation techniques
automation example 186
motion, pasting 185
automation example
about 186
initial state 186
transition begin state 187
transition end state 188, 189
autoplay attribute 325
Autoplay property 109

B

Background Color 56, 65
background color property 108
Background Position Offset X 135
Background Position Offset Y 135
Background Position Units 136
Background Size Height 136

Background Size Units 136
Background Size Width 136
beforeDeletion action 209
bitmap images
  about 140, 141
  animated GIFs, using 144
  importing 142, 143
  types 141
bitmap images, types
  about 141
  GIF 142
  JPEG 141
  PNG 141
Blur radius property 106
Border Color 66
Border Radii property 66
Border Radii units 66
Border Style 66
Border Thickness tool 66

C

Cascading Style Sheets. *See* CSS
category definitions
  Cursive 123
  Fantasy 123
  Monospace 123
  Sans-Serif 123
  Serif 123
CDN 276
Change Language...command 53
Chrome Developer tools
  about 313
  Audits tool 314
  Network tab 314
  other development tools 315
  used, for page load measuring 313, 314
class property 103
click action 210
clipping
  about 255
  Image elements 258
  image elements, revealing 259-263
  text elements, revealing 259-263
clipping rectangle 255
Clipping tool 257
clip property

about 107, 256, 258
  clip 107
Close All command 51
Close command 51
Code command 52
Code panel
  about 206
  code error warnings 207
  full code view 207
colors property 299
col-resize cursor 200
Command + Click (Mac) 81
Command key 61
composition
  post-publishing 301
  pre-publishing 301
  publishing 300
composition actions
  beforeDeletion 209
  compositionReady 209
  creationComplete 209
  keydown 209
  keyup 209
  onError 209
  OrientationChange 209
  Resize 209
  scroll 209
Composition ID property 109
compositionReady action 209
content delivery network. *See* CDN
content grabber 258
context-menu cursor 200
controls attribute 325
creationComplete action 209
crosshair cursor 200
CSS 16
Ctrl+ Click (Windows) 81
Ctrl + G 101
cursor property
  about 105, 106
  cursor 106

D

dblclick action 210
default cursor 200
digital rights management. *See* DRM

Dither solid colors property **299**
Document Object Model. *See* **DOM**
Document title property **108**
DOM
   about 57, 91
   Ellipse tool 56
Dots or Pixels per Inch. *See* **DPI**
Down-level Stage command 110
Down-level Stage panel
   about 287
   custom Down-level Stage, creating 291, 292
   editing 287, 288
   poster image, using 288
Down-level Stage property 109
DPI 299
DPS 281
drawing elements
   duplicating 68, 69
   rectangle element copying, Selection tool
      used 69, 70
drawing tools, Adobe Edge Animate
   about 56
   Background Color 56
   Ellipse tool 57
   Rectangle tool 56
   Rounded Rectangle tool 57
DRM 320

E

easing equation 176
ECMAScript (ECMA-262) Edition 3 16
Edge Animate
   about 15
   actions 193
   advanced CSS treatments 316-318
   animation 161, 162
   application menu 38
   content, integrating into existing websites
      308
   CSS 16
   Edge Inspect, using with 328, 329
   existing web content, modifying 305
   goal 161
   grouping 252, 253
   HTML 15
   JavaScript 16

jQuery, using 16, 17
JSON 17, 18
keyboard shortcuts 49
local fonts, using 127-130
menu items 50, 189, 222, 253
panels 41
playback controls 162
PNG sequences using 270-274
sprite sheet, using 266, 267
symbols 223
Text tool 113
timeline 162
timeline controls 165
toolbar 38
ungrouping 252, 253
video support 318, 319
web fonts, applying 125-127
web fonts, using 122
Edge Animate actions
   actions, applying to individual elements
      198
   actions, applying to Stage 196, 197
   Actions panel 195
   working with 194
Edge Animate Community Forums...
      command 53
Edge Animate Composition
   about 275
   publishing 275
Edge Animate content integration
   about 308, 309
   composition, embedding 309
   content, embedding 310
   content embedding, HTML 310
   content embedding, JS/CSS 310
   content embedding, with static content 310,
      311
Edge Animate element properties
   Clip 107
   element 102
   position 104
   Shadow 106
   size 104
   Stage 108
   Transform 104
Edge Animate elements
   properties 102

Edge Animate Help...command 53
Edge Animate JavaScript API...command 53
Edge Animate Library
    fonts, managing 130
    fonts, viewing within {projectname}_edge.
        js 131
Edge Animate project
    file structure 32
Edge Animate Runtime 278
Edge Animate Stage
    about 88, 89
    Center the Stage control 90
    manipulating 89
    Rulers and Guides 89, 90
    zoom controls 90
Edge Animate Symbol file 148
Edge Animate symbols
    comparing, with Flash Professional symbols
        228, 229
Edge Animate toolbar
    about 38
    Stage panel 38-40
    Timeline feature 41
Edge Inspect
    using, with Edge Animate 328-330
Edit menu, Adobe Edge Animate
    Copy command 75
    Cut command 75
    Delete command 75
    Duplicate command 75
    Keyboard Shortcuts command 75
    Paste command 75
    Paste Special command 75
    Redo command 75
    Select All command 75
    Transform command 75
    Undo command 75
Edit Web Font dialog box 130
element animation
    background, creating 183
    cover art, animating 183
    end stage 184
    title text, animating 184
element properties
    about 65, 102
    actions 103
    Background Color 65

Border Color 66
Border Radii 66
Border Radii units 66
Border Style 66
Border Thickness 66
class 103
ID 103
opacity 104
overflow 103
Visibility 103
Elements command 52
Elements panel
    about 95, 96, 101
    elements, grouping 100, 101
    elements, locking 97
    elements, renaming 99, 100
    elements, reordering 99
    managed elements 98
    static elements 98
    visibility 96, 97
elements responsive way
    about 92
    Global versus Applied 92, 93
    responsive presets 94
    responsive presets, scale size 94
Ellipse tool (O)
    about 57
    using 63, 64
    working with 63
e-resize cursor 200
ew-resize cursor 200
existing web content, in Edge Animate
    animating 305-308
    modifying 305
Exit command 51
Export GIF dialog 298
Export Image dialog 158
external assets
    about 133
    file types, importing 133, 134
    image element types 134

F

File menu, Edge Animate menu
    Close All command 51
    Close command 51

Exit command 51
Import command 51
new command 51
Open....command 51
Open Recent command 51
Preview In Browser command 51
Publish command 51
Publish Settings...command 51
Revert command 51
Save As...command 51
Save command 51
file structure, Edge Animate project
  edge_includes directory 33
  {project_name}.an 32
  {project_name}_edgeActions.js 33
  {project_name}_edge.js 32
  {project_name}_edgePreload.js 33
  {project_name}.html 32
File Transfer Protocol. *See* FTP
Fireworks
  Edge Animate extension, using 153-155
  exporting from 152, 153
  extension, using 155-157
Flash Professional
  about 20
  exporting from 158
Flash Professional, comparing with
  about 20
  Actions 22
  keyframes 21
  Labels 22
  Library 22
  stage panel 21
  Symbols 22
  Timeline 21
Flash Professional CS6
  PNG sequences, generating 268-270
  sprite sheets. generating 264, 265
Flash Professional symbols
  comparing, with Edge Animate symbols
    228, 229
Fontdeck
  URL 125
Fonts.com
  URL 125
FontsLive
  URL 125

Font Squirrel
  URL 125
frame labels 203
FTP 284

G

Generate Sprite Sheet dialog 265
GIF 133, 142
Google Chrome extension
  downloading 329
Google Chrome Frame 278
Google Web Fonts
  URL 125
graphical user interface. *See* GUI
Graphics Interchange Format. *See* GIF
GUI 42
Guides command 110

H

height property 108, 299
help cursor 200
Help menu, Edge Animate menu
  About Adobe Edge Animate ...command
    53
  Adobe Product Improvement Program ...
    command 53
  Change Language...command 53
  Edge Animate Community Forums...com-
    mand 53
  Edge Animate Help...command 53
  Edge Animate JavaScript API ...command
    53
history, Adobe Edge Animate 14, 15
hosted services
  Adobe TypeKit 125
  Fontdeck 125
  Fonts.com 125
  FontsLive 125
  Font Squirrel 125
  Google Web Fonts 125
  MyFonts 125
  Typotheque 125
  WebType 125
HTML 15

HTML5 <video> tag
  about 319
  MP4 319
  OGG 319
  WebM 319
Hyper Text Markup Language. *See* **HTML**

I

iBooks / OS X
  targeting 284, 285
ID property 103
image elements
  about 134
  alt attribute 137
  unique properties 134
image element types
  <div> 134
  <img> 134
Image Source 135
imported assets
  instance, creating 146
  managing, within Library 146
  swapping 146
  Symbol Libraries, importing 147, 148
  working with 144, 145
  working with, considerations 145, 146
InDesign/DPS/Muse
  composition, placing within InDesign 283
  composition, placing with Muse 283, 284
Insert button 295
installation
  Edge Animate 23, 24
interactivity
  adding, to album art 216-218
  adding, to title 216
  adding, to website header 214
  text element, creating 214, 215
interactivity, adding to web header
  bout 214
  composition, completing 218, 219
  text element, adding 215
  text element, creating 214
Interlace property 299

J

Java Runtime Environment 18
JavaScript Object Notation. *See* **JSON**
Joint Photographic Experts Group. *See* **JPEG**
JPEG 133, 141
jQuery
  using, in Edge Animate 16, 17
jQuery actions
  about 211
  focus 211
  mouseenter 211
  mouseleave 211
JSON 17

K

keyboard shortcuts, Edge Animate
  about 49
  dialog, accessing 50
keydown action 209
keyframes
  adding, through application menu 168, 169
  adding, through Properties panel 168
  inserting, right-click used 170
  Timeline keyframe buttons, using 169
keyframes, Edge Animate 21
  about 166
  navigation 167
keyup action 209

L

labels
  about 203
  working with 203, 205
Labels, Edge Animate 22
Layout Preferences tool
  about 70, 71
  Corner Alignment 71
  Height Units 71
  Horizontal Position Units 71
  Vertical Position Units 71
  Width Units 71
Lessons command 52
Library command 52

Library, Edge Animate 22
Lock Guides command 110
loop attribute 325

M

main text element properties
about 120
Align Center 121
Align Left 121
Align Right 121
Bold 121
Font Name 121
Font Size 121
Font Size Units 121
Italic 121
Text Color 121
Underline 121
ManyFonts directory 131
masking concept 255
menu items, Edge Animate
edit 222
Edit menu 190
Help menu 53
Timeline menu 191, 192
Window menu 52
mobile
touch actions, using 219-221
Modify menu, Adobe Edge Animate
Align | Bottom command 77
Align command 76
Align | Horizontal Center command 76
Align | Left command 76
Align | Right command 77
Align | Top command 77
Align | Vertical Center command 77
Arrange | Bring Forward command 76
Arrange | Bring To Front command 76
Arrange command 76
Arrange | Send Backward command 76
Arrange | Send To Back command 76
Convert to Symbol command 77
Distribute | Bottom command 77
Distribute command 77
Distribute | Horizontal Center command
   77

Distribute | Left command 77
Distribute | Right command 77
Distribute | Top command 77
Distribute | Vertical Center command 77
Edit Symbol command 77
Modify menu, Edge Animate menu items
Convert to Symbol command 253
Edit Symbol command 253
Group Elements in DIV command 253
Ungroup Elements command 253
motion
creating 167
keyframes, inserting 167
Pin, animating with 173, 174
Playhead, animating with 170-173
motion pasting, automated animation
      techniques
Paste Actions command 186
Paste All command 186
Paste Inverted command 186
Paste Transitions From Location command
   185
Paste Transitions To Location command
   185
mouse actions
about 210
click 210
dblclick 210
mousedown 210
mousemove 210
mouseout 210
mouseover 210
mouseup 210
mouse cursor
about 198
types 199, 200
mouse cursor, types
auto 200
col-resize 200
context-menu 200
crosshair 200
default 200
e-resize 200
ew-resize 200
help 200

move 200
ne-resize 200
nesw-resize 200
no-drop 200
n-resize 200
ns-resize 200
nw-resize 200
nwse-resize 200
pointer 200
row-resize 200
se-resize 200
s-resize 200
sw-resize 200
text-resize 200
vertical-text 200
wait 200
w-resize 200
mousedown action 210
mousemove action 210
mouseout action 210
mouseover action 210
mouseup action 210
move cursor 200
multiple Edge Animate composition
  embedding, within web page 311, 312
MyFonts
  URL 125

N

ne-resize cursor 200
nested elements
  about 242
  assets, nesting 244
  controls, creating 249, 250
  element Actions, preparing 251
  nested content, controlling 248, 249
  text, nesting 245-248
  working 243
nesw-resize cursor 200
new command 51
no-drop cursor 200
n-resize cursor 200
ns-resize cursor 200
nw-resize cursor 200
nwse-resize cursor 200

O

on Error action 209
opacity property 104
Open...command 51
Open Recent command 51
OrientationChange action 209
overflow property
  about 103, 256
  auto command 109
  hidden command 109
  scroll command 109
  visible command 109

P

panels, Edge Animate
  about 42
  Actions 47
  Code 48, 49
  Elements 44
  lessons 42, 43
  Library 45
  Properties 46, 47
paragraph text 118
Paste Transitions To Location command 188
Pin (P) 261
playback controls, Edge Animate
  about 162
  Show Grid control 164
  time 163
  timeline options 163
  timeline options, auto-keyframes mode(K)
    163
  timeline options, Auto-Transition Mode (X)
    163
  timeline options, Toggle Pin (P) 164
PNG 133, 141
PNG sequences
  about 268
  generating, from Flash Professional CS6
    268-270
  using, in Edge Animate 270-274
pointer cursor 200
point text 118
Portable Network Graphics. See PNG

position property 104
poster image
  about 285
  capturing 286
  saving 286
poster image, using
  image properties 289, 290
  text properties 290
Poster property 109
preload attribute 325
Preloader assets 296
preloader property 109
preloaders
  about 293
  built-in preloader, using 294-296
  custom preloader, creating 296-300
Preloader Stage command 110
preloading
  about 293
  immediate preloading 293
  polite preloading 293
Preview In Browser command 51
Properties command 52
Properties panel 81, 294
Publish command 51
Publish content as static HTML option
  without Static HTML selected 280
  with Static HTML selected 280, 281
Publish Settings
  about 276
  Web / Optimized HTML, targeting 277
Publish Settings...command 51

Q

Q. See Transform tool

R

raster image 140
real time messaging protocol. See RTMP
rectangle elements
  copying, Selection tool used 69, 70
  modifying 66, 67
  properties, modifying 67, 68
Rectangle tool
  about 56-59, 271, 321
  using 59

resize action 209
resolution property 299
responsive compositions
  building 91
  document responsive way 91
  elements responsive way 92
  screen sizes, simulating 95
Revert command 51
rotate property 105
Rounded Rectangle tool (R)
  about 57
  using 60-62
  working with 60
row-resize cursor 200
RTMP 320
rulers 72
Rulers command 110

S

Save As...command 51
Save command 51
Scalable Vector Graphics. See SVG
scale property 105
scroll action 209
secondary text element properties
  Letter Spacing 122
  Line Height 122
  revealing 121
  Text Indent 122
Selection tool
  about 58-81
  appearance 80
  locating 79
  using 81
se-resize cursor 200
Shadow color property 106
Shadow horizontal offset property 106
Shadow property
  about 106
  Blur radius 106
  shadow color 106
  Shadow horizontal offset 106
  shadow type 106
  Shadow vertical offset 106
  spread 107

Shadow type property **106**
Shadow vertical offset property **106**
Shift + Click **81**
Shift key **81, 179**
size property **104**
skew property **105**
Smart Guides
 about **74**
 disabling **74**
Smart Guides command **110**
Smooth property **299**
Snap to Guides command **110**
Spread property **107**
sprite sheets
 about **263, 264**
 animating with **263**
 generating, from Flash Professional CS6
  264, 265
 using, with Edge Animate **266, 267**
src attribute **325, 326**
s-resize cursor **200**
Stage panel, Edge Animate **21**
Stage property
 about **108**
 autoplay **109**
 background color **108**
 Composition ID **109**
 document title **108**
 Down-level Stage **109**
 height **108**
 overflow **109**
 Poster **109**
 preloader **109**
 width **108**
SVG
 about **133-138**
 images, importing **138-140**
 notification **140**
Swap Image **135**
sw-resize cursor **200**
symbol instances
 unique properties **236**
Symbol Libraries
 importing **147, 148**
symbol management, through Library panel
 about **233**
 Delete command **233**

Edit command **233**
Export command **234**
Rename command **234**
symbols
 assets, converting **231, 232**
 creating **229, 230**
 Edge Animate **223**
 exporting **235, 236**
 features **224**
 importing **236**
 managing **229, 230**
 managing, through Library panel **233**
 sharing, across Edge Animate
  Compositions **234-236**
Symbols, Edge Animate **22**
symbols, features
 own Timeline **226, 227**
 Playback Actions, employing **227, 228**
 self-contained **224, 225**
 stage instantiation **225**
 within library panel **225**

T

T. *See* **Text Tool**
Tab Index property **107**
text cursor **200**
text elements
 creating, on Stage **116**
 creating, Text tool used **117, 118**
 main text element properties **120, 121**
 Paragraph text **118**
 point text **118**
 properties **120**
text element types
 <address> **115**
 <article> **115**
 <blockquote> **115**
 <code> **115**
 <div> **115**
 <h1> to <h6> **115**
 <p> **115**
 <pre> **115**
text property retention **119**
text shadows
 about **122**
 Blur Radius **122**

Shadow Color 122
Shadow Horizontal Offset 122
Text tool
about 113, 114, 297
Text element types 114, 115
using 114
Timeline Actions layer 202
Timeline command 52
timeline controls,Edge Animate
about 165
keyframes 166
Pin 165
Playhead 165
zoom controls 166
Timeline, Edge Animate 21, 162
Timeline feature 41
Title property 107
Tools command 52
touch actions
about 211
touchend 211
touchmove 211
touchstart 211
using, for mobile 219-221
touchend action 211
touchmove action 211
touchstart action 211
Transform Origin property 105
transform property
about 104
rotate 105
scale 105
skew 105
transform origin 105
Transform tool
about 82
Edge Animate tool, using 84-87
locating 79
Transform Point, manipulating 84
using 82, 83
transition easing algorithms 177
transitions
composition duration, contracting 180
composition duration, expanding 180
delay 175
duration 175
duration, changing 178

easing controls 176
easing types 177
editing 174
element properties, modifying 175
generating, through keyframes 179
keyframes, copying 179
keyframes, pasting 179
keyframes, selecting 178
multiple transitions, selecting 179
shifting 178
Transparent property 299
triggers
about 201
code editor 201
labels 203, 204
labels, working with 203
snippets list 201
Timeline Actions layer 202
trigger identifier 201
trigger time 201
working with 202
Typotheque
URL 125

U

unique properties, image elements
Background Position Offset X 135
Background Position Offset Y 135
Background Position Units 136
Background Size Height 136
Background Size Units 136
Background Size Width 136
Image Source 135
Swap Image 135
unique properties, symbol instances
Instance ID 237
internal symbol properties 241
playback actions 238
scrub toggle 237
symbol-level events 242
Symbol name 237

V

V. *See* **Selection tool**
vertical-text cursor 200

video support
about 318, 319
Adobe Flash Player 320
HTML5 <video> tag 319
YouTube video, embedding 320-324
View menu, Adobe Edge Animate
Guides command 76
Lock Guides command 76
Rulers command 76
Smart Guides command 76
Snap to Guides command 76
View menu, commands
Actual Size 110
Down-level Stage 110
Guides 110
Lock Guides 110
Preloader Stage 110
Rulers 110
Smart Guides 110
Snap to Guides 110
Zoom In 110
Zoom Out 110
visibility property 103

W

wait cursor 200
web fonts, Edge Animate
about 123
core fonts 124
generic font definitions 123
hosted services 124
using 122
web header
final composition, completing 218, 219
interactivity, adding 214
WebKit 5
Web / Optimized HTML, targeting
about 277
Frameworks, using via CDN option 278
Google Chrome Frame, using 278, 279
Publish content as static HTML option,
using 280
website header
animating 180
asset import 181

element animation, performing 182
project setup 181
WebType
URL 125
welcome screen, Adobe Edge Animate
Clear Recent Files option 27
Create New option 27
Getting Started option 28
Key Features option 28
Open File ..... option 27
Other Options option 28
Quiet option 28
Recent Files option 27
Resources option 28
width property 108, 299
Window menu, Edge Animate menu
Code command 52
Elements command 52
Lessons command 52
Library command 52
Properties command 52
Timeline command 52
Tools command 52
Workspace command 52
Workspace | Default command 52
Workspace | New Workspace command
52
Workspace command 52
Workspace | Default command 52
**Workspace | Delete Workspace command
52**
Workspace | New Workspace command 52
w-resize cursor 200

Y

YouTube 320

Z

Zoom In command 110
Zoom Out command 110
Zoom Timeline to Fit button 166

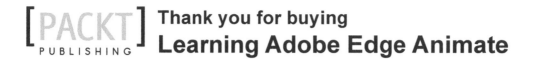

Thank you for buying
Learning Adobe Edge Animate

About Packt Publishing

Packt, pronounced 'packed', published its first book "*Mastering phpMyAdmin for Effective MySQL Management*" in April 2004 and subsequently continued to specialize in publishing highly focused books on specific technologies and solutions.

Our books and publications share the experiences of your fellow IT professionals in adapting and customizing today's systems, applications, and frameworks. Our solution based books give you the knowledge and power to customize the software and technologies you're using to get the job done. Packt books are more specific and less general than the IT books you have seen in the past. Our unique business model allows us to bring you more focused information, giving you more of what you need to know, and less of what you don't.

Packt is a modern, yet unique publishing company, which focuses on producing quality, cutting-edge books for communities of developers, administrators, and newbies alike. For more information, please visit our website: www.packtpub.com.

Writing for Packt

We welcome all inquiries from people who are interested in authoring. Book proposals should be sent to author@packtpub.com. If your book idea is still at an early stage and you would like to discuss it first before writing a formal book proposal, contact us; one of our commissioning editors will get in touch with you.

We're not just looking for published authors; if you have strong technical skills but no writing experience, our experienced editors can help you develop a writing career, or simply get some additional reward for your expertise.

Adobe Flash 11 Stage3D
(Molehill) Game Programming
Beginner's Guide

ISBN: 978-1-84969-168-0   Paperback: 412 pages

A step-by-step guide for creating stunning 3D games
in Flash 11 Stage3D (Molehill) using AS3 and AGAL

1. The first book on Adobe's Flash 11 Stage3D,
   previously codenamed Molehill

2. Build hardware-accelerated 3D games with a
   blazingly fast frame rate

3. Full of screenshots and ActionScript 3 source
   code, each chapter builds upon a real-world
   example game project step-by-step

4. Light-hearted and informal, this book is your
   trusty sidekick on an epic quest to create your
   very own 3D Flash game

Dreamweaver CS5.5 Mobile and
Web Development with HTML5,
CSS3, and jQuery

ISBN: 978-1-84969-158-1   Paperback: 284 pages

Harness the cutting edge features of Dreamweaver
for mobile and web development

1. Create web pages in Dreamweaver using the
   latest technology and approach

2. Add multimedia and interactivity to
   your websites

3. Optimize your websites for a wide range
   of platforms and build mobile apps with
   Dreamweaver

Please check **www.PacktPub.com** for information on our titles

HTML5 Canvas Cookbook

ISBN: 978-1-84969-136-9   Paperback: 348 pages

Over 80 recipes to revolutionize the web experience with HTML5 Canvas

1. The quickest way to get up to speed with HTML5 Canvas application and game development

2. Create stunning 3D visualizations and games without Flash

3. Written in a modern, unobtrusive, and objected oriented JavaScript style so that the code can be reused in your own applications

Mastering Adobe Captivate 6

ISBN: 978-1-84969-244-1   Paperback: 476 pages

Create professional SCORM-compliant e-learning content with Adobe Captivate

1. Step by step tutorial to build three projects including a demonstration, a simulation, and a random SCORM-compliant quiz featuring all possible question slides

2. Enhance your projects by adding interactivity, animations, sound, and more

3. Publish your project in a wide variety of formats enabling virtually any desktop and mobile devices to play your e-learning content

4. Deploy your e-Learning content on a SCORM or AICC-compliant LMS

Please check **www.PacktPub.com** for information on our titles

Lightning Source UK Ltd.
Milton Keynes UK
UKOW07f0042170615

253619UK00004B/232/P